UNRECONCILED

# UNRECONCILED

## Race, History, and Higher Education in the Deep South

ARTHUR N. DUNNING

The University of Georgia Press
*Athens*

A Sarah Mills Hodge Fund Publication

*This publication is made possible in part through a grant from the Hodge Foundation in memory of its founder, Sarah Mills Hodge, who devoted her life to the relief and education of African Americans in Savannah, Georgia.*

Paperback edition, 2026
© 2021 by the University of Georgia Press
Athens, Georgia 30602
www.ugapress.org
All rights reserved
Designed by Erin Kirk
Set in Minion Pro

Most University of Georgia Press titles are available from popular e-book vendors.

Printed digitally

Library of Congress Cataloging-in-Publication Data
Names: Dunning, Arthur N., author.
Title: Unreconciled : race, history, and higher education in the Deep South / Arthur N. Dunning.
Description: Athens : The University of Georgia Press, 2021. | Includes bibliographical references.
Identifiers: LCCN 2020042503 | ISBN 9780820358659 (hardback) | ISBN 9780820358994 (ebook)
Subjects: LCSH: Albany State University—History. | Darton State College—History. | College integration—Social aspects—Georgia. | Education, Higher—Social aspects—Georgia. | Racism in higher education—Georgia. | Georgia—Race relations. | United States—Race relations.
Classification: LCC LD91.A55 D86 2021 | DDC 378.009758—dc23
LC record available at https://lccn.loc.gov/2020042503

Paperback ISBN 978-0-8203-7804-6

To my paternal grandparents Willis Dunning (1858–1948)
and Delia Dunning, née O'Neal (1867–1940),
and maternal grandparents Lev Nobles (1868–1955)
and Mattie Nobles, née Davis (1869–1936).

# Contents

Acknowledgments ix
Prologue 1
Introduction 3

PART ONE. Coming of Age in the Alabama Black Belt of the 1950s 11

CHAPTER 1. The Alabama Black Belt 13
CHAPTER 2. A Sense of Southern Place 21
CHAPTER 3. Navigating Jim Crow 33
CHAPTER 4. The Will to Learn 38
CHAPTER 5. The Great Migration 55

PART TWO. Changing a Life's Perspectives in Places Far from Home 63

CHAPTER 6. It Took Leaving My Country to Find Freedom and Liberty 65
CHAPTER 7. Anger Becomes Resolve 70
CHAPTER 8. Taxes Aren't Segregated 89
CHAPTER 9. Lessons Learned along the Way 97
CHAPTER 10. The Intersection of Race and Higher Education in Georgia 106

| | |
|---|---|
| PART THREE. A Region Paralyzed by Its Past | 111 |
| CHAPTER 11. Albany, the Egypt of the Confederacy | 113 |
| CHAPTER 12. A City Held Hostage by Its Past | 117 |
| CHAPTER 13. A University with Unsinkable Determination | 123 |
| CHAPTER 14. The Calm before the Storm? | 128 |
| | |
| PART FOUR. Never before in Our Nation's History | 143 |
| CHAPTER 15. Pushback in Black and White | 145 |
| CHAPTER 16. A Near Derailment at Square One | 161 |
| CHAPTER 17. When Wounds Go Untended for Generations | 176 |
| CHAPTER 18. Fallout When Unreconciled | 189 |
| CHAPTER 19. Nudges toward Healing | 212 |
| CHAPTER 20. Sometimes It Takes Tough Love | 224 |
| | |
| PART FIVE. What Lies Ahead | 233 |
| CHAPTER 21. Toward Reconciliation | 235 |
| CHAPTER 22. Looking to the Future | 241 |
| | |
| Notes | 263 |
| Bibliography | 269 |

# Acknowledgments

I am grateful for family and friends who made this book possible. First and foremost, I thank my parents and grandparents. I think of my paternal grandparents, Willis Dunning (1858–1948) and Delia Dunning, née O'Neal (1867–1940), and maternal grandparents Lev Nobles (1868–1955) and Mattie Nobles, née Davis (1869–1936), every day. Willis was born a slave. Delia, Lev, and Mattie were born as the Jim Crow system was being erected as a substitute for slavery. Each was born in that isolated region of Alabama known as the Black Belt. None lived to see the end of Jim Crow—they were never truly free. They planted seeds for shade trees of freedom that they were never able to sit beneath.

While their opportunities were few, their vision for what their children could achieve was infinite. They worked tirelessly farming the fertile land of the Black Belt to provide for their families. They each held a vision beyond subsistence—that of securing an education for their children. They succeeded with some even attending college and graduate school.

Much of what I have learned about my grandparents has come through our family's and community's tradition of oral stories. Through those accounts, I learned that each of my grandparents took initiative, demonstrated extraordinary resilience, and worked hard. In a culture that treasured labor, they trusted and treasured intellectual development as well. Their, and my parents', belief in exceptionality for themselves, their children, and generations to come enabled me to write this book.

I treasure my sister, Jean, and our weekly phone calls, where we often reminisce about our youth. While writing this book, I turned to her frequently for details of our family's history, as well as about our parents' household before I came along. My thanks go to all my family, friends, and colleagues who fleshed out my account of various events and conversations, or read drafts of the chapters. Throughout this book I quote liberally from those recollections of verbal exchanges. Although I pride myself on having an excellent memory, such dialogue is necessarily reconstructed. I have, however, tried to preserve the tone and intent of the original and hope you all forgive me for not recalling our conversations verbatim. I've used actual names where full names appear; where only first names or surnames appear, these represent pseudonyms.

I am thankful every day for my wife, Karen. During my tenure at Albany State University, I do not think I could have survived without her by my side. Although she was immersed in her own thriving career, she encouraged me to accept the post. Karen and I are driven by the same values and sense of calling for public service. She is a firm believer that the best avenue for young people of color to live a life of high achievement, performance, respect, and dignity is through education. We both feel that if a young person is from a group that does not have hereditary advantage, success will come down to high performance. A university is the best place to help that young person find the path to achievement. Thus, we could see ourselves in the young people of Albany State.

A graduate of Wake Forest University in North Carolina, the home state of her grandparents, Karen earned her juris doctorate from the University of California, Berkeley. She has practiced law in a prestigious law firm; served as a juvenile court judge and later as a federal court-appointed monitor; dedicated long hours of pro bono work and policy research to help young people in foster care or those that find themselves in the juvenile justice system; directed programs for national, state, and local organizations; and taught university-level courses. Most recently she was a board member and interim president and CEO of the Southern Poverty Law Center.

On the Albany State campus, she supported a number of initiatives, including a program for students who grew up in foster care. For my role at Albany State, Karen was a good listener, always steering me back to my core values when I grappled with difficult issues. She was an objective, confidential sounding board for thinking through all the responsibilities of a, at times very lonely, 24/7 job.

Ours was, and is, a real partnership. I could not have done my job, if she had not embraced the responsibility whole-heartedly. We were equally committed to the task. In fact, Karen treasured her role as first lady, which she played with grace and ease. Then, as now, I treasure her encouragement, support, and insight.

I extend sincere thanks for the invaluable help of Nathan Essex, retired president of Southwest Tennessee Community College, for reading a draft of the book. I also thank Deborah Oliver of Ab Initio for her work editing the book, and Nate Holly of the University of Georgia Press for preparing it for publication. Finally, as I have reflected not only on this book, but the process to bring it to fruition, I am reminded of the words of Nelson Mandela: "There can be no greater gift than that of giving one's time and energy to helping others without expecting anything in return." This is especially true in my case.

When I conceived of this project, I knew I could not complete it alone but would require the assistance of someone to help put my voice, memories, and thoughts on the page. I would need someone with intellectual curiosity, tireless dedication, inexhaustible initiative, and superb research and editing skills. Throughout the course of our professional relationship, Trish Kalivoda has exceeded expectations at every turn. When she agreed to help with this project, I knew without a doubt it would be completed. I am deeply grateful to her for helping me bring this book to fruition.

# UNRECONCILED

# Prologue

It was a surreal moment. In April 2013, I stood on the West Lawn of the White House, watching with other alumni and well-wishers as the University of Alabama championship football team was congratulated by President Barack Obama. Memories came flooding into my mind as though a levee had been breached. It seemed like only yesterday that four fellow students and friends and I joined the same university's legendary coach Bear Bryant football team as walk-ons. We were the first black student athletes to cross the sacred Alabama football field. It was the spring of 1967, and when asked why the team still had no African American players, one of the assistant coaches declared, "I don't ever see a day when a Negro could have the athletic or academic abilities to play football for the University of Alabama."

Standing next to me on the White House lawn, my wife, Karen, took my hand, bringing me back to the present. Forty-five years after my friends and I were walk-ons, here I stood, at the most powerful house in the world, watching today's nearly all-black Alabama team receive congratulations from the nation's first black president. Moreover, Judy Bonner, the first woman president of the University of Alabama, accompanied the team. In that moment, I was deeply proud of the progress that we as a people had made in the state of Alabama, the country, and the world.

Issues of race, history, and culture have plagued our nation since its inception. Alabama was ground zero for the civil rights movement that led to changes in laws, to the integration of schools, and to more access and opportunities for America's people of color, for women, and more recently, for the LGBTQ community. I left the 2013 White House celebration with the strong realization that the world was very different from the one I grew up in. Seven months from that moment at the White House, however, I accepted a call to serve as interim president of Albany State University, an historically black public university in Southwest Georgia. Answering that call propelled me into five of the most difficult years of my career and life. Albany, Georgia, founded in the 1830s after most of its native inhabitants, the Creek Indians, were forcibly relocated, has been mired in ongoing racial animus and de facto segregation since the days when slavery supported the region's plantation economy. Today, Albany is known as one of the poorest areas of Georgia and of the entire country.

Almost two years after my arrival at Albany State, Georgia's governing body of public higher education mandated a consolidation of Albany State University and Darton State College, an historically white two-year college just four miles from Albany State. It would be the first time in our nation's history that such a consolidation would be set into motion without being preceded by a court order. The clash of race, history, and culture came crashing back into my life and made me realize that, as a nation, we have a long road ahead of us to reconcile the memories and devastating consequences of our nation's history.

# Introduction

Late on a Friday afternoon in November 2015, almost two years into my term as interim president of Albany State University, I received a call from a senior administrator with the University System of Georgia (USG), which is the governing body for the state's public colleges and universities. "We are ready to announce to the Albany community plans to consolidate Albany State with Darton State College," the caller told me, "and we want you to lead the process."

The consolidation of these two institutions had been an ongoing discussion in the system office for many years. Even during my tenure as a senior administrator in that office during the 1980s and '90s, I had thought that it made no sense for there to be two separate system institutions in that one location. A final decision would be made for a number of commonsense reasons. The two schools were geographically close to each other, and both were suffering from low enrollments. Consolidation would make for a more efficient use of resources, a reduction of administrative costs, a more seamless transition from associate degrees to bachelor's degrees, and a broader array of course offerings and majors for students. It would also require quieting a community torn apart by the thought of being educated together. It would take place on the heels of the nation being led by its first black president, of changing national racial demographics, and of a resurgence of hate groups.

The USG official closed the call by saying that the public announcement would be made the following Monday. I hung up the phone and drove home filled with a range of emotions. On one hand, I felt sober about the challenges that lay ahead. On the other, I had empathy for a community that needed deep healing and that needed to find a way to reconcile the past—not just about higher education but about issues of race, history, and culture.

When I arrived home, I poured myself a glass of red wine and sat down in the sunroom to discuss this development with my wife. We talked about the feelings, values, beliefs, and experiences that I would bring to the consolidation process and reflected on the impact that my leadership style might have on the success, or lack of success, of the consolidation.

As we talked, I tried to articulate my earliest memories about the values taught to me by my parents. My mom was explicit in these values; my dad was implicit through his behavior. Together, they were insistent, consistent, and always on the same page about what they were doing, which was to teach me, in some easy ways, those values that they felt could sustain a human being in a complex world. I was born in the mid-1940s in the rural town of Sweet Water, in the western reaches of the Alabama Black Belt, just 250 miles west of Albany State. Mine was a close-knit family bent on educating and improving the lives of its children—no easy task for a black family living in the Jim Crow era—a euphemism for nearly a century of racial segregation by law.

At the top of my parents' list of values was personal development, high academic performance and achievement, accountability, and respectability, which included protecting and strengthening the family's reputation. Other values included being independent of thought, demonstrating initiative, and making decisions for the well-being of others, not just for oneself. Two were financial: investing or saving some of one's hard-earned resources and property ownership (my parents were very high on the concept of landownership for the self-sufficiency and independence it provided). Regarding finances, my folks made deferred gratification and self-denial virtues, turning scarcity on its head: "There are certain things you can wait until a different time in your life to have or do. You don't have to have or do everything right now."

As Karen and I talked, I realized that each time I made a decision during the consolidation I would be thinking about, and driven by, each of those values that had shaped me and that have shaped much of America. My values would be my anchor.

From those values, our conversation shifted to the societal environments I experienced after I moved away from home in 1962 at the age of eighteen. Serving in the U.S. military in Taiwan, then attending the University of Alabama soon after it was desegregated, and living and working abroad as a civilian all helped me understand the challenges of race, history, and culture that I would face throughout my professional life. A number of memories, in no particular order, converged.

The first experience that jumped to mind was my arrival on the University of Alabama campus in 1966. I was part of the first wave of African American students to matriculate at this southern flagship university, whose demographics would shift dramatically over the coming decade. The first two African Americans had enrolled just three summers before, in 1963. When I arrived on campus, six weeks went by before I saw an African American student other than my roommate.

At the time, I had just completed four years in the U.S. Air Force. It felt good to be living again as a civilian in my home state. I was excited about being a full-time student on the university's main campus. When I stepped onto the campus quad, I said to myself, "I have earned this space and place." Not long after I arrived, I was walking from the student union building along the west side of the university's quadrangle when someone yelled out from a window, "Nigger, go home!" I walked on, showing no response. Inside, however, I was amused.

On my return to the States, I went home to Sweet Water to see my parents and to walk the land of my childhood. I felt a new sense of geographic place—a sense of southern place. I realized just how much I loved my home and my state. It had taken living in another country to really understand that my roots were in the fertile land of the Black Belt of Alabama.

Hearing the language being hurled at me, which was such a part of Alabama's culture at that time, I said to myself, "Well, I truly am back home." The person yelling at me was talking about racial place. When thinking about the South, many people assume that "place" means "racial place." Already, however, I had redefined "place" to mean "geographic place." The student who yelled out at me had no idea I felt so at home on the University of Alabama campus because it was part of my state—as much as it was part of his.

A second societal experience I was exposed to, as I thought about my military time in Taiwan, was learning that people who have been victimized and marginalized themselves still have the capacity to turn around and debase others with derogatory language. Maybe I should have known this before, but I didn't until one day when I was lounging in my barracks in Taiwan with some other airmen. We were all guests in this country, so when I heard a black man from the Deep South refer to the Taiwanese in disgust as "Chinks," I sat bolt upright. I understood my slice of verbal abuse, but here was someone who had been subjected to the same racial slurs I had, using other racial slurs against yet someone else who looked different. I had long labored under the notion that Jim Crow had given me a sense of grievance, victimization, and innocence that was validated by an environment of laws, policies, and practices intended to devalue. Now I was jolted out of that innocence. Some fifty years later, I would be clear eyed about the capacity of people in Albany, Georgia, in so many ways, to protect their space at the expense of others and to use language to debase.

Another life lesson that came to mind as Karen and I talked was recognizing some of the demons that would be unleashed for a lot of people threatened by the thought of consolidating the city's "black school" with its "white school." There would be challenges ahead and allegations by both sides based on some earlier truths, but mostly based on racial stereotypes and prejudices. Those challenges would be outlined for me in great detail one Saturday morning shortly after the consolidation was announced.

A typical Saturday morning routine for me was to get a haircut, but my visit that day proved to be fateful. Sitting next to me in the barbershop was an African American man who seemed to know who I was and wanted to say something. When I walked out, he followed me. Outside, the man said, "Dr. Dunning, do you have a few minutes? I'd like to talk to you." He then launched into a litany of the challenges that would be raised throughout the consolidation process from the perspectives of both whites and blacks in the community. He was intense, profane, and deeply passionate about his observations and opinions. "Let me give you both sides of this. First of all, you have those people downtown [white business people and white people in the community] who don't wish to see Albany State succeed. They tried to get it closed after the flood of '94. Some of the most prominent white leaders in Albany led that effort with the help of one of the board of regents. So, you just need to watch those crackers. I've been in Albany all my life, and I just think there's a conspiracy going on."

Although the consolidation had just been publicly announced, this man had clearly been observing race relations in Albany over many years and had built up a head of steam about them. He continued, "But now, I'm through with those people. Let me tell you about those Negroes you've got to deal with at Albany State. I hope they've not mismanaged the place as much as I've heard over the years. Sounds like none of their administrative processes work. You've also got some people over there who've hired their friends and relatives. If you question them about it, they get defensive. They just don't seem to want to change or get better at what they do. I know you're working on it, but you need to get all that straightened out before you even think about consolidating. And, when you try to consolidate, you're going to have your hands full. They're proud of being an historically black school. They won't want anything to do with those white folks over at Darton. So, I worry about a consolidation."

He relentlessly blistered both sides. But he accurately portrayed the reality and harshness of the Albany community, highlighting and echoing themes that I was already aware of and would hear repeatedly over the next year from people, both black and white, both on campus and in the broader community.

He had a bead on the stereotypes as well as the raw feelings about, and between, the races in Albany. His assessment was hard edged, hard nosed, and candid. It seemed to me then that this man was speaking in the common voice of the citizenry of Albany. This was a community whose members were caught in an unremitting and unyielding fight about race, history, and culture. He was warning me: "This is the type of community you're in."

Being faced with this man's passion and rage was not a novel experience for me. I had experienced racially charged behaviors and language in the 1960s civil rights era. Fifty years later, I thought I could handle similar behaviors and language from alumni, students, faculty, community and business leaders—even some pastors. I would learn that it was a real challenge, however.

---

I first heard of the opening at Albany State when I was asked to suggest names for a pool of applicants for the position of interim president after Everette Freeman's departure. I knew the school, and the context in which it operated, from my years working in the USG. After some thought and nudging from others, I added my name to the pool. Although comfortable in what I considered semiretirement, the draw of the Albany State position was strong for two reasons.

First, the southwest corner of Georgia, where Albany State lies, is not unlike the Alabama region I grew up in. I could see my teenage self in the students of Albany State. If I was hired for the post, my sole motivation in every decision would be helping those young people earn a college degree and going on to live meaningful, productive lives.

Second, I felt that, regardless of the distractions and pressures, particularly around issues of race, I could focus my attention on choosing the right course for Albany State academically. I would examine issues through the lenses of the academic needs of students and the economic development needs of the region, not through lenses of intense tribalism and racial orthodoxy. I also understood that, if I was selected for the position, my decision-making approach would cause me difficulty sooner rather than later.

What I observed and experienced in Albany, Georgia, was a microcosm of what we are grappling with as a nation today. We are unable to discuss with civility and respect how to shape a common view of the future. It is timely, therefore, that this is a book about race in America. Much of the impasse is caused by divergent interpretations of our nation's history and entrenched vested interests in maintaining the status quo, as well as fears and concerns about current and future shifts in our demographic profile.

The pages that follow delve into not just the feelings and passions that accompanied the consolidation of two schools, but also the feelings and passions still triggered by modern-day integration. Thus, this is also a book about lessons learned and best practices needed to guide our nation toward reconciliation of the past, and to build trust in our future. Each decision I made throughout the consolidation process was built on the values instilled in me as a young man growing up in a loving family and community in the segregated and obscene system of Jim Crow laws in Alabama, as well as on the lessons learned from living and working in other countries, attending college in Alabama shortly after forced integration, and serving for over forty years as an administrator in higher education.

I also hope in this book to convey the complexity of the context into which I found myself living in Albany, Georgia, as I made decisions that would be in the best interests of young adults seeking an education. Perhaps some of the lessons I learned along the way might help readers navigate through our nation's ongoing transformations, which are hobbled by the seemingly intractable divides of race, history, and culture, as well as by a lack of trust in our institutions. Creating spaces for reconciliation, and then leveraging, cooperating, and collaborating across racial differences might just allow us to embrace an ever-changing, diverse, and global world in ways that allow future generations to flourish.

# PART ONE

# Coming of Age in the Alabama Black Belt of the 1950s

My life journey started just southwest of the triangle formed by Selma, Montgomery, and Birmingham, which was the cradle of civil rights change in the twentieth century. The region is called the Alabama Black Belt. Although the term originally described the fertile land of nineteen counties crossing from east to west in the southern half of the state, the designation later also recognized the thousands of African American slaves that tilled the soil, mostly on cotton plantations.[1] Thus, "Alabama Black Belt" describes not just the geology but also the people who worked the land. This land has sustained generations, including three generations of my own family, through farming.

CHAPTER 1

# The Alabama Black Belt

Seventy-five million years ago, the Alabama Black Belt was a seashore. Calcium-rich materials (e.g., shells, phytoplankton) built up over time to form a dense chalk layer. Organic matter settled on top of the chalk, creating the dark soil for which the region was originally named. Native Americans populated the land hunting in its forests and on its open prairies. The French and Spanish explored the region.

In the early 1800s, once white visitors realized the potential of the soil, settlers rushed in to establish claims on the land. The rush was called Alabama Fever. Many of the settlers were cotton planters from states to the east who used slaves for the labor-intensive cash crop. This slave system was supported by a transatlantic slave trade. By 1800, from 10 to 15 million people, mostly from West Africa, were shipped across the Atlantic Ocean to the Americas, where they were sold into permanent bondage, becoming the legal property of their owners.[1]

For me to understand the history of my family living in this plantation economy of the Alabama Black Belt, I had to go back to the beginning—to that transatlantic slave trade. In 1992, I had the opportunity to do so. I accompanied President Jimmy Carter and about a dozen others on an election-monitoring observation mission to Ghana in West Africa.

Our time was spent monitoring the presidential election in the capital, Accra, and in outlying villages. We watched as people walked into the central area of a village to drop their paper ballots into a box. As election monitors, we were on the lookout for irregularities and signs of intimidation, such as soldiers with guns near the ballot boxes. Our job was to determine if the voting process was free and fair, but it also gave us the opportunity to meet and speak with the locals. In one community, in the course of my conversation with a local Catholic priest, I asked for the Ghanaian perspective on the transatlantic slave trade. He replied simply: "visit Elmina Castle."

Europeans built Elmina Castle in 1482 as the first of many fortified trading posts for gold, but in the 1500s demand for labor in the Americas shifted traders' interest to people, who became the latest commodity in an even more vicious trade that continued into the nineteenth century. One of the epicenters in the slave trade of Africans and now a World Heritage site, tourists come to Elmina Castle to learn about the slave trade or seek answers to their heritage, or both.[2]

Touring Elmina Castle, I caught a glimpse of the wretched horror behind the priest's succinct reply. It was heart wrenching to picture the transatlantic slave trade in the very building from which so many were held, sorted, and shipped. The guide explained the process of separating the men from the women, the healthy from the unhealthy. As I looked out across the ocean, I imagined what the voyage was like—the lack of facilities, the lack of food, the illness, the immense suffering. Half would die on the voyage. As the other tourists and I exited the fortress, some dropped to their knees and cried.

The ships carrying slaves from Elmina Castle on the west coast of Africa sailed through the West Indies to Virginia, Maryland, South Carolina, Georgia, and the Gulf Coast, including Mobile Bay in Alabama.[3] The captives were sold to planters and slave traders. Their labor built the South's economy, and by extension the nation's. Today the Alabama Black Belt is populated with the descendants of people from West Africa. They are my ancestors. I knew these facts, but it truly hit me how personally connected I am to West Africa when I participated in a 1992 election monitoring meeting with a handful of Ghanaian dignitaries: a couple of the men bore a remarkable resemblance to my uncle and a first cousin. Not just the physical resemblance but also the dignity with which they carried themselves were striking, and unlike other men I had grown up around.

Driving the slave trade in the United States was the production of cotton for profit. When Alabama became a state in 1819, 30 percent of the state's population was enslaved. That population doubled in each of the coming decades. Although every county in Alabama had enslaved residents, most lived in the counties along the Tennessee River Valley or in the Black Belt. Most had been brought to Alabama from other states.[4]

Indeed, stories passed down in my family tell how some of my ancestors were brought from South Carolina to Southwest Alabama.

Even after the U.S. Congress banned the importation of slaves in 1808, smugglers continued importing slaves illegally, and plantations continued to be established in Alabama and elsewhere, with the rich soil and slave labor creating great wealth and political power for the plantation owners. This is where my known family history begins.

My paternal grandfather, Willis Dunning, was born into slavery in the Alabama Black Belt in 1858, three years before the start of the Civil War. While my paternal grandmother, Delia, was born in 1867, two years after the war ended and after emancipation, she and my grandfather never lived a free existence. After the Civil War, states across the South—Alabama among them—quickly put in place Jim Crow laws, which kept freed slaves in a superior-subordinate caste system—one determined by skin color. After the Civil Rights Act of 1964, de facto separation of blacks and whites continued.

My grandparents never spoke about their early years to us. There were things that people talked about and others they did not, and those years fell firmly in the latter category for them. As far as I know, no one in my family knows how my grandparents met or what they did in the years before my dad's ten siblings and he were born. To get a sense of what those early years were like for my grandparents, I must turn to historians. Howard Zinn writes that after the war, "southern blacks were determined to make the most of their freedom, in spite of their lack of land and resources.... They began immediately asserting their independence of whites, forming their own churches, becoming politically active, strengthening their family's ties, trying to educate their children."[5]

None of this was easy to achieve because whites still owned the majority of the land, which forced most former slaves to farm as sharecroppers on former slave plantations still owned by whites. Tenancy for black farmers was less frequent, with the distinction between it and sharecropping being that tenants supplied their own tools and mules. Chalmers Archer Jr. writes that sharecroppers "were the most dependent on landowners, and their will was subject almost completely to the landowner's will. The practices of the system were passed from one generation to the next."[6]

For the few freed slaves who managed to purchase their own property, landownership was a big deal. It meant the difference between living in perpetual poverty and building a future for one's family. It allowed for respect, for dignity, and for entering the market economy with one's own work. The work at that time was agriculture, and while unpredictable in its ability to produce a reliable income, it allowed a family to be independent. It sustained life.

In the 1880s, my grandparents found a way to purchase land in Marengo County, Alabama, in a region that would become and remain one of the most segregated places on Earth except for the Mississippi Delta. According to family lore, a man who owned several thousand acres returned home from the Civil War with the intention of moving to Texas. He carved up his acreage into sellable parcels. My grandfather bought a 175-acre parcel for twenty-five cents an acre, an amount that was difficult to come by at that time, not least for a former slave.

My grandparents provided for their family's subsistence by raising cattle, by growing cotton as a cash crop, and by planting, harvesting, and preserving their own vegetables and fruits. They did not buy food from a store except what they couldn't make themselves, like baking powder, baking soda, sugar, and salt and pepper.

I have one of my grandfather's receipts from 1896. He had taken a bale of cotton to be ginned, in a wagon pulled by mules, and got a receipt for $4.96. The significance of the receipt is that it showed that my grandfather owned his own land. Unlike a sharecropper, he was able to benefit from the fruits of his family's labor because he was a property owner. He could sell all of his harvest rather than having to give a large share of it to the landowner. Still, it was a modest living. I also have some of his bank statements from the 1910s. Even after he harvested crops, the most I ever saw in his bank account was $918, and that was in a banner year.

People in those days had large families. My grandparents had eleven children, eight boys and three girls. While struggling to enter the market economy with their cash crops, they also had to harvest enough to feed their children. They worked hard. They never went hungry, and they made enough income off the land to secure an education for their children, with most of the sons finishing high school. Some were able to go to college, including my dad, who graduated from Alabama State College in the early 1930s and went on to earn a master's degree in 1949. Owning land and earning a college education gave my dad, and others like him, a measure of dignity. It allowed them to grow up to be confident, thoughtful men who behaved like men of means and substance, which indeed they were.

By the late 1910s and 1920s, when my grandparents' children were grown, all but my dad had moved to the North, where there were job opportunities with fixed wages for a fixed-hour day. In contrast, farmers in the Deep South and elsewhere worked from "can to can't," or from first light until the day's light was gone and they could no longer see.

Because my grandfather died without a will, his property was divided among his heirs. Of the eleven children, my dad was the only one interested in hanging on to the land in Marengo County, to which he had an almost mystical attachment. He spent four or five years traveling to Detroit, New York, and Tennessee to ask his brothers and sisters, or their heirs, to sell him their shares of the inherited property. They all agreed to. They enjoyed more social freedom in the North than in the South, none wanted to move back, and many did not ever want to see that land again. There was a common saying back then by many African Americans who had moved to the North and did not want to return: "If I don't ever see it again, it'll be too soon."

In a cemetery just off Highway 43 in Dixons Mills, Alabama, my grandparents lie buried, along with many of my unanswerable questions. How were they able to get the money to purchase land? How did they marshal an inner strength to harness that land, to have eleven children, and to send some of the younger sons off to college? Farming to eke out a living was hard enough. How did they do it in a society that had laws to keep people from living and moving around freely? The one thing I do know is how important owning those 175 acres was to my grandparents.

My parents, Arthur and J. L. (short for Johnnie Livingston) Dunning (née Nobles), were in the second generation after slavery. Born and raised in the southwest corner of Alabama, they never left the land of their birth. Each came from property-owning families. My dad owned the land of his father. He, in turn, rented some to people in the community who wanted to grow cotton on it. He, as his father had done, raised cattle and sold timber off the land.

My mom grew up on a tiny street in Thomasville, Alabama, a railroad town founded in the late 1800s. The family used to say that her street was "full of preachers and teachers." Her father and brother held good jobs that gave them what was considered a substantial income for black families at that time. At that point in time, her family would have been considered part of the black middle class.

Her father worked on the railroads out of Thomasville. He was part of the hewing operation for crossties. My mom's brother, James, was a railway postal clerk with the U.S. Postal Service for almost forty years, retiring in the mid-1950s. He had one of the most significant and stable jobs for African Americans in his town as a federal worker, which was a great help to his family. Long after my mom had married and moved away from home, James's income supported their ailing father and a sister who surrendered a teaching career in another town to come home and care for their father.

Neither of my parents was a full-time farmer. Each had studied hard to become educators. My mom was an elementary school teacher. My dad began his career as a mathematics teacher. Later, he became the principal of a junior high school and then of a high school. Over their forty-year careers as educators, their salaries were meager but steady. As teachers in the Jim Crow South, they had to do other things to supplement the family income.

My dad's owning the 175 acres was crucial to providing for my mom, my sister, and me. Growing up in the 1950s, I often went with my dad to sell his cattle or timber. We would take cattle to the stockyard in Linden, Alabama, the county seat eighteen miles from home. The timber we took to a sawmill about four miles west of our land. Between their teacher salaries and their profits off the land, my parents were completely self-sufficient. To this day, I can hear my parents' words: "Do things for yourself. Don't expect others to take care of all your needs."

Every summer in the 1950s, my dad and I had a routine. At the beginning of the summer, he and I would spend many days alone in the deep woods repairing the barbed-wire fences and clearing the land on which he kept cattle. Next, we would sometimes move the cattle from one eighty-acre parcel to the other parcel to feed on fresh pastureland. To help move the cattle, my dad would enlist the help of boys in the community. In this communal approach to living on the land, the older boys would drive the cattle while we younger boys ran around opening and closing gates and chasing after a stray cow.

Once the cattle were well situated for the summer, my dad would travel more than a hundred miles northeast to take graduate classes at either Alabama State College (today Alabama State University) or the Tuskegee Institute (today Tuskegee University). The courses typically lasted six weeks. While Dad was away, I remained home with my mom. A voracious reader, she spent her summers reading and doing the abundant chores required of farming life. She quilted, sewed, and preserved fruits and vegetables.

All the while, my mom gave me the freedom to roam by myself. I spent hours walking through our land. Most of that time I mused, lost in daydreams. Often I would visit and help one of our neighbors or watch him while he worked. A veteran of World War II, Mr. Dozier Bouler lived on a forested tract adjacent to ours. To reach his place, I followed a path through the dense forest, the whole time eagerly watching for the deer, wild turkey, foxes, rabbits, squirrels, quail, and partridges that abounded. I would also see hornet or wasp nests, rattlesnakes curled up in the pine straw, or water moccasins dangling from tree branches over Mill Creek. Traversing the creek by means of a large log that had fallen across it, I then had a short walk to Mr. Bouler's house. Over time, those walks helped me develop an intimacy with the land of my father and grandfather. I knew all of its sounds and smells like the back of my hand.

Some Saturdays I went with my dad when he drove Mom to Selma to shop. During the Jim Crow era, in a town like Selma there was no safe place for African Americans to do what could be perceived by whites as "loitering." While Mom shopped, Dad and I usually either sat in the colored waiting room of the Greyhound bus station or in the car in the parking lot. One Saturday, however, we wandered into the Sears Roebuck store. There, I saw for sale a .22-caliber rifle. I pleaded, "Dad. I *really* need this rifle." I explained that I would feel safer when I was alone in the woods. I would only use it if I came across something like a poisonous snake, or for hunting; never would I use it to harm a person.

My dad agreed to buy the rifle under two conditions. First was gun safety. He said, "You must always keep the safety on. Never prop it up against a fence or a tree where it might accidentally discharge." Second, he said, "Never point the gun on anyone." I would become an expert shot from many days walking through our land where I would, every now and then, shoot at a poisonous snake or a tree branch.

I never had to use that rifle to protect myself from another person. I was fortunate in that respect. We lived in a region deeply immersed in the hierarchical, superior-subordinate, and often violent culture that evolved in the plantation economy of the southern United States, which meant that violence against African Americans was common well into the twentieth century. In 1931, nine African American teenagers falsely accused of raping a white woman in Scottsboro were sentenced to death by an all-white jury. By the mid-1920s, the Alabama Ku Klux Klan had almost 150 Klan chapters, and their "vigilante tactics" lent a sense of "lawlessness" to Alabama that was still strong when I was growing up.[7] In 1955, the fourteen-year-old Emmett Till was lynched—beaten and shot and thrown in the Tallahatchie River. There was no doubt that we lived in dangerous times for African Americans.

As children, however, we did not live in daily fear. Our lives were insulated by strong, supportive families and resilient communities. For my grandfather's generation, my dad's generation, and me, our small piece of land in the Black Belt gave us a sense of self-respect as property owners because of the independence it afforded.

There is not a single other place in the world that is more important to me than that family land in Sweet Water, Alabama. It is the land of my ancestors. It is where I came of age. It is the place that nurtured me and taught me civility, manners, respect, and high expectations in one of the deepest segregated places you could find in the United States. As I look back now, I see that everything that I am today I owe to those people who I grew up with in that Alabama Black Belt agrarian community. In my mind, it is the place I come back to every time I have to make a hard decision.

CHAPTER 2

# A Sense of Southern Place

Oddly enough, a tour of overseas duty in the U.S. Air Force helped me appreciate my southern roots. And, just as important was the realization that I had just as much claim to a southern identity as my white contemporaries. Today I respect and treasure my southern geographic place, even though in some ways I have grown beyond it. My southern culture is rooted in the nature of the land, and from lifetimes lived in the superior-subordinate social structure of the Deep South. It is characterized by its close-knit communities, its central role of the church, its cuisine, and—most nostalgically for me—its blues music.

Thomas Holt writes that African Americans "depended on cultural support systems provided by community and kin to survive degradation and oppression" throughout the century of Jim Crow.[1] That was certainly true when I was growing up. Directly across the road from my family was a family who had been there since the 1800s—the same as my family. Mr. Robert Young farmed his own land and sharecropped on another piece of land. He was the go-to person in the community related to all things farming and livestock. He was full of wisdom, knowledge, and information.

Mr. Young and his wife had seven daughters and four sons. The third son, Tat, was a few years older than me and became one of my closest friends. I spent long hours with the family as a child. Many mornings, I would walk to their house, where Mrs. Young would ask me to take water to her husband out in the corn or cotton fields. I would carry a large bucket with its dipper to Mr. Young, who would stop the mules in the middle of the field he was plowing to drink. Then he would tell me to walk to the end of the row and set the pail in the shade so the water would not get too warm.

When Tat was a young teen and had grown in size and strength, Mr. Young would leave him on his own with the two mules to plow the fields. I was always underfoot wanting to help Tat, who kindly showed me how to do everything he was doing. He taught me all the commands to guide the mules gently. If I tugged slightly to the right with the reins, they knew to turn on their own at the end of a row.

Once, when I was about age ten, I learned a lesson about collaboration from Mr. Young that remained with me throughout my life. One morning when I went over to the Youngs' house, Mrs. Young said, "Mr. Young's down about a mile from here cutting firewood with some other men." So, I walked down the road to where I could see that they had turned the mules and wagon off the road and into the deep woods. I followed the wagon tracks, which were deep and muddy, listening for the men's voices for about a quarter of a mile into the darkness of the forest.

When I reached the clearing, I saw that everyone was in full motion doing things. Not wanting to get in the way, I found a freshly cut oak tree just right for a nice little seat for a ten-year-old to sit and watch all that was going on.

When Mr. Young saw me, however, he walked over and said, "Son, everybody down here's working. If you're going to be here, and spend time in these woods with us, you're not going to be allowed to just sit on your ass."

"Yes, sir." I hopped right up.

"Everybody down here has a job. So, here's what I want you to do," he said. He instructed me to pile the cut-off branches to be burned later. By the time they had finished, I had made a huge pile.

When the wagon was loaded high with the firewood, Mr. Young got up on the seat of the wagon, took the reins, and turned the mules to head out to the road on the deeply rutted tracks they had come in on. It all looked very precarious to me. He asked if I wanted to ride in the wagon.

"No, sir—thank you. I'll walk beside the wagon." My mind was already racing ahead, envisioning the mules bolting if a swarm of bees frightened them, seeing in my mind's eye that heavy wagon flipping over.

Once out of the deep muddy ruts and back onto the gravel road, he asked when I wanted to hop onto one of these mules. He meant on my own, while he was driving them, and while they were moving. I quickly gave that question some hard thought, my mind churning back and forth: "It looks awfully dangerous. So, I should walk. But he asked me. I don't want to be disrespectful. He must think I can do it." I decided to give it a try.

I jumped up to catch the collar of one of the mule's harnesses. It took me three swings to get my body up and on the mule. Once up there, I immediately formulated an escape plan. I made sure that one of the reins that connected the bit in the mule's mouth to Mr. Young's big strong hands was tucked up under my leg. I was thinking, "If these mules take off, I'm going to get off the same way I got on. I'll catch the mule's collar and flip down."

Two things come to mind as I recall this incident. First is the whole idea of a work project with a clear goal, and full participation by everyone involved, each with a specific role to play. No one can just hang back watching and not helping. In this case, the common goal was a wagonload of firewood. Sixty years later, the common goal would be the consolidation of a university and a two-year college.

Second, I see that I was a planner already from an early age. I would study the context of a situation, formulate options, and plan ahead for contingencies before acting. What would happen if the mules bolted and the wagon tipped? How was I going to get off that mule in a hurry if need be?

Later, in elementary and high school, my classmates teased me because they said I always had a plan for "what if?" and "what are my options?" As a young adult in the air force, I would assess a job order and determine the most efficient, effective way to complete it. As a university administrator, I would study the pros and cons of action options to address challenges using logic, reason, and data, selecting an option that I thought would be best for the students or the communities that would be affected. Every time I've engaged in an activity, I've developed a plan by studying the contingencies and formulating options.

The Youngs weren't our only neighbors, of course. Wandering my family's land as a young teen, I would often stop in at one of the neighboring farms to help out. I would place my rifle over in a corner and would spend the day there assisting as best I could. My parents accepted my daily excursions because they knew all of these farmers, felt I was safe when I was away for the whole day, and knew I would make myself useful.

The time I spent with our neighbors built on other important lessons I was learning. In that era, knowledge was passed down through storytelling. Communities were insular, with few phones and radios. People received news and information through newspapers, through conversations, and through stories told while sitting on neighbors' front porches, in the churchyard over a Sunday lunch buffet following a morning sermon, or on benches outside the general store while waiting for corn to be milled or cotton ginned. The communal tasks required in an isolated, rural, agrarian community also called the members together to butcher a hog in the fall or help herd cattle from one pasture to another. Women would gather together, moving from house to house, for quilting and for preserving fruits and vegetables. Through all that common work and assistance we learned respect, civility, and how to get along with others—what would today be called soft skills.

In the generations before Facebook, we learned the value of loyalty from childhood friendships that would last a lifetime. Three of my closest friendships were forged in elementary school. We were like brothers then, and the closeness we forged then has continued all these years and I suspect will stay with us for the rest of our lives. Such friendships and continuity of relationships help people develop a sense of self and balance, which helps form the lenses through which they see the world. My friendships have had a huge impact on who I am and how I approach life.

We learned how to respect all the citizens within a community, regardless of social class. My parents had more education than most of the people living around them, but they never put on airs that might estrange them from other community members.

My dad knew and trusted the men in the community, and they, in turn, respected him. Some could not read, so often someone would stop by the house on a Sunday afternoon to ask Dad to read a document—perhaps something like a banking contract. He would study it and then explain by saying something like, "If you sign this, you're agreeing to do these three things..."

On our land, when I was a teenager, my dad decided to build a new house adjacent to the one we were living in. The contractor asked him if he wanted to use siding or brick, with both options costing about the same. My mom and I wanted him to choose brick. He chose siding, telling us, "If we use brick, there'll only be two people in the neighborhood who will be happy with the decision. You and your mom." He did not want his neighbors to think that our family thought we were better than others by choosing what looked like the pricier option.

Finally, the physical proximity of people in the community taught us that each member was visible to everyone else; there was no anonymity. One way for people to cope with living in such close contact was to adopt amplified courtesies. People were kind, respectful, and civil. In reading biographies of Presidents Truman and Eisenhower, both of whom grew up in small towns, I realized I share what they must have felt—that, for good or ill, values become clear early on in life because of the social and physical environment. They become more deeply imprinted than in a less insular, disconnected, urban environment.

Those values took on deeper meaning for families in the sparsely populated, isolated African American communities of the Alabama Black Belt during the Jim Crow era. We lived in a parallel society that was separated and stratified based on skin color. It was an insular community, with only rare interactions with whites. It was not until we left home for the wider world that we had to learn how to function in the white world, navigating it so we would not get hurt.

---

The church has historically been dominant and prominent in African American southern culture. Holt observes that "after kinship, religion was the most important value in southern black life."[2] Church was much more than a place of worship. It was a place for socializing, and for learning the expectations of behavior (e.g., civility, respect, how to relate to each other, how to relate to adults). There was a strong hierarchical structure of children and adults and clear-cut roles for men and women. No one ever spoke outright about it. People just grew up understanding it.

In the late 1800s, my grandfather, together with four or five other men, started the Rock Babylon Missionary Baptist Church on the banks of Mill Creek. Placement of the church near a deep-running stream or a pond was important because, until the early 1960s, rural churches in the Deep South performed baptisms in them. All of my friends and I were baptized in Mill Creek. About a mile from the church, Mill Creek ran right through the middle of my family's land.

Our congregation was fortunate in that our pastor remained with our church for some forty years. He was considered very sophisticated because he had attended a small Bible college in Selma, which was rare in those days. Moreover, there was never ever a hint of scandal with him. He had a wife and two children. His external and internal beliefs and values meshed. He did not talk one life and live another.

One of the most important lessons our minister impressed on his congregation, explicitly as well as implicitly, was the importance of critical thinking. Our preacher would get up and read from the Scriptures. For some of the elderly congregants who had limited ability to read and write, listening to him read from the Bible was the beginning of the thinking process. He also impressed upon us that, yes there were the Scriptures by which to be guided and from which to derive strength and hope, but there was also the life of the mind. He taught us to analyze situations and then to act using good judgment rather than to follow blindly what he or anyone else might try to dictate.

When I was a youngster, the church service was held on the first Sunday of each month. Sunday school happened each Sunday. On those Sundays when Sunday school was followed by the sermon, church was an all-day affair. Because people had little time to get together during the workweek, those first Sundays of the month were special. Everyone would catch up on each other's news over church meals after the sermon. The adult men and women would gather—separately—and share news or tell stories.

The largest church gatherings occurred in August, starting with revival on the first Sunday of the month. Our pastor always invited ministers from Birmingham, Mobile, Montgomery, or other places to come and preach. One year he brought the pastor of the 16th Street Baptist Church in Birmingham. Some ten years later, that church would be the target of a racist bombing. Most of the visiting preachers were college graduates, and it showed in their sermons, which both challenged and uplifted our congregation, as many members had little or no schooling.

It was to our pastor's credit that he endeavored to expand our world in this way. Indeed, preachers and church life were cherished throughout the rural South during the days of Jim Crow. The values instilled in me by my parents, extended family, and community were reinforced through living, working, and attending church together.

---

The southern diet of my childhood was tied to the land. Our meals generally consisted of meat that was raised or hunted, fish, and homegrown vegetables and fruits. My favorite foods then were squash, okra, and collard greens. Lard rendered from locally butchered hogs was used in baking as well as to fry the pork chops, bacon, chicken, and fish we ate.

Rounding out our diet were corn, flour, and molasses; what little refined sugar was available was generally used to sweeten tea. The high-calorie fare was needed for the strenuous labor done from dawn to dark, often in the blistering southern sun.

Into the 1930s, the plantation economy functioned much as it had before, although the number of farms increased dramatically as many freedmen established their own small farms.[3] As late as the 1950s, African American families in the Alabama Black Belt relied heavily on what was hunted or produced on the land. In the Alabama Black Belt, where gender roles were clearly defined, men hunted quail, partridge, turkey, rabbit, and deer. Men also did most of the fieldwork. Cotton was a cash crop, but they also grew corn and sugarcane; some grew peanuts. Women were in charge of preserving fruits and vegetables, and of food preparation, though children of both genders were frequently recruited to help.

Cornmeal and corn pone had been dietary staples since the days of slavery, which meant that corn was an important crop for farm families in my community. Our neighbor, Mr. Young, would allow his son Tat and me to take two mules with a load of corn in the wagon to Sweet Water to have the corn milled.

We would drop the corn off at the mill, and just could not wait to get to the general store, where the most massive sugar high awaited us. The southern delicacy for rural kids in the 1950s was a stage plank—two pieces of a molasses gingerbread with nothing between—and a moon pie, washed down with a Coke or a Nehi orange soda. Every now and then we would cut all that sugar with some salted peanuts. We would sit on a bench in the general store with our snacks and wait for the corn to be milled, along with the African American farmers waiting for their cotton to be ginned or their corn milled. The general store was where everyone gathered, deep in conversation, with their mule-drawn wagons tied up in the shade. Listening to the adults around us, Tat and I felt as if we were quite grown-up and on a great adventure.

Returning to the mill, we picked up the corn in huge sacks. Besides cornbread, the milled corn was used in our community to make grits—cornmeal that is boiled and flavored with butter, salt, and pepper. I did not know that grits were a signature southern dish until I was in the air force. There one day, as I was making my way through the mess hall queue, one of the line servers yelled out, "All you southern boys, we have something for you!" Next to me in line was an airman from Mississippi. He teasingly yelled back to the line server, "What is that white stuff? I've never seen that before. Is that ice cream?" The line server shot back, "Alright, you SOB, you know what it is. Get some and get out of here."

Sugarcane juice was extracted and slowly boiled to make molasses, which was used for sweetening and flavoring foods. My family got our molasses from Mr. Bouler. I would often go to help him for two or three hours at a time. As a thank-you, he would give me a tin cup of sugarcane juice.

Most all families had large gardens. It was primarily the domain of the women to care for the gardens except when heavy labor was needed to plant and cultivate. Families grew several types of peas and beans, melons, squash, beets, turnips, radishes, cucumbers, tomatoes, collards, sweet potatoes, white potatoes, and kale. Everyone grew okra, a vegetable brought to the Americas from Africa. As the produce ripened, my mom and other women in our community put up vegetables and made jams and jellies. Like many families, we had an orchard with peach, apple, pear, and fig trees, as well as a scuppernong arbor.

Harvesting and preserving the fruit was a big job supervised by the women of the household. My mom would get the neighborhood boys to pick the peaches. She allowed us to eat our fill, and still there was plenty. Out in our yard, she would set out huge tubs of the freshly picked fruit. We boys would peel the peaches before she cut them in half, boiled them, and put them up in jars to use throughout the winter.

Tied up in the cuisine of the Alabama Black Belt was the concept of communal affairs, where everyone gathered to help out and in so doing created bonds among people. Putting up peaches was not just a matter of pulling a peach off a tree and processing it; it involved conversation, laughter, and learning how to develop relationships with people of all ages. I'm not sure children today have the same opportunity I had to work with one another and to engage with adults. It seems as if almost all children now have a device that they are constantly looking at whether they are standing alone or sitting with others, even in a restaurant.

Most farm households had a couple of dairy cows to provide milk and butter, or to sell. My dad's brothers and their sons raised milk cows and did the milking. Dad, however, had about thirty head of beef cattle, which he would sell to make extra money for the family. Since nearly everyone had a few hogs and a flock of chickens, diets were naturally heavy on pork and chicken. Harvesting and butchering were always communal affairs, with families gathering to help each other with the labor-intensive processes. All would go home with a portion of the fruits of the labor.

One such activity was the butchering of hogs in the fall. Mr. Young was in charge, assigning everyone—men, women, and children—their specific job in this daylong process. One of my earliest memories is of standing in line waiting my turn to turn the handle of a grinder clamped to the edge of a table to make pork sausage. All us kids thought it was great fun, but we lasted only about five minutes at the crank, when our arms wore out and the next child eagerly took our place.

Almost nothing of the hog was thrown away. The intestines are boiled down to make chitlins and are then fried and seasoned. The skin, to which a layer of fat is still attached, is fried to make cracklings.

The hog meat itself was often preserved by smoking. My grandfather and Mr. Young had smokehouses. There they would hang hams and other cuts of the hog to cure, extending the shelf life of the meat without need for refrigeration.

When the harvest was complete and people had a break from toiling in the fields all day, families would fish for brim, perch, and catfish. One technique for catching fish was to build cotton baskets where the fish could swim in but could not swim out. People would drop the baskets down in the deep section of a creek. Another common practice was called muddying the waters. After heavy rains, the creeks would flood their banks and make temporary ponds that fish would get caught in. Families would gather on one end and, with hoes stirring the water, start walking in a long line straight across the pond. Choking in the muddy water and needing to breathe, the fish would raise their mouths up at the pond's surface. Then, everyone would scoop up the fish in makeshift sieves made from buckets punched with nail holes. I did this many times as a child. All the fish that were caught from bucket traps or from muddying the waters of a temporary pond were cleaned by the men of the community and prepared by the women.

I wasn't afraid to participate in muddying the waters, although I knew that when my dad was about fifteen years old, he had been bitten by a water moccasin while muddying in a pond. Feeling a sting, he lifted his foot and hanging from it by its fangs was a water moccasin. The family took him home to apply a home remedy, as was common in a community with little financial resources, scant trust of the medical system, and a tradition of self-reliance on natural remedies. In this case the home remedies didn't work, resulting in a nasty infection. Fortunately, my dad's older brother Richard insisted that the family take him to a doctor, which they finally did. The doctor tended to the wound, gave him a shot, and the leg eventually healed.

Desserts generally appeared only for special occasions. Known for her pound cakes, my mom would make them for church revival picnics. During my childhood in the 1950s, families would arrive at church in cars, others in mule-drawn wagons or horse-drawn buggies. Everyone sought out the shade so the food they had brought for the post-sermon meal would not overheat in the hot sun. Still, the food sat out for a long time while we listened—some of us restlessly—to the sermon. Today, knowing the importance of refrigeration for foods, my sister, Jean, and I laugh as we reminisce about those hot summer church meals and express our mutual astonishment that no one ever got sick.

Jean especially remembers celebrations of Emancipation Day in the 1930s. An entire hog would be roasted over an open pit for a communal barbecue to recognize the anniversary of President Abraham Lincoln's signing of the Emancipation Proclamation on January 1, 1863. Everyone who could from the community would attend these celebrations.

Today, a meal of fried chicken, collard greens, squash, corn, and okra evokes memories of more than just food-to-sustain. It brings back good feelings of family and community. I grew up eating a diet that had been shaped by race, history, and culture. As I grew older and was exposed to knowledge and information from being in the military, traveling around the world, and going to college, I began to understand the relationship between cause and effect, which in turn allowed me to apply logic and reason to a given situation, rather than just lean on culture and history. That was rarely easy. It can take willpower and mental gymnastics to have reason win out over culture.

Developing a cross-cultural appreciation for how food is prepared and consumed allowed me to think about optimal weights and a health-conscious way of life, as well as the types of things that can happen when people develop lifestyles different from those in the past (e.g., today's sedentary lifestyle leading to obesity, high-sugar diets leading to diabetes).

---

As I've noted, my closest friend growing up was Tat. He loved my mom and dad, and they, in turn, liked and trusted him. From a young age,

Mom would sometimes let me hang out with him, and through Tat I first started listening to music.

Before desegregation, juke joints were one of the few places African American adults could congregate after a hard workweek. Like old working-class Irish pubs, juke joints were places to eat, drink, and listen to music. On Friday nights when I was about ten years old, I would walk with Tat to Peggy's Place that was about a mile down the road from our house. My parents didn't frequent the place because of their roles as teachers in the community, but many of the patrons knew my family, and I knew them.

Our county was dry, but the juke joint owners got around the prohibition by making their own whiskey and beer to serve the hardworking people who had toiled all week with the endless chores of farming or working in sawmills. As in many cultures, often the workers came to the pub directly from the fields or from the mills. The basic fare sold there was fried chicken or fish served with hot sauce and white bread.

Tat and I usually didn't get there until after dark. Since I was too young to go in, I would find a place to sit across the road to wait for Tat. I would sit on the dewy grass, and with eyes closed, legs crossed, and leaning against a bank that was shaped like a berm, soak up the music from a distance for the couple of hours Tat was inside. I loved the music, and I loved listening to the stories the songs told. Most of the songs captured our southern agrarian culture or told about faraway places, leaving me to daydream about leaving Marengo County and seeing the outside world.

Having first been exposed to blues at Peggy's Place, I started listening to a Nashville radio station. WLAC was a pioneer in the early 1950s by airing rhythm and blues.[4] Later, my sister bought me a record player. Almost eleven years older than I, Jean began her teaching career and married in the mid-1950s. With her first paycheck, she bought me a record player from the Sears, Roebuck and Company in Selma. I started buying my own 78s—what people now call "vinyl." I would order the albums from Randy's Record Shop or Ernie's Record Mart. The first album I ever bought was B.B. King's 1955 release of "Every Day I Have the Blues."

The records were of what was then called "race music." Muddy Waters, John Lee Hooker, Elmore James, Howlin' Wolf, B.B. King, and Jimmy Reed all hailed from Mississippi, where the blues were born. The same type of music, sung by southerners who came off the land, was being played in Southwest Alabama during my childhood. When it started being played on radio stations like WLAC, it became more widely integrated into the lifestyle and culture of the people.

As a young teen, I just loved the music. As an adult, I studied its history and developed an appreciation for its genesis from slavery. The people delivered on the American continent to be sold into slavery came from many different backgrounds. They had no common language, literature, or culture. Out of their common bondage, and over time, a musical genre was created in the South that was uniquely American. The music was mostly vocal music often accompanied by guitar and sung by self-taught black men, though many of the early recordings were by women. It grew out of work songs, "field hollers," and church music.[5] The music by artists in the Mississippi Delta would become a major influence on later genres.[6]

Between listening to the music at Peggy's Place, listening to WLAC, and purchasing records from Randy's and Ernie's, I developed a lifelong love of blues. The stories, the feelings expressed, and the soulful sounds of blues captivated me then and now. For me, blues reflected black culture. It grew out of work, marginalization, anger, hatred, love—all the human emotions and conditions. The rhythms and sounds are spellbinding, but what is really powerful for me are the lyrics, the story behind each song. Blues has stayed *in* me, helping me to get through hard times and to celebrate good times.

Perhaps like many teenagers, I felt that there was a certain incongruity about my life. I was immersed in an agrarian community surrounded by hardworking people who toiled all day in the hot sun of the South and relaxed at Peggy's Place after sundown. Too young to go in myself, I reveled outside listening to the earthy soulful blues playing inside. Later that night, I would be back home in bed, reading every book I could get my hands on until almost dawn. Juke joints and blues, and reading books were not natural allies, and maybe I thrived because I relished both. I not only loved the land, the people, and the music of my community, but I also loved access to my country, the world, and the universe through books.

Blues, southern foods, gatherings of family, friends, and neighbors during the communal tasks of farm life and at church in the mid-twentieth century in an isolated corner of Southwest Alabama form the foundation on which I became an adult. I've carried the values instilled during those years with me throughout my years as a university administrator. They became particularly relevant as I worked to understand the cultural underpinnings of Albany and its university some sixty years later.

CHAPTER 3

# Navigating Jim Crow

Many people younger than those in my generation are unaware of what life was like for nearly a hundred years after the U.S. Civil War. They are not aware of the rules, laws, customs, policies, and regulations slapped into place to control the lives of African Americans. With slavery legally abolished after the Civil War, whites got creative with the legal system to continue to oppress and marginalize African Americans both physically and socially. In addition to the laws, whites used practices, customs, and codes—backed up by ready use of violence—to maintain a caste system based on skin color.

In my home state of Alabama, between 1865 and 1965 almost thirty Jim Crow laws were passed, including amendments to the state's constitution, statutes, state codes, and city council ordinances and resolutions. We can think of those laws as being organized in a pyramid, with the most egregious—even deadly—laws at the apex, and the most petty and pitiful at the bottom. At the pinnacle of the Jim Crow pyramid of laws were those that encroached on the most personal aspect of human interaction. In the 1860s in Alabama, the first Jim Crow laws banned interracial marriages, but it was by no means the only state, and not the first, to institute antimiscegenation laws. Some states even criminalized officiating at interracial marriages.

The airman who had the bunk above mine when we served together at Tainan Air Station in Taiwan was from Philadelphia of Italian descent and married a Taiwanese woman. When he and other airmen, soldiers, and sailors who married women of "other" races were rotated back to the United States in the 1960s, they couldn't be stationed in the South, where antimiscegenation laws remained in place until the U.S. Supreme Court *Loving v. Virginia* ruling in 1967. Alabama was the last state to remove antimiscegenation language from its constitution—in 2000.[1]

A handful of Alabama's Jim Crow laws dictated that blacks and whites could not be educated in the same schools, and libraries were also segregated. When I was growing up in the 1950s, the only public library nearby was in Linden. It was for white patrons only. Access to public libraries would become one of the rights that people pressed for during the 1960s civil rights movement. Nonviolent attempts to secure library cards were frequently met with violence. In the fall of 1963, two African American ministers entered the all-white public library in Anniston, two hundred miles northeast of my hometown, to apply for library cards. They were met by a mob of angry whites who "struck the ministers with sticks, fists, and a chain." The two tried to escape in a car but were blocked. They then ran on foot, where they were picked up by a passing motorist and taken to the hospital.[2]

The extent and detail of Jim Crow laws reached far beyond schools and libraries into mental facilities, prisons, public transportation (e.g., railroads, buses) waiting rooms and seating, hospitals, restaurants, restrooms, and entertainment venues, creating a social structure that permeated every aspect of life. As I've already mentioned, there was no safe place for African Americans to wait or be at rest in a city, unless we stayed put in a place designated for "coloreds." In Selma, the "colored" waiting room of the Greyhound bus station was the only public area where we could wait without being molested by police or white passersby. When Mom was shopping in Selma, either Dad and I sat in the car and waited, or we sat in this colored waiting room. Blacks did not dare wait in the street or sit on a public bench. The extreme limitations on our movements made a great impression on me growing up in the 1950s.

When blacks and whites did come into contact, strict codes and customs governed interactions. For example, when I was about twelve years old, a young white doctor, freshly graduated from the University of Alabama, but originally not from the South, set up a practice in Linden. Not long after arriving, he was walking down Main Street. On the sidewalk stood an African American man. The young doctor stopped and spoke with him, and then shook his hand. As in a scene from the *Andy Griffith Show*, all the white shopkeepers peered out of their windows, watching as the young doctor shook this man's hand. Those shopkeepers made such an uproar over the next couple of days that the doctor had to make up a story that he was handing the man something, not shaking his hand. Any human-to-human gesture that resembled equality was taboo because it went against the code of superior-subordinate.

Life for African Americans in the South continued to be dangerous long after slavery and the Civil War ended. When I was growing up in the 1950s Alabama Black Belt, my family subscribed to newspapers and periodicals that informed us of the African American schools vandalized, churches burned, and innocent people tortured and murdered by whites in lynchings around the South. These horrors ricocheted around the nation, especially in the black press.

I began to realize that I had been living in a safe, close-knit community, protected by my family and neighbors. The more I read, the more I appreciated how exposed people were in rural areas. One June evening in the mid-1950s, I experienced the fear of racial violence firsthand. A man pulled his pickup truck up very close to our house on the farm. No one had ever driven right up to the front door of the house, across the lawn. In those days, families often sat outside in their yards. Our family would sit under a huge pecan tree in our front yard. Anybody who came up, like someone from the power company to read the meter, would park away from the house. So, it was strange to have someone park so close to the front door.

My parents and I were inside the house that time of night. When I looked out the door, I saw a white man, a neighbor, getting out of the truck. He was angry, menacing, and clearly intoxicated. I called to my dad, who went out to meet him. I followed Dad outside, but he directed me to go back in the house, and I obeyed.

In the few seconds that it took my dad to walk out to the man, three feelings welled up in me at the same time: fear, anger, and resolve. I felt for the first time the danger of living in the Alabama Black Belt. Images of Emmett Till and of the Scottsboro Boys sprang to mind. I sensed that my dad was in danger. I thought the man had a gun, since everyone in those days had a gun rack in their pickup truck.

I got out my rifle. From my perspective as a young boy, this man coming up to the house presented a danger and a challenge of abuse and hostility. My dad was out there with an angry white man. The two men were standing close. Dad was calm, the other belligerent. I had no idea where this was going to lead.

I put one cartridge in the chamber and ten in the magazine. I stood right by the door where Dad couldn't see me. I had become an expert shot at snakes and squirrels, but in that moment I knew I would have shot the man had he done anything to hurt my dad. Fortunately, after about ten minutes, Dad turned and walked back toward the house, and the man got back into his truck and drove off. I quickly put away my rifle so my dad didn't see what I was prepared to do.

My dad never mentioned the incident to me, then or even years later. At that time, parents protecting their children involved not talking to them about the realities of the world or about difficulties and traumas. I, in turn, never told him that I had fetched my rifle. Had I ever told him, he would have been angry because he knew then what I have since learned. My life's whole trajectory would have changed completely and irrevocably had I fired the weapon.

My dad had told me, "You go back in the house, and I'll take care of this." Although I trusted him, I didn't trust what the other man might do. This was our land, and this white intruder was on it. I was fully aware that the situation could unravel. Still, kids are kids, and they don't always do the right thing, nor are they always cognizant of the consequences of their actions, no matter how well-intentioned. I understand now that I had a knee-jerk, fight-or-flight response to what I perceived as a threat to my family and our land, knowing no one was there to step in to help us. My dad, on the other hand, took a rational, nonthreatening approach to de-escalate the situation and calm the man down.

The isolated section of Alabama we lived in was not a friendly environment for African Americans. No one at that time would have ever considered calling the county sheriff. On the rare occasions the sheriff did come down from Linden, people knew they were going to get a bad deal, so they did whatever they could to avoid calling the constable. Unless things really got bad, they tried to self-regulate. It was a self-policing environment, not least because African Americans who wound up being charged with a crime, particularly a violent one, knew their chances of being acquitted by the inevitably all-white jury were zero.

The short answer to the question of what had set off that white neighbor on that long-ago June evening is that he felt that his superiority over a black man was being threatened. At that time, his access to his property was on a dirt road that ran through the middle of our property, causing a lot of damage to the land. While the man had a right-of-way to access his property, he had no right to dictate where the road was located.

My dad had explained to him his plan to move the road over to the fence line, where the damage would be minimal. Dad's plan would actually benefit this man because after laying out the new road, he would provide a deed for the man to own the road. The man could then build the road up with gravel and maintain it over time.

The neighbor was already simmering over a black man having the right to change something that affected him, a white man, but drinking set him off that evening. My dad was in no way denying our neighbor his rightful access to his own land but was merely asking him to drive instead on the new road—ultimately a better road. He defused the volatile situation that June evening by remaining calm and saying quietly but firmly his intention to go through with the plan to move the road.

The point of this story is threefold. First, it represents the minefield that blacks negotiated in the course of their daily lives in the Jim Crow era. Second, it exemplifies the stereotype of the day that African Americans who owned land were "uppity" and rejected their place in the superior-subordinate system. Finally, an understanding of what African Americans had to endure under Jim Crow provides some insight into the feelings of Otherness, marginalization, and victimization that many blacks still endure today.

Martin Luther King Jr. captured the essence of what this life was like, and why people were pressing hard for change, in his 1963 "Letter from Birmingham Jail": "when you are harried by day and haunted by night by the fact that you are a Negro, living constantly at tiptoe stance, never knowing what to expect next, and plagued with inner fears and outer resentments; when you are forever fighting a degenerating sense of 'nobodyness'—then you will understand."[3]

The deep scars left from generations of degradations that persist today explain the unreconciled intensity of race in this country. I have seen these feelings of past wrongs surface over and over again in the workplace. In my years working in the University System of Georgia headquarters in Atlanta, and as president of Albany State University, I witnessed firsthand the emotional wounds of Jim Crow in how some African Americans interacted with whites, even half a century after the end of legal segregation.

CHAPTER 4

# The Will to Learn

The history of education for African Americans in Alabama and around the South is almost hard to believe. During slavery, antiliteracy laws made it a crime for blacks to learn to read and write and for anyone to teach them.[1] Among the mandates of the Freedmen's Bureau, established by the U.S. Congress toward the end of the Civil War, was helping freed people establish schools. In the seven short years that the bureau operated, some three thousand schools were established for freed slaves across the South.[2] Church missionaries and northern white philanthropists founded schools for African American children in an attempt to compensate for the state's lack of interest and support.

In Alabama after the war, the state eventually created a dual system of education, one system for black students, and one for whites. Both systems were poorly funded, so there were almost no educational opportunities in Alabama for my grandparents' generation after the Civil War. My grandmother could sign her name, and she could write letters. My grandfather, when asked to sign something (e.g., ownership of his cattle and wagon), had to put an "X." He could neither read nor write. For my grandparents, raising a family in Marengo County in the 1910s, the catalyst for providing education for the community's black children was a mutual respect and friendship cultivated between two men, Booker T. Washington—the freed slave who became an education advocate and activist—and Julius Rosenwald, a northern philanthropist.

Washington and Rosenwald met in 1911 and became friends.[3] To celebrate his fiftieth birthday in 1912, Rosenwald made a number of philanthropic gifts, including one to Washington at Tuskegee. Concerned about the lack of education for the South's black children, Washington asked to use some of the money to build elementary schools near the Tuskegee Institute. Rosenwald agreed, and the first Rosenwald school was built close to Tuskegee in 1913. Over the next twenty years, Rosenwald, through his Rosenwald Foundation, partnered with communities to build more than five thousand schools in fifteen southern states.[4]

The Rosenwald schools are one of the most well-kept secrets about the education of African Americans in the Jim Crow South. Rosenwald and Washington came up with the simple concept that everybody who benefited from a school should have skin in the game. There were no free lunches, so to speak. Thus, the state and the community had to each contribute funds to the project. It was a magnificently simple process using an almost universal principle: to nurture people of strength, people have to have invested in it themselves.

In 1918, my grandfather and two other men in the community pooled their resources to purchase a plot of land for $300 as part of the partnership with the Rosenwald Foundation and the state to build a Rosenwald school in Marengo County. I still have the 1918 letter that George Watson, the superintendent of schools in Marengo County, Alabama, sent my grandfather setting out the terms of the project. That first Rosenwald school built in Marengo County in 1919 served grades one through six. The curriculum focused on the foundations of a liberal education: reading, writing, and arithmetic.

Some of my grandparents' eleven children attended the Rosenwald school. There they engaged not only in an academic process but also in a socialization process. Many of the children came from families eager to enjoy the pleasures of leisure time (e.g., social gatherings, dances, movies). Teachers at the Rosenwald schools helped by elevating the children's social skills. To do so, on Saturday evenings, the school's two teachers would open the schoolhouse as an entertainment venue. The lead teacher, Miss Carrie Carter—as everyone always called her—organized the activities.

The Rosenwald school was about a mile from our family farm. All of the children in the area, accompanied by two or three adults, would walk down to the school on Saturday evenings. Mr. Young ushered people through the door and kept order inside. He was kind but firm. If he walked up and told us, "Boys, you need to calm down," no one disrespected him.

The program for those Saturday entertainment nights always had three elements. First, they almost always showed a movie—mostly westerns—

on a film projector owned by a community member who was a veteran of World War II. Then they showed an episode from a serial film. Popular from the 1910s through the 1950s, these were films carved up into a dozen or so "chapters." There was a hero who usually had a sidekick and who gave orders to his henchmen. The stories involved plenty of action. So, for example, a chapter might end with the hero riding off a cliff, making us wait until the next week to see what happened to him. We children would get all energized and excited about what was going to happen each week.

The last item on the program was blues played on a record player that someone had brought. Some of the children would dance, others would run outside and play. In the midst of showing the movie and listening to the music, the adults put out food. Typically, they served white bread, fried fish, and hot dogs. The entire evening lasted no more than a few hours because the children had to get home, and the adults were tired. Today, the simplicity and predictability of those evenings would be almost unthinkable.

Apart from the educational programs they offered, the Rosenwald schools were the only places where African American youngsters could congregate to socialize and relax. Adults had the juke joints; we children and teens had the Rosenwald schools.

Learning the history of Rosenwald schools and the significance of them to my family helped me understand the importance of cooperation, collaboration, and leverage, a crucial life lesson. This example was front and center in my mind throughout my career as an educator, and most importantly when I was president at Albany State.

As the world entered the twentieth century, education in Alabama was poorly funded, the system for black children abysmally so. Rural black children had it worst of all: in 1924, white urban schools of Alabama taught about 174 days per school year; black rural schools about 87 days.[5] In other words, African American rural children received half as much educational opportunity each year as their white urban peers.

Another life lesson that has stuck with me is the lengths people and families will go to educate themselves and their children when the cards are stacked against them. Family lore held that my grandfather was the labor provider for food, shelter, and clothing; my grandmother was the thinker and doer about scholarship. A story has been passed down in my family about how the two found a way to educate their children.

In the 1890s, a circuit preacher would ride in on horseback to spend a week in town for the revival held at their church. The deacons provided the preacher food and lodging. During one such revival, the preacher spent time at Delia and Willis's home. As the adults sat on the porch on those hot August evenings, they watched and listened to the children playing in the yard. The preacher, observing the children, said to my grandmother, "Delia, are you going to do much with those children? They seem to be very apt. There's a school down in Thomasville that they're just starting for coloreds. You ought to think about sending them there."

Delia replied, "Parson, I don't plan for my children to stay around here. I don't know quite how to do this, but if you can help me talk to the people down there and see if some can work in the kitchen washing dishes and helping 'round the school to help pay—we don't have much money. What you said to me is exactly what I'd like to do. Get these children, especially my boys, away from here to study."

"I'd be glad to do that," he answered. And so Delia orchestrated a sequence. One son would go to the school in Thomasville, about fifteen miles south of Sweet Water. Once settled in the school and working there, he would pave the way for the next son by saying that another brother would be coming, and "Could he do the same kind of jobs to help pay his way?"

Grandmother was determined that her sons not grow up to be farmers. She herself had never been far from home, but she knew she wanted her children to get an education and get out of Marengo County, even though it would ultimately mean the end of the family's way of life, as the farm could not survive without men to do the labor.

The state of Alabama's education for African Americans in the early 1900s can be seen through the story of two of my grandfather's eight sons. Richard was my grandparents' fifth of eleven children. My dad, Arthur, was a couple of years younger. When Richard completed the sixth and final grade in Sweet Water's Rosenwald school, he attended a boarding school in Thomasville that continued through the ninth grade.

There was no high school for him to attend in Marengo County, so Richard had to travel over a hundred miles northeast to Montgomery to attend the Alabama State College Laboratory High School. The Lab High School was a teacher training school within Alabama State Teachers College, what would become Alabama State University. There, black teens from rural areas got a high school education while adults were trained to become teachers through on-the-job practice teaching.

While in school there, Richard boarded with a local family, as did many young people from rural areas. Families in Montgomery provided housing in exchange for chores. A Jewish family gave Richard a bunk in the basement of their home in exchange for his keeping up the yard and house and maintaining the coal furnace. When Richard completed high school, Arthur was right behind him. Richard asked the family if Arthur could have the same arrangement. They agreed.

After high school, Richard secured a summer job as a Pullman porter on the transcontinental railroad from Quebec City to Vancouver. Between this summer job and a job during the year in the university's cafeteria, Richard was able to attend Fisk University in Nashville, which in the 1920s and 1930s was considered part of the Ivy League of black universities. After he graduated, Richard went on to a sales career in the life insurance industry.

Arthur, after graduating from the Alabama State Laboratory School, attended Morehouse College in Atlanta. It was, however, so expensive that after only one semester he had to return to Alabama to continue his education at Alabama State College. Richard had asked the railroad's hiring agent to consider hiring his brother. In that way, Arthur came to work summers as a Pullman porter in Canada, as his brother had, making beds and serving food on the trains, in order to pay for his first two years of college.

In the late 1920s and early 1930s in the Alabama Black Belt, students could begin teaching in rural black grade schools after having completed only two years of college, which was in any case far beyond what most in those communities had achieved. Many children had to stop their schooling at about the fifth or sixth grade to help on their parents' farms. Teaching in such grade schools was how Arthur, my dad, started his career, and how he earned enough money to complete his college degree.

His first teaching position was as the sole teacher in a one-room schoolhouse in Cuba in Sumter County, Alabama. He roomed with a landowning family, and the community provided food. A receipt—a piece of paper torn from a legal pad—shows that he made $27.50 per month. He returned to Alabama State every summer until he earned his undergraduate degree. He became a lifelong educator.

My mom was also resolved to get an education. Born in the first decade of the twentieth century, she, too, was raised in a family where scholarship was essential. Not satisfied with the school options in Thomasville, my mom's parents put her on a train for a fifteen-mile trip to the adjacent Wilcox County, where she attended a boarding school for African American children. The school was established and run by a group of missionaries from the North. There, her parents felt, my mom would be exposed to a broader curriculum. Having graduated from that school, she went to college at Alabama State. Like my dad, she started her teaching career after two years of college, studying in the summers to complete her degree in the early 1930s.

Before I came along, when my parents headed off to Montgomery for the summer to take classes, my sister would stay with my paternal grandparents. To help them make ends meet while they were away, Grandmother would load them up with food from the garden. Years later, my mom told me, shaking her head with a smile, "One time we looked like folks heading out from Oklahoma during the Great Depression."

"I'd have been embarrassed to do that," I cringed.

"Well you wouldn't have eaten, then!," Mom chuckled.

It is interesting to me how every summer they went back to school. They were determined to complete their degrees. Even after my dad earned his bachelor's degree, he took summer graduate courses. He did that for many years, earning a master's degree from Alabama State in 1949. Theirs was a tale of individual and mutual endurance and persistence.

When I came along, my parents were teachers in a two-room schoolhouse in Putnam in Marengo County, about ten miles from my grandfather's farm. In many farming communities, the largest landowner typically provided a place for the teachers and their families to stay, because that family generally had the means to assume the additional burden. So, as my dad had done when he taught in Cuba, Alabama, in Putnam the three of us boarded with a landowning family (my sister was away at boarding school). They owned five hundred acres of rich bottomland on the Tombigbee River and had three children who attended the school. On weekends, the three of us returned to the family farm in Sweet Water.

Closer to our family land was the Rosenwald school that my grandfather had helped found. A second Rosenwald school, the John Essex School, had been built in 1925–26. Originally a two-room schoolhouse that served grades one through eight, it later expanded to provide schooling through the twelfth grade.

When I was about six years old, my parents left the Putnam school and moved to the John Essex School, where my dad was both the principal and a math teacher, and my mom taught first grade. After four years, my dad became principal at Linden Academy (later renamed George P. Austin High School) about twenty miles from our home. Linden Academy was a first- through twelfth-grade school. Again, my mom followed him. For her entire career she taught first grade and my dad was her supervisor.

Each of these schools was segregated under the doctrine of "separate but equal." They were anything but. There were two school systems both governed by a white superintendent and school board. The black schools were given paltry funding and little supervision. Throughout their careers, my parents struggled to navigate young African American students from elementary through high school with almost no resources from the county or state.

For the white high school in Linden, the county purchased one set of books for the year. At the end of the school year, the used books would be sent over to the colored school. A lot of the books were written in, damaged, or had pages torn out of them.

By the same token, the only school furniture colored schools had access to was whatever was deemed no longer usable in the white schools. My dad led an annual ritual in the fall. Gathering a dozen or more teenage boys, they would ride in a friend's truck over to the white high school in Linden to collect the used, often broken, unwanted desks. Carpenters in our community would repair the desks for Linden Academy.

This allocation of resources and distribution of broken-down educational materials occurred throughout the Alabama Black Belt and elsewhere across the South. All county school systems were run by whites, who were not about to purchase anything for the African American schools, which were supposed to make do with the cast-offs.

Teacher pay for African Americans was far below what white teachers made. My dad often told the story of how, one day in the mid-1950s, he was listening to Big Jim Folsom, who was running for governor. A large, tall man, Folsom was well-known for being a heavy drinker and a womanizer. He ran on a populist platform, appealing to African Americans by saying, "If you elect me governor, I'll raise the pay of colored school teachers equal to that of white teachers." At the time, that would have brought the monthly wages up to about forty-six dollars. My dad had a wry sense of humor. He laughed, "If I made that much money, I wouldn't know what to do with it all."

My parents remained stoic about the low salaries for teachers. Unlike the uncertain fortunes of farming, a teacher's pay was a predictable wage.

Their neighbors, who were farmers, had hit-or-miss incomes depending on how the cotton was coming in and how much it brought at market. We were fortunate because my parents were able to supplement their regular teachers' salaries with raising cattle, growing timber, and renting some of their land to farmers in the community.

Despite their salaries being almost half of what white teachers earned, my parents were dedicated teachers. They were resilient and creative in their efforts to secure their own education and later to educate the African American children of Marengo County in the Jim Crow era.

My dad always said that he and my mom were "teachers seven days a week." For decades, he taught teenage boys in Sunday school in the church that his father helped establish. My dad had a real gift for connecting with young teenage boys. My mom taught Sunday school to the adult women of the church.

When I think back, I am awed at how members of our community revered and respected my parents. A local boy, my dad had gone off to college, done well, and returned to Marengo County to help educate his community. So, anything he said about the education of children, people paid attention to him. Likewise, my mom enjoyed the respect of Marengo County residents.

In later years during my travels, especially in Africa, I saw again how scholarship can flourish in remote rural areas. In the villages there was always a headmaster of the local schools. The children wore uniforms, and all obeyed what the headmaster said. We had lived out on the land in one of the most remote places of the United States. My dad functioned very much like those African headmasters. If he said something, the children paid attention. He was the decision maker.

I learned from my parents and extended family that living in a closed, segregated system of disenfranchisement was no excuse not to try to excel. In fact, I was acculturated to understand that, in an integrated world, being average was definitely not sufficient for blacks. My dad modeled that living up to high expectations was just what we were supposed to do. His philosophy was, "You're supposed to be doing well. It's just what you do." My parents both instilled in me the idea that I could work to be elite—being very good at something—without being elitist, which would have estranged me from my community. This was the philosophy I took with me to Albany State University in the 2010s. It is a philosophy, however, that would be challenged in ways I could not have anticipated.

About the Jim Crow system, my mom always said, "You have all these choices you can make. These other things are going to take care of themselves over time." My dad's position was that "the system of legal segregation cannot sustain itself. It will crack under its immoral stance. In the meantime, there is something called 'personal development' for performance academically and for achievement that you do have control over."

One avenue that allowed us to engage in friendly competition with one another with the goal of improving ourselves came in the form of oratorical contests sponsored by the black Elks Club. Contestants were judged on public speaking skills of delivery, articulation, pronunciation, and topic. We weren't judged against a phony standard of white speech, since we were rarely in contact with whites. So, rather than these contests being an exercise in affectation, they gave rural blacks an opportunity to work on self-improvement.

---

My education in the 1950s was a combination of formal schooling, learning hands-on from people in our community, attending 4-H summer camp, and reading on my own. One of my earliest memories is of accompanying my parents as they walked to their jobs in the schoolhouse in Putnam each day. As we walked, children would be waiting along the road to join us. We walked along a wooded area, crossed a stream, and continued along fields with barbed-wire fences. One farmer had built a set of stairs for his children to climb over the barbed-wire fence, rather than having to duck under. I was too young to start school but was placed under the wing of a woman who taught the other first-grade section. My mom expected me to observe quietly and stay out of the way, but when I got in the class I started participating like the rest of the students. Soon the teacher told my mom that I was doing extremely well. She said, "He's not but five, but he could go into first grade." The schools were segregated, and the Marengo County School Board certainly didn't care that one African American child started first grade before time, so I started school early, with my mom teaching in the adjoining room.

What undoubtedly put me ahead of my peers was that my dad had been reading to my sister and me since we were very young. After each bedtime story, he would explain the moral of the story. It was our earliest introduction to the skills of critical thinking.

After first grade in Putnam, I attended the John Essex School and later Linden Academy. My parents were teachers in each of these schools, but I think they saw to it that I was never taught by either one of them. My dad was also the principal, but that never caused a problem.

Throughout my school years, I had more men than women as teachers. Many of the teachers in my high school were U.S. military veterans of World War II or the Korean War. Military service had been a means for many southern black men to get out of the South and experience the world. Once they returned home from Europe and Asia, the GI Bill financed college educations for veterans, black and white. In the South, African American veterans attended the Tuskegee Institute, the Alabama Agricultural and Mechanical College, Alabama State College, or other universities. Many of them settled in small towns or out on the land. With few other job opportunities for educated black men during the Jim Crow era, they often became public-school teachers, going on to be leaders in their segregated communities. Together, military service and the GI Bill helped these men become members of a black middle class.

Having such distinguished men for teachers was an extraordinary gift for me and my classmates. From studying math, chemistry, and English with these gifted teachers, I learned and understood the skills of problem solving, analysis, and communication. Each teacher stressed reaching for a high standard of excellence. A student who was striving was never accused of "trying to be white," not least because we had no idea what that might entail. In those segregated days, we had no idea what they were doing in the white schools, so we were able to navigate through difficult subjects without holding ourselves up to that comparison. Instead, we were working toward a universal standard.

---

Outside of school, I learned a lot by helping our neighbor farmers, whether piling up branches that Mr. Young cut off when preparing firewood or helping our neighbor, Mr. Bouler, produce molasses. Much of what was done on the land was skills driven, and it was passed down from generation to generation.

Mr. Bouler was unusually wise but also taciturn, so he didn't talk much in public. When it was just the two of us, however, he opened up and we had good exchanges. He and I had a mutually beneficial relationship: I helped him, and he was among my elders who taught me how to think critically.

As a nine-year-old, I watched Mr. Bouler commandeer creativity and ingenuity to improve his processes on the land. When he made molasses to sell, I would watch as he experimented by varying the size of the cooking pans in order to find the ideal depth and width for cooking molasses in the shortest period of time. Mr. Bouler modeled thinking deeply about innovation.

A hundred yards or so beyond Mr. Bouler lived the Smiley family. After helping Mr. Bouler, I would often walk over to visit the Smileys, who had several children considerably older than me. The family kept cattle and horses on their forty acres. I spent a lot of time at the Smileys', much of it riding some of their horses.

Mr. Smiley was an extraordinary storyteller in the southern tradition. He would keep us teenage boys in stitches with his stories. The stuff he would tell would not come close to being risqué today, but every now and then he would say something racy enough that Mrs. Smiley would come out on the porch and tell him to temper it.

Mr. Smiley was also a gifted farmer and hunter. As he grew older, his eyesight failed, but he had acute hearing and understood the sounds of the land. We would be sitting on the porch and he would detail to us what he was hearing. One day, he told his son, "Robert Lee, go in the house and get the rifle. The dogs are getting ready to run that deer across the road."

None of us kids had seen or heard a deer, though we could hear the dogs barking excitedly. Robert Lee, who was an exceptionally good shot, obeyed his father. Mr. Smiley gave precise instructions to his son about exactly where he should stand and exactly when the deer would be close enough for a clear shot. When the deer leapt into view just where Mr. Smiley told his son it would be, Robert Lee hit it in midair with a perfect shot.

Mr. Smiley's keen knowledge of the land had just provided venison for the family. He was wise and participated in the tradition of transmitting his knowledge to the next generation through stories and instruction. Not having had the chance to attend school for long, Mr. Smiley respected education, as did everyone in my community. He found some of the things I would come up with from books I was reading amusing. He enjoyed hearing about my book learning, but teased me, "Boy, they're going to keep you in school so long you won't be fit to do anything."

In many ways, my worldview of blackness and of work ethic was shaped by World War II veterans like Mr. Bouler and farmers like Mr. Smiley who lived deep in the forested areas of the Alabama Black Belt. They had an intense work ethic coupled with a strong sense of self and family, and of respectability and responsibility.

Indeed, a strong work ethic and desire for self-improvement ran deep in our community and throughout the Alabama Black Belt despite the scarcity and lack of educational opportunities. People had to work hard to sustain life at the most basic levels—food, shelter, and clothing. But that drive for self-improvement could make good things happen, too, if a person was just given half a chance. A cousin of my dad married a young man who had been raised by our neighbor, Mr. Young. The young man had a little land but was also a sharecropper. As soon as our cousin married him, she encouraged him to make a move a few miles away, where her family gave them a parcel of land for their own. Once they owned their own land, they thrived because they were dedicated and prepared to work hard.

I learned mostly through the efforts of my parents and teachers and through books. To encourage us to think for ourselves, my parents would lay out small opportunities for me to run with. For example, the summer I was ten, my dad returned from his graduate courses in Montgomery with an orange basketball goal, knowing I loved playing basketball. He handed it to me, saying simply, "Here's your goal. You guys go out and figure out what to do with it." My friends and I found some old lumber to create a backboard. Then we went and cut the two straightest trees we could find and put up the goal in the yard.

We boys played so much that we turned the lawn into dirt. Realizing pretty early on that I would never be tall and big enough to be a basketball superstar didn't stop me from playing or diminish my enthusiasm for the game. At night, with the lights on, I would shoot that ball for hours.

Naturally right handed, I decided to learn how to shoot with my left so someone, knowing I was right handed, couldn't overplay me on the right side. I wanted to surprise them by using my left hand. I ordered a book about how to make yourself ambidextrous. To train myself to use my nondominant hand, I started doing simple things with my left hand, like opening doors and tying my shoes. I kept at it until I could shoot a layup and a short hook with either hand. It gave me an advantage and made me more of a whole player. I ordered a lot of books about sports, especially basketball, so that I could learn how to improve things like my jump shot, layup, and hook shot. I would see later how consistent and persistent efforts at self-improvement would pay off.

One organized educational opportunity for young people presented itself in my teen years. In the mid-1950s, the Tuskegee Institute started a 4-H summer camp for African American youth. When I was thirteen, my dad sent me to the two-week program even though I really wanted to stay home. He, however, was of the generation of parents that didn't discuss decisions with the children. It was a very hierarchical family structure, with the men in charge. When my dad said, "You're going to spend two weeks at Tuskegee," that was as much of a discussion as there was going to be. I went. Telling him that I didn't want to go didn't even occur to me.

Each summer of my teen years, Mr. Charles Forman rounded up all the young boys (me included) and girls to pack into two cars to drive to Tuskegee for the two-week 4-H camp. I think he saw a bunch of youngsters with potential who lived in an isolated section of the state and who needed some exposure to the larger world. A kind, thoughtful, soft-spoken man, Mr. Forman was another World War II veteran who had a major impact on my life.

He had a 1954 Chevrolet and enlisted a second driver for a rented Ford. The boys were in one car, the girls in another. We drove 150 miles northeast from Marengo County to the Tuskegee Institute in Macon County.

I remember being awed by the magnificent physical set of buildings on the campus. To me as a young teenager, the Tuskegee Institute was a very elegant place. Students came there from all over the country because of Booker T. Washington's renown. The place was a big deal. Despite my initial resistance to going, once I got there I loved the program.

For a young teen like me from a rural region where most people had little or no education, the Tuskegee campus and all it offered and represented was almost overwhelming. Tuskegee had a wide variety of academic programs as well as air force and army Reserve Officer Training Corps (ROTC) programs. Among Tuskegee's ROTC graduates was Daniel "Chappie" James Jr., who became a U.S. Air Force fighter pilot and later the first African American to rise to the rank of four-star general. Going to Tuskegee and seeing African Americans at Tuskegee in the 1950s in army and air force ROTC, men with doctorates in science, technology, engineering, and math (STEM)—people who were not struggling and working from sunup to sundown on the land—was a powerful experience.

These men had earned their degrees from universities in the Northeast and Midwest. They wore coats and ties; they spoke self-confidently and knowledgeably. In some way maybe I had taken for granted the education my own parents had gotten. Certainly, during those summer 4-H experiences, I started to connect to the educational process and to understand what education could do for a person.

Back home, my routine was to read almost all night. I liked books, all books. As a young teen, I was especially keen on detective novels by Mickey Spillane and Erle Stanley Gardner, the author of the Perry Mason series. I would lie in bed until all hours with a book in my hand and the radio softly playing WLAC.

The crowing of Mr. Young's rooster around four in the morning was my signal to turn off the light and sleep for a few hours. As I was drifting off, I could hear Mr. Young getting his mules ready to head out to the fields. I would sneak in about two hours of sleep, and then go out to catch up with Tat, who was out working the fields with the mule-driven plow.

The more I read, the more interested I became in words, in the use of words and language, and how language could shape human lives, organizations, communities, and countries. I bought a thesaurus to help me understand unfamiliar words I came across in my nightly reading. This practice allowed me to read more complex literary works because I became nimble with words. I continued that practice for decades, even during my military years in Taiwan.

Before I went off to college, however, between my well-traveled veteran schoolteachers and my reading, my imagination carried me all over the world without my ever having left Marengo County, Alabama. For me, reading was a form of personal development and self-sufficiency that had nothing to do with the superior-subordinate world I lived in.

---

Reading was vital to me as a youngster, but it took some doing to gain access to books. Unlike today, when anyone can walk freely into their local library, in my youth the "separate but equal" doctrine prevented African Americans from using their local libraries. We had no place where we had equal access to information. My dad, therefore, used the U.S. mail to order books because the job of the U.S. Postal Service was to deliver without discrimination. So, if my dad ordered something, it came through the mail, and the letter carrier delivered it.

The U.S. mail was the access point for information for which there could be no barrier placed between information and a family, regardless of race. Also, when we ordered reading material to be delivered through the U.S. mail, we ordered brand-new books and periodicals, unlike the used and out-of-date books black schools received once white schools were done with them.

Our parents subscribed to a number of periodicals in order to stay informed of current events. *Look* and *Life* magazines connected us to what was happening in the nation in general. *Ebony*, *Jet*, and the *Pittsburgh Courier* kept us up to date with the nation's African American community.

*Ebony*'s articles highlighted African Americans in a positive light. I remember features about Lena Horne, Harry Belafonte, and Martin Luther King Jr. In my day, *Jet* leaned toward sensationalized headlines. When Emmett Till was slaughtered and his body found in the Tallahatchie River, the Mississippi authorities wanted to bury the body quickly; they tried but failed to prevent his mother from opening the casket.[6] She, however, wanted the nation to see what had been done to her son, so she held an open-casket funeral and allowed photos to be taken of her son's mutilated body. *Jet* was among the few venues that took the risk of printing that grotesque and sobering picture. When I was a teen, the *Pittsburgh Courier* was one of the top black newspapers, covering news about African American communities from one end of the country to the other. The two magazines together with the *Pittsburgh Courier* were popular with many middle-class African American families. Since we were denied access to the local library, the U.S. Postal Service was a portal to escape the isolation of a segregated rural community.

My dad also ordered a set of the *Encyclopedia Britannica* by mail order. Although he was probably the only person in the community that had the encyclopedia, many other schoolteachers supplemented their lack of materials through the same process.

The dedicated teachers in African American schools saw to it that bright children graduated from high school rather than drop out to work. In the early 1960s, blacks graduating high school in the Alabama Black Belt had only four options. First, they could move to the North to find work. If they did that, the men had to register with the selective service, which meant they could later be drafted into the army. Second, graduating men and women could enlist in the military, which meant that they could likely choose among the services. Third, they could enroll at a segregated college: the Tuskegee Institute, the Alabama Agricultural and Mechanical College (now Alabama A&M University) in Normal, or Alabama State College. A fourth option, which I can remember no one choosing, was farming. After twelve years of education, no one said to themselves, "I've seen my parents struggle as sharecroppers all these years—gosh, I think I'll follow in their footsteps." The political, economic, and social system of Jim Crow made it too risky even for a hardworking African American landowner to be successful and sustain a family solely through farming.

Today's black graduates have a few more options than they did in my day. For one there are more colleges to choose from. There are, however, fewer farms, and unfortunately still a lot of minimum-wage work. The educational marginalization imposed by whites on blacks is taking generations to overcome. My grandfather could not sign his name, but he was a landowner, which helped provide an income to educate his children. My grandmother was the one who was aggressive about encouraging her children to go on to college, if they could. My grandparents were like so many families of their generation—they cherished education and wanted their children to succeed.

The challenge for my grandparents', parents', and my generation was access to information because access to schools and libraries was legally circumscribed. Today's African American youth still struggle with access, some because of policies and practices, but many more because of economic challenges. Student loan debt hits students of color significantly harder than it does white students. The whole situation speaks volumes about the value that our country places—or fails to place—on the education of its young people.

One of my high school friends, William Curry, an extremely bright man, was our class valedictorian. We were in the military at the same time, though he was in the army. He went on to serve on the Marengo County Commission and the Linden School Board. Not long ago, William and I reminisced about education during the Jim Crow era. We talked about how many bright African American children there were during our school years, how many of those bright youth left Linden and left the South, and how much more might have become of those young people if only there had been anything remotely like a level playing field. But there wasn't such a thing. When the 1896 *Plessy v. Ferguson* U.S. Supreme Court ruling dictated "separate but equal," there was nothing "equal" about it, especially in Alabama.

For African Americans educated in the Alabama of the twentieth century, almost everything we had in the way of support was "less than." Still, in that sparse environment, I was among those with the will to learn. Despite the roadblocks they faced from the county, state, and federal governments, my parents and teachers succeeded in nurturing in me an insatiable intellectual curiosity. The habits of mind they fostered have in turn sustained my lifelong commitment to education.

CHAPTER 5

# The Great Migration

Separate and unequal schooling was just one factor driving the exodus of six million African Americans from the South between 1910 and 1970 known as the Great Migration. People in my high school class weren't the only ones to see that the "separate but equal" system was anything but, with migration the only way out. The Jim Crow superior-subordinate social system also extended to the sharecropping and tenancy agricultural systems, which guaranteed poverty for those who remained in the South. Fear for the safety of oneself and one's family in the face of continued violence against blacks was a strong impetus to escape the South. Finally, agricultural mechanization and the devastation caused by the boll weevil made sharecropping and farming even less of an option than they already were. Jobs with steady wages in other regions of the country were a strong draw. Isabel Wilkerson describes the Great Migration as "a turning point in history" that "would transform urban America and recast the social and political order of every city it touched. It would force the South to search its soul and finally to lay aside a feudal caste system. It grew out of the unmet promises made after the Civil War and, through the sheer weight of it, helped push the country toward the civil rights revolution of the 1960s."[1]

In 1910, almost 90 percent of all the African Americans in the United States lived in the South. At the end of the Great Migration in 1970, almost half lived elsewhere.[2] Today scholars tell us that there were, in fact, two waves of the Great Migration, one 1910–40, and the second 1940–70. My generation was part of the second migration. My uncles and aunts were part of the first.

The boll weevil infestation had engulfed most of Alabama by the mid-1910s, devastating the state's cotton economy. Many farmers could not switch to other crops quickly enough and were ruined. Landowners were forced to sell out. Sharecroppers and tenant farmers moved north and west to find work.[3]

The First World War opened up an escape path. In the 1910s, as the war was starting, northern industries needed workers. The black press, including the *Chicago Defender*, advertised jobs paying steady wages in the factories, steel mills, and slaughterhouses of the North.[4] Chicago, Detroit, New York, and Philadelphia were among the cities that saw the greatest influx of African Americans.

The railroads that crisscrossed the country were the primary means of escape. From the Mississippi Delta, the Illinois Central Railroad took people to Chicago's South Side. In Alabama, many went to Detroit on the L&N (Louisville and Nashville) Railroad. People in Georgia and Florida took the Atlantic Coast Line and the Seaboard Air Line Railroads to Philadelphia, Washington, D.C., and New York. Still others made their way to Texas, where they boarded the Union Pacific Railroad for California.[5]

My paternal grandmother encouraged all of her children to go to school and later to explore other parts of the country to make a living. She was essentially saying, "Don't try to make a life in Marengo County." It took a lot of grit to watch them leave home, but she felt strongly about education and opportunity. She felt that education was the path to leave behind a life of toil on the land. She also thought that leaving home was the surest way for them to have the opportunity to live their lives with dignity and respect, as opposed to enduring the superior-subordinate system of Jim Crow. Education and the promise of a better life were their catalysts for leaving.

In their new homes scattered across the country—Mobile, Birmingham, Detroit, and farther afield—my aunts and uncles worked hard, raised families, and thrived. I doubt any of them regretted having left Marengo County, though they returned for family celebrations.

The Great Depression of the 1930s slowed the migration, but with new wars starting in China and Europe in the late 1930s, the North once again needed more labor for factories. California industries were also drawing African Americans.

Where I grew up, working from sunup to sundown sawing timber and hoeing cotton netted about two dollars a day. Entire families worked at that. Moreover, income was unpredictable for sharecroppers—bad weather reduced crops and therefore income, and landowners were not always fair in settling up after a harvest. But people I knew who moved to Detroit to work on the Chrysler or Ford assembly lines earned steady wages for a fixed day of work.

Agricultural mechanization came to the Alabama Black Belt in the 1940s and 1950s. In the mid-1940s, many landowners were buying Ford tractors. In the 1950s, the mechanical cotton picker was introduced, drastically reducing the need for workers to pick cotton by hand.

My generation had more educational opportunities than the previous generation had, and more young people were graduating from high school in my time than ever before. The Rosenwald and missionary schools, though basic, provided enough education to endow people with the mental processes needed to understand fully their environment and how limited their possibilities and opportunities were. We all learned about cause and effect and were able to apply that knowledge along with simple math to understand the sharecropping system: sharecroppers don't own the land, they get only a portion of what they make through their hard labor, and they are further disrespected by being called Boy, Uncle, and John by white landowners and the rest of the white community.

Sharecroppers throughout the Alabama Black Belt were some of the most exploited people in America. I saw it. I saw landowners take half— or more—of what sharecroppers had earned. Sometimes sharecroppers got no money at all, despite all their work. It was a system of credit, so there was no way to get ahead.

Although many of my friends' parents could not read or write, my friends could, and they certainly understood what was happening: their parents were being had. I remember children appealing to their fathers to review the landowners' math and to stand up for a fair assessment. But the parents would say, "No, no, no. Don't create a problem." The "education" the parents had been subjected to was to endure the generational systemic exploitation, whereas their children had fortunately received another education.

Thus, by the time these bright young people finished high school, they left as quickly as they could, and they encouraged their parents to stop sharecropping. Some did. Those who were still able-bodied would move to industrial cities like Birmingham or Mobile to find work. Farms closed down. Sharecropper shacks were abandoned. People left in the middle of the night. Otherwise, especially in places like Mississippi, if people were caught at the train station they would be locked up for vagrancy. Tat, who could always make me laugh, said that the trains were so full of people escaping the South that when they approached a hill, everyone had to get out and push.

By the late 1950s and early 1960s, people were weary of being denigrated and disgusted with the obscene Jim Crow system. There was a feeling among young blacks that they were no longer going to be held to the system. At the federal level, segregation laws were slowly beginning to change. At the state level, especially in the South, whites were defiant against change. A quiet resistance gradually became more visible, where more and more African Americans said "I will no longer abide by this." So, they left with heads high, knowing that where they were headed they would not have to look down and reply "yes, sir" or "no, sir" to white men. They wouldn't have to step off the sidewalk into the street when white people passed by. Even a ghetto in Chicago was preferable to staying in a sharecropper's shack in Alabama.

Even as the country was changing, white Alabamians clung to custom and practice. African American families lived under the constant threat of violence for the slightest misstep. The most innocent interaction with a white person could lead to verbal abuse, jail time, or worse.

In the 1950s, one of my childhood friends who was about eleven years old, started working for a Jewish merchant in Linden. David was paid a dollar each day he worked after school, sweeping up. When he was about thirteen, the teenage daughter of one of the white sales clerks started working in the shop, too. As David worked, Linda would pester him by running past him and snatching his hat off his head. David did what any other thirteen-year-old boy would do in that situation: he chased her to retrieve his cap.

Later, David's brother got into a fight in the street. David was not involved, but they both had to appear in court in Linden. David raised his hand and said, "Judge, I wasn't in the fight."

The judge said, "You shut your mouth. I hear you like to play with little white girls. If you open your mouth one more time, I'm going to give you a year in jail."

Even at thirteen years old, David knew to keep quiet. The judge was threatening him with the juvenile jail—in this case Mount Meigs in Montgomery County.

When David got home, his mother packed everything he owned in a box and put him on a bus to Mobile to live with her father. She knew Jim Crow well enough to sense what was ahead for her son: "If you stay here, you're going to go to jail. I'm getting you out of here."

David stayed in Mobile for a year or two and then made his way to Cleveland, where he became a truck driver. Eventually he started his own trucking business and became a contractor for the U.S. Postal Service. David never returned to Linden. We talk by phone frequently, and to this day he harbors some anger at the way he was treated in Linden.

Another friend, John, and I went into the service at the same time, he into the U.S. Army. Back in high school, he had a job during the Christmas holidays at a shop in Linden assembling bicycles for people who had purchased them for their children. A white girl, Mary, who worked the front register would frequently leave her post to chat with John while he worked in the back. They both went to segregated schools, and to make conversation she would ask what he was doing in school. He told me later that most of the time he kept his head down, continuing to work on the bikes, answering Mary's questions as briefly as possible, "yes" or "no." John noticed, however, that the shopkeeper would walk up behind them to watch the scene closely. "I could see him out of the corner of my eye, but I didn't look up to acknowledge that I saw him." In Alabama in the 1950s, whites felt their superiority threatened simply by blacks looking them in the face. John realized that the shopkeeper was just waiting for him to make a comment or a gesture that would have been deemed over the line and "uppity."

Several years later, when John returned home from the army, he happened to be in a Linden clothing store when he realized that Mary was working there. She brightened when she saw him, saying, "I didn't know you were back! Where've you been these last few years?"

"I've been in the army."

The two visited for a short while, and then John left the clothing store to visit his mother, who worked at a café across the street. Later, he was walking home down Highway 28 toward Thomaston when Mary pulled up beside him in her car and asked if she could give him a ride. John politely declined, noting that it wasn't a good idea, so she drove on.

A few days later, after having visited his mom in the café, John was again walking home when Mary pulled up in her car to again offer him a ride. Again he declined: "No, I'm alright. If I did, there may be problems. I could get into trouble."

"You're going to have more trouble if you're seen standing here on the side of the road talking to me," she replied. The fourteen-year-old Emmett Till had been brutally murdered in 1955, and blacks throughout the South knew that the mere appearance of impropriety was sufficient "proof" for whites to act violently against them. With that, John got into her car, and Mary drove to his house and dropped him off.

In this small community, it was inevitable that some would see John riding in Mary's car and that word would get around quickly. The next week, John met up with about ten friends who were just finishing a day of work laying sod for a new nursing home nearby. As they all walked back toward town, he tried to talk them into a pickup basketball game. A white man pulled up beside them; he had been drinking, and a pistol was visible on the back seat.

The man lurched out of the car, demanding, "Which one of you boys been talking to that girl that works in the clothing store in town?" Everyone looked around at one another in confusion, not knowing what he was talking about. John remained silent.

Later, the owner of the café where John's mother worked pulled her aside to warn her that word on the street was that her son was dating the girl. When John's mother got home that evening, she gathered up everything her twenty-two-year-old veteran son owned and stuffed it in a suitcase, just as David's mother had done a decade earlier. Then she walked across the highway to ask the family there if John could ride with their son, who was visiting and about to return to his home in New Jersey. From New Jersey, John could then make his way to a brother on Long Island. They agreed, and the young men set out together.

Rather than risk going into Linden, where the white men at the service station, which also served as the bus station, would surely see them and make their presence known more widely, the two waited at a bridge over a bogue—a small river—about five miles out of town to flag down the bus on its way out of town. In those days, Greyhound buses still stopped along the route to pick up passengers. The two took the bus to Birmingham and from there continued northward. John made New York his home for the rest of his life, working in the aircraft industry there. It was several years before he dared return to Alabama even to visit his family.

Each of these friends intended to leave Marengo County at some point, but neither planned to leave under those circumstances. In the South, white men controlled every aspect of life. White women were given special status. The white European standard of beauty required protection. Thus, since the days of slavery, the worst crime a black man could commit was to have any sort of relationship with a white woman, even a platonic one. These stories show what life was like under the pyramid of Jim Crow laws, with the most dangerous being those dealing with relationships between the sexes. The mere fear of a "relationship" between the races was sufficient to endanger any black man seen interacting with or in the vicinity of a white woman. David was only a young teenager when a judge threatened him in an open courtroom for having been seen in the proximity of a white girl. John was in danger for having ridden in a white woman's car. The violence visited upon the Scottsboro boys, Emmett Till, and anyone trying to secure voting rights for blacks is well known, but I share with you the stories of David and John, both of whom I grew up with, as examples of my personal knowledge of the volatility of southern small towns.

---

There were pushes and pulls for out-migration from the South. David and John were two young men who were pushed out, leaving under the cover of darkness in fear of their lives. Others were drawn by the pull of industrial wages over uncertain sharecropping wages.

At age eighteen, I too joined the Great Migration. I felt stifled coming of age in the South. I had wonderful teachers in high school, men who had seen the world through their military service. Summers at the 4-H camp at the Tuskegee Institute opened my eyes even wider to the possibilities that education provided. I had read books about all corners of the world, and was eager for a physical, emotional, and intellectual change in my environment.

Education has enormous power to change the expectations of young people. In Alabama in the mid-twentieth century, even though the state had invested only paltry resources in blacks' education, that investment had been multiplied by dedicated, educated, and passionate teachers. As a result, bright high school graduates abandoned sharecropping and left the South, taking that investment to other parts of the country. That mass migration was human capital that the South could not afford to lose. Education not only changed the South, but it also changed the Northeast, Midwest, and West. The South lost human capacity, whereas the other regions benefited. Many of my contemporaries who moved north after graduation often discovered that they were better educated than their northern peers. They also brought a different work ethic with them. They worked hard, and that served them well outside the South. The residual effects of the Great Migration together with the anger that comes from feelings of Otherness brought on by life under Jim Crow remain the two greatest challenges facing the South today.

William, my valedictorian high-school friend, lamented in our conversation about how so many of our class left. "Think of the loss of human capital in this country because of a system that was designed to provide an inferior education by policy, laws, and practices. It was designed to do that! What have we lost as a nation? We are paying a price for it in many of our communities."

Today, Alabama's rural Black Belt includes some of the poorest counties in the United States. It remains a sparsely populated agricultural region with high unemployment, poor access to education and medical care, substandard housing, and high rates of crime. When I arrived in Southwest Georgia in the 2010s to lead Albany State, I saw once again the devastating effects of the Great Migration.

In fact, the region looked almost identical to that of Southwest Alabama, which was one of the reasons I was attracted to the position. Once I was there, people would say that I did not understand them or Albany. They could have challenged me on my ideas for developing the human capacity of Albany State's students or the economic capacity of Albany. There was no denying, however, that I understood what it meant to come of age in the Jim Crow Alabama Black Belt. For each decision I made while at Albany State, my goals were to help students get good educations, and to create economic and employment opportunities for graduates so they didn't feel pushed to migrate to other parts of the country to find jobs.

# PART TWO

# Changing a Life's Perspectives in Places Far from Home

In 1962, I chose the military as the way out of the oppressively segregated South. I joined the air force, serving two years at Tainan Air Station in Taiwan and two years at Maxwell Air Force Base (AFB) in Montgomery, Alabama, where being on base was a reprieve from the surrounding Jim Crow community. After the service, I matriculated at the University of Alabama in Tuscaloosa, where I earned my bachelor's and master's degrees. I wanted a career tied to education and international programs. The path led me to Thailand and later back to the University of Alabama, where I worked in Academic Affairs while I completed a doctorate in higher education administration. From there, I built a decades-long career in education, some in the classroom teaching, but mostly as an administrator. My interests lay in creating sustainable programs and infrastructures to enrich the student experience and to support economic development of communities locally and internationally. When I left home at age eighteen, I had no magic window into the future, but, looking back, I realize that joining the military and serving in East Asia were vital in helping me realize my career dreams.

CHAPTER 6

# It Took Leaving My Country to Find Freedom and Liberty

With tensions rising in Southeast Asia, all of my male friends and I knew we could either join the military voluntarily or wait to be drafted. Enlisting gave us a measure of control over which service to enter, whereas all draftees wound up in the army. I made the decision to join the U.S. Air Force.

Not long out of high school, I boarded a bus heading to Lackland AFB outside of San Antonio, Texas, for six weeks of basic training to become an airman. Other than accompanying my dad on his annual visits to a sister in Birmingham—where I could see the southern peaks of the Appalachian Mountains—I had previously traveled outside Marengo County only to Louisiana and Tennessee. When I boarded that bus to Texas, I was venturing farther from home than I ever had before.

Basic training involved deliberately traumatizing the new recruits, but in a good way. Information was put in front of me that I had never seen before. What we were being told in effect was that whether we hailed from Hobbs, New Mexico; Upstate New York; Kansas; or Sweet Water, Alabama, it didn't matter. We were all United States Air Force airmen. Expectations were laid out for us: "This is what excellence looks like." Nothing was hidden, or unstated, or not what it appeared to be. Everything was out in the open. This transparency was intoxicating.

By joining the U.S. Air Force, I discovered a whole new world. In 1948, President Truman had integrated the military. Some were still getting adjusted to that new reality, but by 1962—with the Cold War well underway—the nature of our mission did not allow for issues of race or religion to interfere. High achievement was demanded of everyone. We were expected to collaborate and cooperate as a unified team to accomplish the mission. The military experience was so intense that the officers didn't have time to worry about skin color. There was no time to think about how to disenfranchise some while showing preference to others.

It was perhaps an unintended outcome that the military normalized high expectations for all those who served. There were performance measures whether it be of physical fitness or of classroom achievement, and performance achievement was race neutral. Many new white recruits, especially those from the South, were offended by this system, which simultaneously invigorated many of the black airmen with a new sense of worth. Nonwhite airmen had never experienced competing with whites on a level playing field.

The drill instructor in basic training was tough on everybody. He wondered how each and every one of us "sorry souls" had gotten into his air force. He was harsh on everybody, whether we were rich and white from Manhattan or poor and black from North Carolina. Basic training was the most rigorous six weeks of our lives, on the field and in the classroom.

The approach the air force took reminds me of some football teams like the one at the University of Alabama, where the coach, Nick Saban, tells his players, "We don't play against other teams—we play against our standard." Coach Saban sets an expectation of excellence for all on his team by saying that "if you come here to play, this is the world you're going to live in." In the air force in 1962, you came to perform against uncompromising expectations. There were no pluses or minuses for skin color.

After basic training, I was given a choice of where to be stationed. Most of my friends chose Europe. In my mind, however, the cultures of European countries were too similar to that of the United States. I longed to step completely out of my comfort zone so that I would experience dissonance. I wanted to be forced to rethink everything I knew, and to have all my assumptions about the world challenged. I was energized rather than distressed by the prospect of exploring a completely new environment. So, I chose Asia. Given the choice of the Philippines, Korea, Japan, or Taiwan, I chose Taiwan. When I told the officer in charge, he chuckled and said, "I don't think that'll be a problem." I didn't know at the time that few airmen volunteered to go there.

Another reason for picking Taiwan was that I needed, at least for a short time, to get as far away as humanly possible from the Alabama

Black Belt. At age eighteen, just thinking about what was euphemistically called plantation agriculture (i.e., forced labor camps), slavery, lynchings, Jim Crow, day-to-day racial discrimination, the sharecropping system, and persistent poverty was disheartening and enervating for me. Later in the sixties, when I could look at it all more objectively, it seems to me that the lyrics to Albert King's "Born under a Bad Sign" captured the convergence of all these things that had been done to a people because of the color of our skin. In it, he sings about having had bad luck since he was born and of having to struggle his whole life. The song summed up my feelings about living in a region with so much disharmony, strife, and brutality. Home was where, almost every waking hour during the day, people were reminded by law, policy, practice, and custom that they were "less than." All schools: segregated by law. The library: couldn't go in and certainly couldn't get a library card.

After basic training, I went home on leave before starting the long journey to East Asia. The first leg of the process was to travel by bus from Thomasville two hours south to Mobile, where I would board a cross-country train to Los Angeles. On the way, I was twice reminded of the superior-subordinate southern culture I had grown up in. The first reminder came less than an hour into the ride, when we stopped in the little town of Grove Hill. I got off the bus to get something to eat at a small establishment there. As I approached the front entrance, a woman came up to block me from entering. As I stood there in my U.S. Air Force uniform, she said, "I'm sorry. This is for whites only. You have to go 'round back. There's a place for you there."

Walking around to the back, I found a garage. There, a couple of African American men were draining the oil from old cars propped up on cinder blocks. They directed me toward a doorway. It was a colored waiting room the size of a closet. Crammed inside were two chairs and a window cut through the wall. The same woman came up to the window. I could barely see her face. She said, "Can I help you?"

"No, ma'am. I think I'll just get back on the bus."

When I reboarded the bus, we drove on for several miles. More out of habit than anything else, I resumed my seat in the back of the bus and began to read. The back half was now full of African American passengers, although there were open seats in the front half of the bus, traditionally the white section. The driver stopped along the route to pick up an elderly African American woman. She was holding two grocery bags of turnips and collard greens in one hand, and a beat-up old suitcase in the other. She boarded the bus and walked past the empty white section toward the back. There was nowhere for her to sit. I said, "Ma'am, would you like my seat?"

"Oh yes, young man. Thank you so much," she replied. I went up to the front and sat right behind the bus driver. In an instant, he pulled the bus over to the side of the highway. There I was in my U.S. Air Force uniform, and he said to me, "You can't sit up front. We have laws of segregation on this bus. You'll have to stand up in the back." I very politely responded, "Sir, right above your head is a sign that reads, 'Interstate Commerce Commission.'" The sign on the front of the bus showed that the route originated in Nashville, making it an interstate route. Just a year before, the U.S. attorney general, Robert F. Kennedy, had seen to it that interstate buses could no longer segregate passengers. Buses traveling within a state could, but buses that crossed state lines were subject to the new Interstate Commerce Commission regulations. I calmly told the driver all this.

He glared at me as if he was ready to forcibly kick me off the bus. I stared back at him. Finally, he said, "Oh, just sit here." I retook my seat behind his, and he continued on to Mobile. He knew I was right, and he wasn't prepared to risk his job by going up against the federal government. Still, if the bus had originated in Birmingham, or anywhere else in Alabama, I could have been arrested and thrown in jail for refusing to sit in the segregated section.

Once in Mobile, I took a train to Los Angeles and then a bus to Travis AFB, northeast of San Francisco. There, with those two recent reminders of my racial place in Alabama still in mind, I boarded a turboprop plane for Honolulu. From there, we hopscotched across the Pacific Ocean to Wake Island, Guam, the Philippines, and then on to Taiwan. It was my first time flying, as well as my first time experiencing air turbulence. I was exhilarated knowing that I had no idea what I would find when we landed.

What I found when I arrived in Taiwan was true freedom. Up until then, I hadn't even known that for the first eighteen years of my life in my home country I had not experienced liberty. What an astounding irony that it took traveling more than seven thousand miles from Sweet Water, Alabama, to feel freedom. I found that in Taiwan I could act, feel, and think in ways that I had never been able to do before because of the constrictions that whites and white laws placed on my race. My movements weren't limited by the signs reading "COLORED" or "WHITE" that were all over my home state and throughout my home country's Deep South. I could enjoy being outside without fearing that someone would arrest me for "loitering." Half a planet away from all that was happening in my home state, I was seen and welcomed by the Taiwanese as an American airman, not as an African American man.

On my days off, I felt free to move around the island as I wished. I would ride a bike off the base and into the villages to observe and talk with the Taiwanese. There was a pattern to these excursions. I would bicycle into a village. An elder would greet me, ask me to sit, and offer me some rice wine. We would drink for a few minutes. The elder would summon a young bilingual person to sit between us to facilitate our conversation. They asked, with genuine interest, about my life.

I thought, "This liberty and freedom stuff feels good." Experiences like these with the Taiwanese are why, to this day, I have a deep passion for that part of the world. Moreover, this new sense of freedom and liberty, in the uniform of a U.S. airman, led me to proudly add "American" as part of my identity.

CHAPTER 7

# Anger Becomes Resolve

The first time I experienced the intersections of race, history, and culture was in Taiwan. It happened around work, sports, and barracks life. We were a microcosm of the United States—thrust together in a way that had not happened to any of us before. We were strategically placed on Taiwan to carry out the foreign policy of our country, yet at the same time we experienced the convergence of different cultures, and the "different" cultures turned out to be our own.

Over time, living and working around men from all over the United States, I came to understand that in addition to my identity of being black and male, I had deep in my core another identity—that of southerner. I had thought when people from other states talked of southerners, they were referring to whites. But then I heard black airmen from Chicago and elsewhere talk about me and some of the other black southern airmen as "you boys from the South." I knew I was geographically from the southern United States, but it was dawning on me that I was also *culturally* southern.

Up until the early 1960s, blacks in America were viewed as a monolithic culture. A black person from any part of the country, and of any education level, or socioeconomic class was viewed the same by whites. All blacks were seen collectively as "less than." Similarly, whites from the South were lumped under one stereotype by others around the country.

When in Taiwan, I came to understand, however, that mine was a southern identity of an African American living in a sparsely populated agrarian region of the Deep South. It was not the southern identity of, say, a person growing up in Appalachia. Nor was it like that of the white planter class in Alabama. There were southern aristocrats living close to Sweet Water who sat on the front porches of their antebellum homes and sent their sons off to state or elite universities. Those young men had a very different sense of homeplace than I had.

I discovered that growing up black in the South was also different from growing up black in other parts of the country. My African American identity was tied to blues and to the lifestyle and cuisine of a southern farm. In the service, I met African American men from Los Angeles, New York City, Chicago, and elsewhere. Their cultures were not remotely close to mine. They denigrated blues as "slave music." They would ask, "Why you listening to that nigger music?" In those days, even for blacks not raised in the South, blues was too earthy and too profane.

They preferred the more urbane sound of jazz artists Ramsey Lewis and John Coltrane. They considered blues artists like John Lee Hooker and B.B. King to be lower class, an embarrassment to African Americans trying to fight their way out of marginalization and shed the stereotypes of being poor and black in the agrarian South. To my nonsouthern black colleagues, the music characterized a culture they were trying to distance themselves from, even though perhaps their parents had been born in Mississippi or Alabama. They thought that I should aspire to shed myself of what they considered to be undesirable traits and that I "shouldn't listen to that plantation music."

That was my first realization that music and culture are tied to geography as much as they are to race. This was reinforced when I befriended an African American airman from Hobbs, New Mexico. I teasingly told him, "I didn't know there was a single black person in New Mexico." His love of music had Latino roots. He grew up in a town with a significant Latino population, very few whites, and a handful of African American families. I was intrigued by the kind of music he played in the barracks, music I'd not heard before and didn't know existed.

Although I had loved music as a child, now as an adult I was beginning to appreciate the solid cultural underpinnings that music gives people. I think of the music of Appalachia and what it means to people who grew up there, of New Mexican music with its Native American and Hispanic influences, of Miami Latin music, and of the blues of my Deep South.

Although others in the barracks berated my choice of music, my friends never did. Indeed, I never surrendered my embrace of the music that reflected the people of modest means who sang, danced, and played that music in the rural South of my childhood. Today, my wife points out that I am still thin skinned when people talk about blues as race, plantation, or slave music. I bristle when people characterize the blues as second class, marginal, or "less than."

I observed these differences in U.S. culture while stationed on a small island in East Asia. I felt them acutely one night on a stopover in the Philippines on my return to the United States from Taiwan. Flying from Taipei, we landed at Clark Air Base on Luzon Island in the Philippines. There, we would stay three nights before flying on to Guam and then Hawaii. One evening, three other airmen and I left the base and went to a bar in Angeles in central Luzon.

While on Taiwan I had observed that when we were on duty, we were integrated. When we socialized off duty, however, airmen tended to self-segregate.

I was overcome with nostalgia when I walked through the doors of that bar on Luzon Island. The bar was full of U.S. paratroopers, airmen, and sailors. All were young African Americans; not a single one was white. The women there were all local Filipinos. The first thing I heard was a recording of B.B. King singing "Sweet Sixteen." Then I smelled the food. The whole experience transported me back to Southwest Alabama.

It had been two years since I'd eaten southern food. So it was something of a miracle to me that, thousands of miles from Alabama, Filipino cooks in a Filipino-owned bar were serving up black-eyed peas, collard greens, and pork chops. I could not imagine how they obtained, never mind learned to cook, these foods in this small corner of Southeast Asia. What I saw, heard, and smelled that night exemplified for me the power of culture. It carried me directly to my core memories and feelings about my socialization—my coming of age—in Southwest Alabama.

As I think back to that evening today, I wonder over how even to the other side of the world we military personnel had transplanted our social norms dictated by race, history, and culture. We lugged our U.S. experience overseas and segregated our social lives in our off-duty hours. Entrepreneurs in Taiwan, the Philippines, and wherever else U.S. military personnel were stationed quickly perceived what we were doing and adapted. Eventually, establishments catered to the self-segregating U.S. service personnel to the point where businesses were segregated just as they were back home.

Even though in the two years I was on Taiwan we had self-segregated when we weren't working, that evening on Luzon Island showed me the resilience of social conventions and the difficulty of implementing real social change. In that era, serving in the military was one of the main avenues for African American men to live lives not shackled to the superior-subordinate environment of the South. Somehow I realized that the real challenge would come when we returned home. It remained a question whether we could reenter the U.S. status quo, and the South's extreme version of it, without frustration, anger, and impatience at white opposition to social change.

---

Before I went into the air force, I behaved as if I were a renter in this country. I came out of the military as an owner. Michelle Obama got in trouble when one sentence was taken out of context from a 2008 presidential primary event speech she delivered. The sentence seized upon was, "For the first time in my adult life, I am really proud of my country." The context was that she felt the nation was coming together during the campaign to look past difference in order to make the United States a better place for all of its people.[1] I knew just what she meant. Before the air force, the only thing I felt deep ownership for was my family's land. I felt no ownership of Alabama or the South. When I left the military, I felt like an owner of the entire country. I was not willing to be closed out any longer from liberty and freedom.

In many ways, mine was a journey intellectually and emotionally as much as it was a geographic one. It started when the plane took off in California heading for Taiwan. My anger was at its peak then. On Taiwan, I saw that the Taiwanese and the Chinese had their own racial and societal challenges. I found out that this superior-subordinate stuff that goes on in human society was not just a black-white thing in Alabama. It popped up on Taiwan and all over the world, where people engaged with one another in struggles for land, power, status, and economics.

By the time I returned to the States, I had been transformed intellectually and emotionally into an immigrant to my own country. I returned with three traits that many immigrants hold. First was a strong sense of superiority that manifests itself in a calm, quiet demeanor of having a special status. With all I learned from my parents, and what I experienced abroad, I felt proud about what African Americans were accomplishing. They were persevering and enduring with a strong work ethic while dealing with systematic, entrenched exploitation. It gave me a sense that, given what we were already handling, we could do just about anything if we set our minds to it. I have seen this trait in many other immigrants, including a number of international faculty who I would later work with at Albany State. They did not let skin color or race limit them.

Immigrants also often bring with them a sense of insecurity, since they constantly encounter people who think they are not, and never will be, "good enough." This was something African Americans understood quite well. They had been a scorned people since the days of slavery right up through legal segregation. But thrown in with forty to fifty other guys in East Asia, I saw the melting pot of feelings, thoughts, and emotions from every corner of the United States. Even if the U.S. Air Force as an institution didn't discriminate on the basis of race, some individual members found it difficult to unlearn a lifetime of biased thinking. Our off-duty self-segregation wasn't just a natural tendency to congregate with people like ourselves, but perhaps also an expression of those ingrained biases. Among the airmen coming from all over, the most universally scorned were southerners, black and white. As a southerner from Alabama and even worse, one from the Alabama Black Belt, I had an additional burden in off-duty settings; the guys in my barracks criticizing my preference for blues was the most benign expression of this.

A third trait that many immigrants bring with them is impulse control. Accepting the necessity of deferred gratification was a trait that my parents turned into a virtue. Though we lived in a farming community and so never experienced hunger, we still lived frugally. My mother made all her own clothing, not only because she was an excellent seamstress, but also because most clothing stores didn't allow African Americans to try on clothes before they purchased them. My parents owned their own home, though it was modest, on land they owned. They also saved whatever money they could. We never, however, felt or complained that we lived in a less-than environment.

The Jim Crow legal system offered a primer for blacks in impulse control and deferred gratification. Back home in Sweet Water, the black press brought to my family's doorstep the atrocities being committed against African Americans around the country in the 1950s and early 1960s. On Sundays, our pastor preached from the pulpit about the Christian faith and being equal in the eyes of God. I would go to Selma to the Greyhound bus station and see signs saying, "COLORED" and "WHITE." I developed a painful recognition of how wrong segregation was.

As an idealistic teenager, I struggled in a world that did not make sense. I was surrounded by honest, decent people who were toiling through life. They worked hard to provide food for their families and to ensure their children's education. They did this despite the fact that life for African Americans entailed a string of daily degradations that constantly reminded us of the inferior-subordinate social status that pervaded every aspect of our lives.

---

Sometimes the dissonance of that reality overloaded my mind, and it fueled a pent-up anger. By the time I left the Alabama Black Belt in 1962, I was tied up in knots. While stationed on the island of Taiwan from the end of 1962 through part of 1964, I continued to read as much as I could. I stopped by the base library every morning to read the *New York Times*, *Time* magazine, and the *Wall Street Journal*. I saw that things were blowing up back in the States. Some of those events are seared in my memory.

In May 1963, in Kelly Ingram Park in Birmingham, Alabama, police and firemen deployed police dogs and fire hoses to assault young African American student protesters (mostly children and high school students). Their peaceful protest was part of the nonviolent Birmingham Campaign, an organized effort to bring attention to the struggle to end legal segregation.

The next month, on a Tuesday with the heat approaching 100°F, Alabama governor George Wallace defied a presidential executive order by preventing two black students from registering at the University of Alabama. He infamously "stood in the schoolhouse door" to read a statement that ended with, "I do hereby denounce and forbid this illegal and unwarranted action by the central government."[2] Wallace finally stood aside when he was faced with a hundred Alabama National Guard troops called in by President Kennedy.

The next morning, President Kennedy made a nationally televised address about civil rights. Hours later, the thirty-seven-year-old Medgar Evers was killed by a white supremacist and Klansman in Jackson, Mississippi. Evers, a college graduate and World War II army veteran, was a vocal civil rights activist. He and his family had been living under constant death threats. That morning, as he was walking up his driveway from his car to the house, he was shot in the back. His wife drove him to the local hospital, where he died.³

Three months later, on a Sunday morning in September, four Ku Klux Klansmen blew up the African American 16th Street Baptist Church in Birmingham, killing eleven-year-old Carol Denise McNair and fourteen-year-olds Addie Mae Collins, Carole Robertson, and Cynthia Wesley. Addie Mae's younger sister, Sarah, survived the explosion but was permanently blinded in one eye by glass fragments flying into her face. More than twenty others were injured in the blast.

These events unfolding at home while I was in uniform abroad merely intensified my anger. Living and working side by side with other U.S. airmen, however, I was learning that people from the same country could hold radically different worldviews. Often those views were 180 degrees different from mine. Which brings to mind another incident.

In our barracks, we airmen pooled our dollars together to pay a Taiwanese boy to clean. On a late November day, this houseboy shook me awake, crying "The president is dead! The president is dead!" I thought he was referring to the president of the Republic of China, Chiang Kai-shek, whose government was then based in Taipei. He said, "No! No! The American president." I got up quickly and raced into the hallway. There, I found two airmen laughing and cheering, "We got the son of a bitch!" One of the airmen was from Morrow, Georgia, and the other was from Huntsville, Alabama. These two young men wanted no part of the desegregation and civil rights for African Americans that President Kennedy had been working for. In that moment, watching those two airmen celebrating our president's assassination, I realized just how deep the fault line was between blacks and whites, especially in the South.

I felt rage rising inside me. There I was, serving my nation on foreign soil, while back home, children were being attacked by dogs, two young African Americans were being escorted across the quad of the University of Alabama by U.S. Marshals just so they could get a college education, innocent people were being shot, children were being blown up in a church, and a U.S. president championing civil rights was shot to death. All the while, I was in Taiwan to protect the Taiwanese from the Chinese.

My bitterness must have shown. I had a native Hawaiian supervisor, Sergeant Wong, who knew firsthand about oppression and discrimination. One day he said to me, "You're one of the bright ones in my squadron, but you have a chip on your shoulder. You can't fix everything back in the States, you know."

"Little girls are being slaughtered in a church!"

"I get that! But you have to learn to manage your anger if you want to get ahead. When you wear that uniform you represent the United States to the rest of the world, so get your act together."

Those few words from the sergeant jolted me. It made me recognize that I would have to engage robust mental gymnastics to not use grievance and victimization as a crutch. I remembered what I had learned from my mom: "Performance and achievement. Those are generic."

In the insulated environment of my family, I had developed a healthy sense of self-worth and confidence. I had been brought up in a culture of high expectations for A's from me in school. Until age eighteen, I had not yet experienced living and working among white people where I would have been told that I was "less than." Not accepting this reality would have been backed up with violence.

Still, it took me a while to understand that my bottled-up anger would get me nowhere. I slowly realized that when I returned to the States, I had to be able to manage segregation, which was still the law of the land. This process of identifying the problem and realizing how I needed to modify my behavior in order to solve it served me later in life. Being in a leadership position meant that I would have to look across the table at people who were different than me. I would have to see them for who they were, and I would have to understand the lenses through which they saw the world.

It took leaving Marengo County, leaving the South, encountering a level playing field in the military, and observing my country from the outside to understand my place in the world, and to understand those with different worldviews. If all those things hadn't fallen into place just so during my years in the air force, I could have easily ended up a man consumed by anger, which would not have been sustaining in a complex society. I remain grateful that my military time did not expose me to the hardships and trauma that soldiers, airmen, sailors, and marines face in wartime. Being in the military instead exposed me to the experiences and learning that finally dissipated the anger built up in me.

Others in my squadron also struggled with coming to terms with their anger. One was Thomas, a six-foot, 220-pound airman from Tennessee. He and I were the two starting African Americans on the base's basketball team. He played center and I was point guard. Thomas was a great guy, but growing up under Jim Crow had fostered in him a deep and overt contempt for white people, whom he frequently referred to as "Mr. Charlie" or "Chuck." He would complain to me sometimes, "Man, there're just too many Chucks here," meaning he was irked by having so many white airmen around him. He would needle them by telling them something like, "I'm working with Chuck tonight."

"Chuck? We don't have anyone named Chuck here," the white airmen would respond, clueless. He was doing what slaves had done over the generations: use code to communicate with one another. The expression had been used by slaves to talk about their white overseers and bosses. It was a passive-aggressive way for a subjugated people to feel some sense of dignity. Having grown up in the superior-subordinate culture of the South, where white men spoke to all black males, regardless of age, as "Boys," Thomas referred to white men as "Chuck" or "Mr. Charlie" as a way to release his anger.

Thomas's use of "Mr. Charlie" as a code name wasn't unique. As a youngster, I heard black men in Marengo County use it behind the backs of overbearing, condescending white men. Sammy Davis Jr. even used the term when he covered "Blues for Mr. Charlie" on his 1965 album. The song recounts the suffering on the transatlantic slave ships, the greed of the planters (aka Mr. Charlie) killing their souls with dreams of gold reaped from slave labor, and of people living and hoping for freedom and dignity.

As I reflect on this particular practice, I think that finding small avenues through language and music to push back against whites helped African Americans and other oppressed populations maintain a measure of self-respect while living under an unequitable system.

Thomas's resentment often put him in dark moods, even on the basketball court. Because I had an excellent outside shot, Thomas, who played down low close by the goal, would always try to get the ball to me when I was open. In the course of one game, even though I was almost constantly covered, Thomas still refused to pass the ball to the other guys on the team. During a time-out I took the opportunity to say privately to him, "It's getting obvious what you're doing out there. I'm being covered, so you can't pass to me. You've got to pass the ball to the other guys."

"Well, I don't give a damn. If you don't want to shoot it, I'll shoot it myself."

"That's not what I'm talking about. We're playing as a team. Pass the ball to one of the three other guys. They're open."

This was 1963, when the racial violence back home was burning up the news. Thomas and others weren't immune and walked around as if with lit fuses. They began to react to every little thing as if it were a racial issue. Sergeant Wong tried to be a broker about all this. For some of us, his words helped; for others, it fell on deaf ears.

One strategy to deal with the pent-up frustration was humor. Humor and comedy can powerfully challenge authority, change societal views, and push for social justice. In our barracks was an African American from New York. William was very dark complected but had naturally straight hair. He was self-conscious about this and would correct people's impression of him by saying, "I'm not a Negro. I'm Blackfoot," meaning that he was descended from one of the Blackfoot Native American people. He endured a lot of good-natured banter about that, but some guys ribbed him ruthlessly. St. Julien, an African American airman from New Orleans, was a little older than the rest of us. He was gifted at his work, but he frequently got into trouble for his off-duty carousing, and so had been reduced in rank a couple of times.

One afternoon there were about thirty of us lounging on our bunks in the barracks when St. Julien returned from yet another off-duty drinking binge. He yelled from one end of the barracks to the other, "Hey, William, you say you're Blackfoot?"

"Yeah, yeah. That's what I am," William responded. St. Julien continued, "Well, let me tell you something. When you get home, you take your black ass down to Georgia to one of those all-white swimming pools. When you jump off the diving board, yell one of your Indian 'Waa-whoos!' and see what they're going to call you when they haul your black ass out of that pool. See if they call you Blackfoot then!"

St. Julien had the whole barracks—young black men and young white men of many different backgrounds—in hysterics. We all knew that Jim Crow was in effect and that it would have been unheard of for a person of color to even attempt to go to an all-white swimming pool in any of the southern states. Yet St. Julien was able to turn that serious situation into something the rest of us could laugh about, although unfortunately it was at the expense of one of our buddies.

St. Julien was indiscriminate and unsparing in his ribbing, poking fun at everyone regardless of their race. To the white airmen from the South, he would say things like, "You say you're from the South? I'm surprised you white boys have all your teeth. The air force must have fixed them for you." St. Julien was like a stand-up comedian taking on painful, powerful realities and stereotypes.

---

As my anger and frustration subsided, I was able to better observe and learn from the behavior of others. I was particularly struck by the power of language, and by how quickly certain words can bring out the worst in people, even escalating the danger of a situation or event. When I came in from duty, I would remove my combat boots and lie down on the bunk. To unwind, I would read for about thirty minutes, still in my fatigues.

One day, I was reading while surrounded by other airmen in conversation. By then I had gotten used to hearing white airmen use ethnic slurs like "Chinks" and "Gooks," but that day I heard an African American airman complain about being so far from home just to help "garlic-eating Chinks." His words jolted me out of the naive notion that no one who has been the victim of racism would ever use racial slurs about others.

Today, I recognize that people have different notions about the semantics of the words "racist" and "racism." Some people say it is impossible to be a racist unless there is power and authority to back the words. Without power, the words are just words. This rationale is a nonstarter for me. Something my mom always said explains why: "Two wrongs don't make a right." There's no question in my mind that derogatory terms about other people are inappropriate and insulting, no matter who is saying them.

In another instance while I was in the air force, language escalated to the point of life and death. On the base there were a number of Butler buildings, which were basically large, pre-engineered metal buildings. Some served as hangers for aircraft; others stored nuclear weapons. The buildings were surrounded by manmade bunkers so the enemy could not get close enough to shoot at the buildings. Fencing cordoned off the perimeter, and an alarm system signaled if there was an incursion or other threat.

One night I was assigned to a strike team, which meant that even when we were off duty we had to sleep in our fatigues and keep our weapons at the ready should the alarm sound. In the middle of the night, it did. The six or eight of us grabbed our M2 carbines and jumped in the back of a large military truck. When we got out to the scene, we saw that airmen who were working in the area had detained a Taiwanese man who had gotten too close to where nuclear weapons were stored. They had his hands up against the chain-link fence. They had searched him, and they had scanned the perimeter of the storage area to make sure no one else was with him.

Airman Hansen and I from the strike team were tasked with taking the man to a nearby runway, and another airman already at the scene would drive us there in a large truck. We would then wait to turn him over to the Taiwanese military police.

We got the captive up on the back of the truck. There he squatted with his back up against the truck's cab and with his hands in the air. He was clearly terrified. Hansen was down on one knee, his rifle aimed directly at the man's chest. I, too, was down on one knee, with my right hand just slightly above the trigger of the carbine and with the barrel resting in my left hand.

As we were riding to the meeting point, Hansen started yelling at the captive, swearing and using racial slurs. Even if the man didn't understand all the words, he certainly understood the tone and the facial expressions. I knew how incensed I became at racial slurs and was concerned about what our captive might do in fury or sheer terror. I was particularly worried because Hansen habitually got drunk when off duty, and I suspected he was still pretty drunk from his last off-duty binge. Certainly he was acting unhinged, and it seemed to me that he was deliberately trying to provoke our captive into reacting so that Hansen would have an excuse to shoot him. But I knew that shooting an unarmed captive would almost certainly get us court-martialed.

I kept telling Hansen to stop provoking our captive and to calm down, while at the same time making calming gestures toward our captive. My mind raced trying to figure out how to keep the situation from spiraling out of control, but one thing the air force hadn't trained us in was what is known today as de-escalation. I was just a heavily armed nineteen-year-old kid with another heavily armed nineteen-year-old, standing guard over a terrified captive. So I just kept repeating to Hansen, over and over, "Calm down! Calm down a minute!" As the only one on the back of the truck maintaining some semblance of calm, I felt it my responsibility to not just make sure our captive didn't escape but also to not allow harm to come to him while under our watch.

We finally arrived at the designated runway and held the man there until the Taiwanese police came and hauled him away in a military jeep. Afterward, Hansen and I never spoke of what transpired that night. I still don't know how the three of us made it through that awful night without something disastrous happening. It was, however, the height of the Cold War. Everything was hair-trigger and exacerbated by alcohol, bigotry, and blind fear.

That night in Taiwan was one of the most tense and terrifying moments of my life, but it helped me understand that when people come under significant stress and strain, all kinds of things are revealed about who they are. Some people lose some of their humanity, and in so doing take away the humanity of others, as well.

The incident framed my approach to working in stressful conditions. It helped me recognize that when I was pushed to the limit, with human lives at stake, I did OK in some ways. I also learned that when the dynamics of gender, race, religion, history, culture, and politics are piled onto an already tense situation, some people will find it almost impossible to function calmly and rationally.

---

Early in 1964, after two years in Taiwan, I was transferred to Maxwell AFB in Montgomery. At the time, the Civil Rights Act was still pending legislation that was being fought over in Washington and around the country. The South was still segregated, not just by custom and practice, but by law—Jim Crow laws. My home state had become ground zero for social change in the United States. Violence against blacks in Selma, Montgomery, Tuscaloosa, and Birmingham, and protests by blacks and whites in those places in large part led to President Johnson signing into law on July 2, 1964, the Civil Rights Act that would codify into law freedoms and protections for all, regardless of race. Standing behind the president to watch him sign that landmark legislation were Martin Luther King Jr. and the Rev. Ralph Abernathy (who was born and raised in Linden). But I didn't know any of that would happen when I was on my way back to Alabama.

What I did know was that I could not return to the United States and voluntarily surrender the freedoms I had experienced by reverting to the severe limits of segregation. I was done with that. The scorn that whites had for blacks was their problem, not mine, Jim Crow or no Jim Crow.

Those were my thoughts on the flights from Taiwan back to the States. I got off the plane at Travis AFB and boarded another plane bound for New Orleans, Louisiana. From there I, together with other airmen, took a Greyhound bus along the Gulf of Mexico coast, east through Mississippi, and home to Alabama. At a stop in Biloxi, Mississippi, I knew we were really back in the Deep South when I saw the "COLORED" and "WHITE" signs segregating the bus station waiting rooms. There was an orthodoxy about obeying those signs, about staying in one's racial place, which, despite my earlier resolve to not resubmit to segregation, I knew I could not breach without creating trouble for myself and for others.

For the past two years I had been free to move about without restrictions based on race, but now I had returned to a place where everywhere I went off base was mired in Jim Crow dangers. It did not matter that I was wearing a U.S. military uniform. I was returning to a country on the cusp of social change. Federal legislation was the hope on the horizon. Customs and practices would lag far behind, however. In fact, with the slow, pulsating death of Jim Crow, extraordinary violence would continue.

In mid-June 1964, another tragedy struck the Civil Rights movement. Three men in their early twenties were harassed by local police and then murdered by white supremacists in Mississippi. James Chaney, who was African American, was from Meridian, Mississippi. Andrew Goodman and Michael Schwerner were white and Jewish young men from New York who were in Mississippi to help register African Americans to vote. As the three were driving from one community to another, they were pulled over by police on the pretext of a traffic violation. They were taken to a jail and detained for several hours. As they drove out of town shortly after their release, they were abducted, shot, and buried in an earthen dam outside of Philadelphia, Mississippi.[4]

With such hate crimes on the rise, especially by members of the Ku Klux Klan, my dad was concerned for my safety and cautioned me, "When you drive through Selma coming home, don't come at night. You could get hurt. You know what happened to those young men in Mississippi!" It was a scary time.

At the time of those murders, the Civil Rights Act was being fiercely debated in the U.S. Senate. The road to passage was not easy and included the longest Senate debate in history (sixty days) with southern senators filibustering. The act addressed a number of unequal practices, but in essence it ended legal segregation. It would begin to change U.S. society.

The stroke of a pen, however, did not end the violence, nor did it end segregation in social customs or practice.

Not long after the Civil Rights Act became law, I was reminded of how long it would be before real social change would come to Alabama. I made a visit home to Sweet Water. Two childhood friends were the first to greet me. One was Tat, and the other was Steve, the son of one of the few white families that lived around us. To celebrate my return, they decided to get some beer. Marengo County was a dry county, so we drove up to Perry County to buy several six-packs. We brought the beer back and went down to the Tombigbee River, where we submerged the cans in the water to keep them cool and hidden. The three of us sat on the riverbank late into the evening, having a great time catching up.

As the beer took effect, Tat mused, "If there weren't any black women overseas, could you date anyone while you were there?" The interracial challenges between black and white ran so deep, that neither he, nor any of my other friends, could imagine the possibility of having a relationship with a woman of another race. He and Steve were astounded when I told them about two of my airmen buddies. One had married a Korean woman, the other a Japanese woman. What Tat and Steve did believe was that neither airman could be stationed in a southern state because of the antimiscegenation laws. For their entire military careers, these airmen had to be stationed on the West Coast or in the Asian Pacific region.

When it got late, Steve said he knew some young women who lived nearby. We drove to where they lived, and he said, "I'm going in to spend the night. Do you guys wanna come, too?"

A red flag instantly went up for me. Visions of the Scottsboro boys, Emmett Till, all-white juries, and my plans for college and for my future all flashed before me. There was no way Tat and I were going to spend the night in a house in Alabama with white women. I said to Steve, "What have we just been talking about! Hand me your car keys. We'll come back and get you in the morning."

After spending almost two years in Taiwan, where I had experienced freedom and liberty from racial restrictions, I was prepared to stand up for myself, but I wasn't going to be stupid.

---

Even after the Civil Rights Act was enacted, throughout the South, violence continued to ratchet up against those on the side of peaceful social change—white supremacists were not going to surrender Jim Crow without bloodying those working to tear it down. Particularly in Alabama in the early 1960s, it seemed as if blacks and civil rights activists were more or less live targets. I watched as more of my contemporaries left the South for other parts of the country that held more promise for equality—and safety. I, however, was still stationed on the base in Montgomery, with fewer than two years left to fulfill my enlistment commitment.

While I was at Maxwell, the February 1965 death of Jimmie Lee Jackson in the Alabama Black Belt town of Marion at the hands of state troopers was just the latest in a string of unprovoked and unjustified murders.[5] The twenty-six-year-old Jackson was beaten and shot while trying to protect his eighty-two-year-old grandfather from police and state troopers who were beating and clubbing people after they had departed a peaceful meeting at the Zion Methodist Church and marched to the nearby county jail to protest the detention of a civil rights activist there.

Civil rights activists responded to Jackson's murder by organizing a march from Selma to Montgomery in March 1965. Their intention was to peaceably cover the fifty-plus miles from Selma, the epicenter of the violence against demonstrators in Alabama, to the state capital, Montgomery, to bring national attention to voter suppression and the need to protect voting rights. Before they had walked even a mile, the six hundred peaceful marchers on the first day of the march were brutally attacked on the Edmund Pettus Bridge by Alabama state troopers and others with billy clubs and tear gas, in what came to be called Bloody Sunday.[6]

When the marchers started again two days later, Martin Luther King Jr. was in the lead, but this time the group turned back, respecting a hastily signed court order prohibiting them from continuing. Despite the peaceful action, that night one of the marchers, a white minister from Boston, was beaten by white extremists and died from his injuries.

The twelve days before the third attempt at the march saw a sea change across the country, highlighted by a national address in which President Johnson made a strong case for passage of the Voting Rights Act. On Sunday, March 21, the march to Montgomery began once again from Selma. By then it had garnered some twenty-five thousand participants from all over the country willing to risk life and limb to support the cause. This time the march, which took several days, was protected from Selma to Montgomery by the federalized Alabama National Guard.[7]

The marchers reached Montgomery on Wednesday evening. A few of us airmen at Maxwell asked if we could go into town to watch the end of the march. We were given permission to go for the evening but were instructed to wear civvies. We watched the marchers gather behind the St. Jude Educational Institute, a Roman Catholic high school south of the downtown. After holding a rally, they camped on a huge recreational playing field behind the school. Dr. King spoke. It was the only time in my life that I heard Dr. King speak in person. After his speech, Sammy Davis Jr., Harry Belafonte, Tony Bennett, Joan Baez, and Peter, Paul, and Mary were among a number of well-known singers who performed to the crowd. We returned to the base after all the festivities that evening.

The next day, Thursday, March 25, 1965, the massive gathering continued the rest of the way to the steps of the Alabama State Capitol. There they heard Martin Luther King Jr.'s inspiring speech, "How Long, Not Long." Dr. King could reach people intellectually and affectively, his message transcending class and culture. His philosophy and delivery resonated with people from university professors to domestic workers. The marches had been an exercise in civil disobedience by a coalition of people assembled not by race, but by cause. Supporters had come from all over the country to highlight the evil of racist laws, policies, and practices.

Still, life for African Americans living in the South did not measurably improve after passage of the Civil Rights Act in 1964 and the Voting Rights Act in August 1965, five months after the Selma-to-Montgomery marches. My response to the violence around me was two pronged. In the short term, I would ensure my physical safety with the purchase of a .38 Smith and Wesson for when I was on the road once I separated from the air force. I was prepared to push back if someone tried to control my freedom and movements, and to defend myself if someone threatened me with violence. In the long term, I was determined to get a college education.

On the base, I had a desk job that required working all three shifts on rotation, three days on each shift before three days off, after which the cycle started again. Despite my fluctuating work schedule, I was determined to take college classes during my time off. The officer at the base's education office suggested I enroll at the Montgomery Center on Bell Street. Now no longer there, the Montgomery Center, in the early 1960s, was a small satellite location of the University of Alabama.

The director of the center, Robert Springfield, was a retired air force colonel. There were no African American students at the center, so he was dubious. "But, let's see what we can do. If we can figure out a strategy . . ." He thought for a moment and then continued, "When you come to class, wear your uniform. Don't come here in civilian clothes. In uniform—they're less likely to bother you." That strategy worked. I enrolled, taking two classes at a time. Although I was indeed the only African American taking classes at the center, no one questioned it or harassed me. In fact, most of the men taking classes there were veterans or were on active duty. There was a respect for the uniform.

My boss at the base was Sergeant Tucker, a career enlisted man from the Appalachian region of East Tennessee. On my night shift, he often saw me reading textbooks. One night he said, "Listen—I think I can make your studies a little easier for you. I'm going to change your work schedule so that you're on day shifts only. But keep this between the two of us. Don't go around bragging about it." He did it just like that. With nights off, I could spend all that time studying. My buddies asked, "How'd you do that?"

But I played it cool. "I have no idea. Sergeant Tucker just told me this is what I have to do." Privately, however, I was in shock. Because Sergeant Tucker was southern and white, I hadn't even thought it worth asking him for some flexibility in my work schedule. But here he was initiating assistance without my ever asking.

Sergeant Tucker and I never had another conversation about it, and as far as I know, he never mentioned it to anyone else. He simply changed the work schedule. Only years later did it occur to me why my white southern sergeant was so circumspect in his kindness toward me. In Alabama at that time, anyone caught helping an African American in a public way was called names like "nigger-lover." Even in the U.S. Air Force, he couldn't risk what his colleagues and superiors would think about his gesture of helping a twenty-one-year-old black man further his education.

Certainly, Alabama governor George Wallace was a role model in denigrating anyone who treated blacks with respect. It was a strategy of fomenting hatred between groups of people so as to maintain control over them. What I discovered fifty-odd years later in Albany, Georgia, was that whites weren't the only ones to use this tactic.

I made the most of my time while stationed in Montgomery, meeting my air force obligations while taking college classes at the Montgomery

Center. Four times a year an airman was selected as Outstanding Airman of the Quarter. One quarter, I had performed well on duty and so was being considered for this distinction. As part of the selection process, I stood before a group of officers while they asked me questions. To probe about my well-roundedness, one asked me, "What do you do on your off-duty time?"

"I'm taking economics and political science classes, sir." The officers looked at each other, since that was one response they hadn't heard. They were well aware of the "let the good times roll" subculture that permeated off-duty life in the military. I felt, however, that I did not have any time to waste. My goal was a college education. But in the meantime, I was named Outstanding Airman that quarter.

In 1966, when my tour of duty ended, nearly four hundred thousand soldiers were deployed to Vietnam for the war's ground offensive.[8] I had loved being in the military. It was the only place that I knew of where all the standards and expectations were put equally in front of everybody. At my reenlistment interview, however, I saw that others who reenlisted were being sent straight to Saigon. I also knew that I wanted to earn a college degree as fast as I could. Those two factors made me decide not to reenlist. My next step would be to become a full-time student.

CHAPTER 8

# Taxes Aren't Segregated

As the date of my discharge from the air force approached in 1966, I started looking at colleges all over the Northeast and Midwest to attend on the Vietnam-era GI Bill, which would pay for tuition. I was looking seriously at the Ohio State University, Michigan State University, and Pennsylvania State University.

It didn't occur to me to consider a university in Alabama. For one, George Wallace was still governor, and his position on segregation hadn't changed: "segregation now, segregation tomorrow, segregation forever!"[1]

But the director of the University of Alabama Montgomery Center, Colonel Springfield, once again had sage advice for me. He asked, "Why would you want to go to these universities in other states?" He explained that if I went north to college, I would have to pay out-of-state tuition. "The GI bill will pay your tuition, and residence hall and meal fees. But paying out-of-state tuition will leave you with very little left over."

"Well, sir, you make a good point. I didn't realize that. I'm a little hardheaded. I went into the service against my dad's wishes. So, I'm not going to ask him for money now that I'm twenty-two years old."

Director Springfield proposed a strategy. "If you enroll at the University of Alabama, you will have in-state tuition. You've already been admitted to the university—when you enrolled in classes at the Montgomery Center. All you have to do is request to transfer to the main campus in Tuscaloosa. Over these last two years, you've already earned twelve hours of credit at UA."

"I need to go home and talk to my dad. He's a high school principal in Linden, and I don't want there to be any retribution on him. I don't want him to lose his job." The retribution I was worried about was happening all around Alabama. The Jim Crow system was determined to skirt the 1964 Civil Rights and 1965 Voting Rights Acts by exerting social pressure on the *parents* of young civil rights activists. Friends in Marengo County who were challenging segregation couldn't legally be punished. But their parents, who owned a service station, were put out of business when the suppliers retaliated by stopping delivery of gas and food items to the station.

So naturally I consulted with my dad on my next visit home. I asked, "What are your thoughts about my attending the University of Alabama?" I laid out Director Springfield's strategy, and my concerns about retribution on the family. My dad said, "Well, I've been paying taxes in Alabama for as long as I can remember. I don't think they have black taxes and white taxes. I think they took my money and supported Auburn, Alabama—all of those schools. So, you have just as much of a right to register at the University of Alabama as anyone else."

"What about your job?"

"I have enough time in the system that I can retire. I don't have any debt." Debt was considered almost a sin to his generation. "So, if you're going up there means I lose my job, I'm OK with that. You do what you need to do. I'll be OK. I'm secure."

The strategy worked. My transfer to the Tuscaloosa campus was approved. I registered for the summer session, which was set to start on June 1, 1966. No one in Marengo County but my parents knew that I was enrolling in the majority-white, flagship state university in Tuscaloosa. It was almost a covert process.

I was scheduled to be discharged on June 13, 1966. The air force, however, gave me a "thirty-day early out" so that I could matriculate on June 1. I was discharged on Friday, May 27. I headed for Maxwell's Day Street gates with two things in my car. One was my final payment for military service, a check for $508.12. The other was the Smith and Wesson .38, loaded and within easy reach.

As I cleared the gates, I had under my belt four years of working in a military system, with two of those years living in freedom and liberty abroad, and I reentered civilian life in a state where the governor led the talk about the sovereign state of Alabama—proud of its segregated system. I had in my mind the killing and abusive nature of life in the South—the three young men murdered in Mississippi, Jimmy Lee Jackson, the bombing of the Birmingham Church, and the murders during the civil rights marches from Selma to Montgomery. Those were the times.

I had then and still have the highest respect for Martin Luther King Jr. and for Mahatma Gandhi, but after four years of military service, I knew I was not suited intellectually, emotionally, or socially for nonviolence. Even today there is nothing I am more proud of than having served my nation, doing it well, and being honorably discharged, but I was very serious—determined, even—about not letting anyone commit a violent act against me. I felt almost a duty to protect myself because I had stopped the clock on my life and given four years to my country.

I drove the 110 miles southwest to see my parents in Sweet Water. The following Monday, I was in Tuscaloosa on the main campus of the University of Alabama. I had two days to transition from military to civilian life.

There were two things I felt deeply as I viewed the future that I saw for myself. First, I was not going to live a segregated life. Second, I was not going to leave the South in order to do so. Living in the North held no attraction for me. I was going to capture my space and my humanity in the land of my birth. I was not going to leave. I was going to insist that my life journey of self-discovery would take place in the South. The facts that my parents owned their land, had beaten the odds to get an education, and had toiled for years making meager wages as African American teachers was a graphic model for me. Their determination to live contented, fulfilled lives under an oppressive legal and social system kept me grounded in the conviction that Alabama was as much my state as it was George Wallace's.

I was determined not to be marginalized in any way. I felt strongly that, whatever I chose to do, I would be successful at it. Walking onto the University of Alabama campus, I saw a lot of options before me, even though I was one of about ten black students on the main campus at that time. I was there for about six weeks before I saw any other African American students besides my roommate.

My roommate, Larry, and I were assigned to Paty Hall, a brand-new residence hall named for Raymond Ross Paty, the seventeenth president of the university.[2] The five-story building held some five hundred men. We were assigned to the fifth floor on the end of the building. Years later, Larry and I still laughed at our room assignment. We would chuckle, "The algorithm they used for room assignments was kind of strange. How'd it do that—put the only two black students as far away as possible from the white students?"

Life on an historically white campus was quite an adjustment for me after growing up in a mostly African American community and then serving in the integrated air force. When I would sit down in a classroom, some students would get up and walk out. I thought, "Good luck with that! I'm not going anywhere. I worked in a weapons area in Taiwan where we had to get planes off the ground to support the Taiwanese. So, whether you're from Eutaw or Mountain Brook, have at it!" Eutaw, Alabama, was one of the poorest places in the state, and Mountain Brook one of the wealthiest. In any case, I had sharp elbows navigating the campus. I did realize, however that I still needed to be careful. Today, people ask if I ever got angry about the way I was treated at the University of Alabama, in those days. I can honestly say that between my coming of age during Jim Crow and my living abroad at an early age, I developed an extraordinary and perhaps exaggerated inner strength. My feelings were not at the mercy of what people said to me.

While in college, I routinely went down to the Citizens Club, a nightspot that played blues to a house full of mostly African American college-age students. Young people from Stillman College, an historically black liberal arts college in West Tuscaloosa, would be there, along with the handful of African American students from the University of Alabama.

One late afternoon I entered and saw, sitting at the bar, Ralph, a former airman I had served with in Taiwan. He greeted me, "Hey man, what're you doing here?"

"I'm a student at the University of Alabama. What are you doing here?" This was an all-black establishment. Ralph was the only white person there. At that time, blacks could not have entered a white club. But he was white, so he had the freedom to go wherever he wanted—in this case a black blues club.

Ralph asked, "Do you know any girls in here?"

"I think I know three or four of them."

"What're ya doing tonight?"

"Well, I'm going to be here for a while. I'm expecting some friends to show up."

"How about we get a couple of these girls and go somewhere else to get something to drink?" By now, I had moved from being angry about Jim Crow to being lucid, logical, and rational. So I said, "I'm going to be here for two or three hours. Why don't *you* go find a couple of *white* girls and bring them back here, and then we'll go." That instantly ended the discussion with him, as I knew it would. Antimiscegenation laws were still in effect in Alabama, but they were most frequently used not against white men associating with black women, but against black men who associated with white women.

Throughout my college years, African Americans remained at risk of violence from whites, including from law enforcement. Entering the criminal justice system only further exposed blacks to more violence. My dad would warn me every time I traveled between home and campus: "Don't unnecessarily provoke a policeman who sees you sitting at a traffic light in a small town driving a car that has a University of Alabama sticker on it. He's bored. He may pull behind you and turn the light on. You might say something that provokes him. Later, it's your word against his. Guess who's word they're going to take?"

Back then, there were no interstate highways, so to travel from Tuscaloosa to Sweet Water to visit my parents I drove through small towns, taking either State Route 69 through Greensboro, or another road (now U.S. Route 43) from Eutaw down through Demopolis. Both were secluded. The Smith and Wesson was available in the glove compartment at all times. I did not plan—having served my nation—to be shot or harmed because I was black.

All I wanted was the right to be left alone. I did not care about other people's races. I, in turn, did not want to be bothered, harmed, or killed because other people cared about mine. Give me the freedom to become a contributing member of society.

The mid-1960s, however, were tough times for young black men coming of age, trying to manage their lives, to get college educations, and to be safe. That required them to constantly engage in decision-making. They had to make smart choices. They also had to make sure that if they were minding their own business, not bothering anybody, that they had a way to mitigate the violence that could still be coming in their direction at any moment.

As part of the first wave of African American students at the University of Alabama, first and foremost we were committed to our academic studies. We also advocated for civil rights academically, politically, culturally, civically by voting, and socially. We tried to make space for diversity in every corner of the campus. In hindsight, I think we were trying to help whites realize that white southern history was not the only version of southern history, that there was more than one southern identity, and there was room—in the late 1960s—for both.

One year, a handful of students and I visited the university's president, Frank Rose, in his office to share with him our feelings about a fraternity float with the theme of "the Old South" in the homecoming parade. The women were dressed in antebellum-style dresses, the men in Confederate uniforms. They had little black boys on the float fanning them. We were incredulous that the university had approved this float that so grotesquely romanticized Alabama's history of slavery. We appealed to Dr. Rose: "We are Alabamians and we are from the South. We are university students here, and we just don't think this is right." The president listened attentively, thanked us for coming to meet with him, and said he would see what he could do. We never heard anything back, but at least we had made our position heard.

We were more successful in our effort to open up athletics at the University of Alabama. In 1967, four other African American students and I attempted to join Coach Bear Bryant's football team as walk-ons during spring training. We had heard that one of the assistant coaches had said that blacks had neither the academic nor the athletic ability to play football for the University of Alabama. We'd heard that before: "Not smart enough. No physical ability."

With our goal to say, "Nothing is off limits to us! We are not inferior because of the color of our skin!," we all recognized the significance of football at the University of Alabama. We walked onto the field and said, "Coach Bryant, sir. Sign us up!" All five of us had played football in high school, but only a couple had real interest in staying on the team. I had absolutely none. Some people teased me later about it: "You were just out there to raise hell."

Alabama football then, as now, was a big deal. Jackie Sherrill, who later coached at Washington State, the University of Pittsburgh, Texas A&M, and Mississippi State, was a graduate assistant for the team. Ken Stabler, who would go on to a career in the National Football League, was the quarterback.

In about the second week of spring training, Coach Sherrill ran some drills where he stood behind us yelling while we ran plays against the first-string defense. In my last run, I felt like I was in a movie with everything happening in slow motion, each blow painful in its detail and intensity.

The next morning, I was supposed to get up early for a biology test in Gallalee Hall, but I felt like I couldn't get out of bed. My entire body ached from being brutalized by the previous day's rigorous drills. Samuel, one of the other five walk-ons, came to my dorm room and said, "Art, Coach Bryant and the others are looking for you. They have your uniform."

"Let me tell you what they can do with that uniform!" I proceeded to use some colorful language.

"No! You can't say that to Coach Bryant."

"Fine—then you say it. My future is in passing this biology class. It's not on that damn football field." And I did make it to that biology test. For me, passing and getting my bachelor's degree from the University of Alabama was my future. I had enjoyed football since playing in high school, and had done my part to help integrate the Alabama team. A career in football, however, was not my goal. In the end, two of the five walk-ons stayed on the team and three of us left. Coach Bryant went on to recruit black athletes for his University of Alabama team.

I kept on with my studies, completing a bachelor's degree in cultural anthropology in three years, graduating in 1969. I chose that major partly because I wanted to understand the human hardships that characterized the Alabama Black Belt. The B.B. King song "Bad Luck" captured how I felt about the region I grew up in: there were few opportunities, and few avenues out of a life of "bad breaks."

I wanted to understand how people in such a place could endure so much. So I studied how people exploit resources around the world. It could be land. It could be human beings. The exploitation of land could be in the form of stripping the land of valuable minerals or of the nutrients and water that support the growth of crops. The exploitation of human beings could take the form of paying people starvation wages, thereby enslaving them. The Alabama Black Belt had its own version of human exploitation.

After completing my bachelor's degree, I stayed at the University of Alabama to enroll directly into a master's program, which I completed in 1970. From there I took a job with the Tennessee Department of Education in Nashville. While working there, I took some graduate classes at the Peabody College of Vanderbilt University. I wanted to go on for a doctorate, but I needed to get out of the South for a while and get more work experience. Not much interested in living in the North or West of the country, I was attracted to the possibility of going back to Asia.

In 1972, I accepted a position as chief executive officer of District 3, in the Pacific-Area Department of Defense Dependent School Programs in Bangkok, Thailand, thereby returning to Asia as a civilian. The post allowed me to experience life in another country in a completely different way than when I was an eighteen-year-old airman in Taiwan.

CHAPTER 9

# Lessons Learned along the Way

I arrived in Thailand as a self-confident and eager twenty-eight-year-old. There, I was keen to observe how the culture was structured, and to compare it with other countries in the region and with mine. For me, the most powerful takeaway of that experience was the realization that the superior-subordinate relationship was a human condition. It was not a Demopolis, Linden, or Sweet Water, Alabama, issue. I found that when people are immersed in their slice of a superior-subordinate society, they personalize it. When I was able to observe other cultures objectively, I could see that many countries dealt with the same questions of difference and Otherness. That helped deepen my understanding of the human condition.

My second experience living abroad came in the early 1970s. This time I was older, held bachelor's and master's degrees, and was working as a civilian. In my new role I was responsible for anticipating and providing for the postsecondary educational needs of two thousand U.S. Department of Defense dependents through relationships and agreements with more than a dozen tuition-fee and two correspondence schools servicing people all over Thailand. The work touched on all aspects of education (e.g., finance, governance, instructional methods, student support).

Those two years in Thailand gave me tremendous experience administering educational programs. They inspired me to return to the University of Alabama in 1974 to work toward a doctorate in higher education administration. There, I took classes, did research, and wrote my dissertation while working in the office of the vice president for academic affairs, where I was responsible for administering a grant-funded university-wide career development program for students.

After I completed the doctorate in 1976, I held a joint appointment at UA as an assistant to the vice president for academic affairs and as an assistant professor of higher education. I loved being part of a university as both staff and educator—pushing the boundaries of knowledge, passing that knowledge on to students, and applying knowledge to strengthen communities locally and globally.

I particularly enjoyed the existing international reach of the university. Through a partnership between UA and the Monterrey Institute of Technology and Higher Education, I spent one summer teaching senior academic administrators at the institute's Mexico City campus. There, I observed the benefits to all concerned of such university collaborations, which helped inform my role in developing international programs for students and faculty.

In 1983, I left Alabama again, but for once didn't travel very far. I accepted the post of dean of Graduate Studies and Sponsored Research at Kennesaw State University in Marietta, Georgia, thirty miles north of Atlanta. There I was responsible for providing leadership for graduate studies, promoting international studies, and building relationships with external agencies like the local Chamber of Commerce. After four years at Kennesaw State, I took on a new challenge in the University System of Georgia headquarters in downtown Atlanta as vice chancellor for Services.

With thirty-four campuses in the USG at that time, my duties included policy development on all matters related to public service, outreach, and international programs. I served as liaison with state and local governmental agencies on public service and outreach needs and managed the system-wide international intercultural studies program with fiscal and budgetary responsibility for eighteen study-abroad programs in ten countries.

After thirteen years at the USG in Atlanta, I left for a post at the University of Georgia in Athens, where I spent ten years working to extend the institution's public service and outreach programs before circling back to where I had started almost fifty years earlier. I had first experienced life at the University of Alabama as an enlisted airman taking night classes. In 2010, I returned to the University of Alabama as a vice chancellor for International Programs and Outreach, senior research fellow, and professor. Over that almost half-century, I learned lessons too many to count that would later help me understand the context of Albany State University in the mid-2010s.

Over the years I've traveled to more than thirty countries, mostly for work or service, but some for the sheer pleasure of experiencing other cultures. Each time, I found ways to get out of cities and into small villages where I could feel the rhythms of the rural areas. When I was young in Taiwan, I would ride off the base alone on a bicycle. Later in Thailand, I hired a driver. Wherever I went, I would meet and speak with the locals, observing the life around me. In those days, of course, there were no electronic technologies to interrupt our interactions. It was much like what I had grown up with back home.

Once, in Cameroon, Mr. Ndam, a Cameroonian who worked with the United Nations, drove me from the capital Yaounde west about 170 miles to the largest city, Doula. Along the way, we stopped at a small store. Inside, there was African music with a blues sound playing. A woman who was probably a little tipsy was dancing alone. It reminded me of the juke joint back home where if people thought the music sounded OK, the whiskey tasted right, and the spirit moved them, they just got up and danced. No partner required.

That scene and other scenes along the way reminded me how people in all parts of the world find ways to enhance life with music and simplicity. I watched how human beings find generosity, kindness, and respect when living in close proximity under difficult conditions—much like my childhood. Having had such experiences in Sweet Water, Taiwan, Thailand, Cameroon, and other parts of the world, I'm sad to think of how, today, too many people turn to technology instead of one another to find a sense of peace and connection with others.

I've learned more about myself and my home country when I was away from it, but maybe that's not so paradoxical. When I was in the States, I was too busy working and doing to take time for contemplation. While living abroad I had time to think deeply about place. In Thailand, I could see elements of Sweet Water: people working hard, raising their children, trying to take care of their health and their jobs—just as we did back home in the Alabama Black Belt.

Helping people, especially students, experience the power of living or studying abroad became one of my primary goals as a university administrator. I hoped through providing strategic and administrative support,

I could help faculty members develop and lead programs for secondary-school and college-age students. My desire was to help those young people get experiences abroad while they were still shaping their attitudes, beliefs, and values about others. I wanted to help them understand different cultures by giving them experiences to compare their culture with others.

Living and working abroad helped me develop a broader, even global, perspective of the human experience. I was heartened to discover that people around the world have more in common than they do differences. It was sobering, however, to find that people everywhere have the capacity to form stereotypes that can harden into an orthodoxy and metastasize into tribalism, whether about religion, gender, ethnicity, or race. I wonder if leaning into stereotypes leads some to turn against education and critical thinking. Power seekers manipulate others by using anti-intellectualism in order to get otherwise smart people to engage in dysfunctional, destructive behaviors.

---

Deep in my core from about the age of thirteen or fourteen, I developed—most of the time unconsciously—an ability to push back against racial orthodoxy about what it meant to be black or white. My nature pulled me to use logic, reason, and facts to understand and to operate in the world, rather than to rely on the politicized environment of race. By the time I arrived at the University of Alabama, I had moved away from being circumscribed by color. I was open to any group that showed kindness for and respect to others.

Racial orthodoxy is tied to notions of loyalty to a group. Race in our country has led to what some call tribalism. One negative effect of tribalism that I have witnessed many times is the mindset of what is commonly referred to in the African American community as "crabs in a barrel" or "crabs in a bucket." L. Douglas Wilder sums up this attitude as "If I can't have it, neither can you."[1]

I first experienced the essence of this metaphor when I was stationed at Maxwell AFB and taking evening classes at the Montgomery Center. Sometimes after class I would go to the Laicos Club, where airmen typically hung out, arriving about ten o'clock. One night, after my economics and political science classes, the guys started in on me, "Why are you taking those classes? Are you trying to be better than everybody else?"

"Hell, yeah, I am," I responded. One of the guys, Tommy, leaned back and laughed. "So, what did those white folks teach you in those classes tonight?"

"They told me not to hang out with good-for-nothings like you."

We all enjoyed this good-natured banter. There were no hard feelings when I would tease back, "I hang out down here with you, but you've got a look of going nowhere fast, man. I'll have a beer or two with you, but I'm not going to take on any of your bad habits."

I began to understand, however, what sentiment such exchanges conveyed. When a person in a community started to get ahead, the rest would try to pull the person back down. People feared that, the longer a person stayed in school, the more they might become estranged from the community. Tommy's philosophy was that "real" black men had to have grown up in the ghetto, been arrested, and gone to jail. The successful, well-educated would lose their black purity and would no longer be "black enough." They would lose their identity with their tribe.

Tied to racial orthodoxy and tribalism is the issue of class, even if people don't want to call it that. My earliest memories about class concern the standards of beauty, which for far too long hewed to fair skin and straight hair. *Ebony* magazine used to advertise products to lighten one's skin color and straighten one's hair. As a child of nine or ten, I thought this was about the craziest thing I had ever heard. But I would hear mothers talking about whether a child had good hair or bad hair. "Good hair" meant straight; "bad hair" meant a child had natural African hair. In the 1940s and 1950s, even men, especially those who thought they had to make their way in a white world, processed their hair.

As a child, I didn't have the sociological language to frame what I saw, but what I was observing was that skin color and hair texture were tied to caste and class. As an adult, I would come to understand that African Americans had been socialized to remake themselves to try and achieve a prescribed standard of beauty in order to elevate their class.

This unnatural standard of beauty persisted into the early 1960s. In yearbooks from that time, almost all the homecoming queens at historically black colleges and universities are light skinned or biracial. I remember hearing a story from someone that went to Alabama State in the mid-1950s, who one day was sitting at the cafeteria table when a fellow student walked up and announced that she was going to run for homecoming queen. Everyone at the table erupted in laughter. They thought the idea was ludicrous. They said, "Don't you realize what they look for in a homecoming queen? You sure don't fit that! You're too dark skinned."

The Black Power movement of the 1960s and 1970s was largely responsible for shifting the needle. People started to refer to themselves as "black" or "African American," and James Brown and others started singing about loving oneself. The Afro hairstyle came into vogue, making it OK to have black, kinky hair. James Brown's 1968 song, "Say It Loud—I'm Black and I'm Proud," says it all.

As blacks turned away from white standards of beauty, other designations of class, like education level or church affiliation, took hold. When Karen and I moved to Albany, our choice of church affiliation caused a stir with some in Albany's African American community.

One morning as I walked from my car to my office on the Albany State campus, a woman stopped me and after a few pleasantries said, "You've joined the wrong church. That's not where the big Negroes in Albany go." My response was, "Well, the church has a great pastor. He gives good sermons. We like him and his family. We just really like the feel of the church." Our education levels and the nature of our jobs made us part of the black upper class, so people thought we should be members of the church they considered appropriate for upper-class African Americans.

I have worked hard to mitigate issues of class, always thinking back to how my parents comported themselves within their community. I am guided by the memory of my dad choosing siding over brick for his new house.

---

One human condition that has always struck me is the thread of anti-intellectualism and anti-education that runs through many cultures. Education levels tied to class have been in the past, and continue to be, weaponized in political discourse. An incident from 1962 comes to mind. While waiting to board a bus to leave for Taiwan, I happened to find myself standing on the fringes of a campaign event for George Wallace at the very same bus station in Thomasville, Alabama. It was an unintended opportunity to hear his political rhetoric in person. Wallace had lost the Democratic gubernatorial primary in 1958 to then state attorney general John Malcolm Patterson, who had the support of the Ku Klux Klan. In 1962 Wallace was running again, this time on a racist pro-segregation platform.

I watched as Wallace climbed up onto the back of a flatbed truck shortly after a country western band had whipped the crowd into a frenzy. His speech was pure demagoguery. He railed for about thirty minutes against "those scallywagging federal judges, Yankees, hippies in denim shirts, and professors with beards and pipes." He hit right to the core of the southern white working-class inferiority complex. He went on, "And by the way, all of them think they're better than you. They'll call you 'red neck' to your face. But we have states' rights. That's what we've been fighting for since the Civil War. We want autonomy—I know you all don't like that fancy word, but it means 'Do what we want to do, when we want to do it.'" The crowd loved it.

In hindsight, it seems both amusing and sad at the same time. Wallace was expert at political theater. He could get up on a stump and have the crowds laughing at his jokes, or he could flat out lie, and the crowds would believe him. Wallace was playing to southern whites' pent-up anger, seizing an opportunity to win votes from those who seemed forever shamed by the loss of the Civil War a century earlier.

Today, some of our national leaders use the same tactic when railing against "the elites." We see it in fearmongering about illegal immigrants stealing jobs, or rhetoric against environmental science and data. I would see the same strategy play out in Albany during the consolidation process.

An encounter that impressed on me the long memories that people have about race, history, and culture occurred while I was working at the University of Georgia. I was meeting with board members of one of the public service and outreach units. I opened my remarks as I generally did by providing context for the board's discussion that afternoon. I said something about Georgia's history and about the Civil War. After the presentation, we were at a social hour. One of the board members, an elderly woman, came up to me and said, "Dr. Dunning, let me tell you something. You know that Civil War you were talking about? That was the war of northern aggression."

Somebody in her circle of relationships, family or friends, had defined the Civil War as an aggressive act by the North toward the South. She was still holding on to that interpretation. I imagine that since childhood she heard family members tell stories along the lines of "General Sherman brought troops to Atlanta and destroyed Georgia by burning down towns from Atlanta to Savannah. It set us back a hundred years. We've had to bring the economy back from ruins." She carried that perspective of the war all her life.

I heard the same sentiment when I was stationed in Taiwan. I would hear southern white airmen complaining about "those damn Yankees telling us what to do." I finally realized that they still deeply resented, and were even embarrassed about, the fact that the South lost the Civil War.

Diametrically opposed passions about the Civil War run deep and strong even today. Many people have observed and written about the underlying cultural reasons that southern football, especially state college football, has become almost a civic religion. Fans relish the traditions surrounding the game and swell with pride in their devotion to their team.[2] When Alabama played Notre Dame in 2013, I heard that there were some folks yelling, "We're going to beat those damn Yankees." It wasn't just a football game to them.

Over the years, I have developed an understanding about people's sense of loss. I came to understand the other side of this racial divide, rather than just knowing my place in the story—of my grandparents and slavery. Still, it fascinates me how some people cling to memories, whether they are of the Crusades of the Middle Ages, the Civil War of the mid-1800s, or the civil rights era of the 1960s.

The lenses through which people look at life—their gender, race, history, culture, and politics—help create their opinions. People can experience the same events on the same land and yet come down on different sides of them. Some will glorify them, while others will feel degraded. Memories of the past may be an elixir for some, as when people romanticize about the times of Robert E. Lee. For others, those memories only conjure the pain of slavery going back to 1619.

For more than 80 percent of the four-hundred-year history of African Americans living in what became the United States, whites have either owned or controlled black people's lives, devising a series of legal systems in order to grind out any exceptionality in people. Think about it. Laws made it a crime to learn to read and write. Lynchings were used to control and terrorize. Law enforcement frequently condoned, if not actively participated in, violence against blacks. No wonder that outsiders looking in say that today some African Americans have almost a defeatist attitude. They may emote high self-esteem, but their achievement levels speak of generations of being ground down to being "less than." This phenomenon can happen not only to individuals but also to organizations.

Throughout this long period, the inferred rule has always been, "You obey and respond and stay in your place." President Johnson signing the Civil Rights Act didn't produce instant change. There was no process for reconciliation. As a result, you still have people who are saying, "Now, wait a minute. Somebody needs to say something about this." On the other side, others are saying, "Get over it! Let's move on."

Divergent memories of history in our country explain why, today, it may feel that there is always an undercurrent of anger—on both sides, white and black. Neither side seems to be able to get it out of their system. I have spent decades trying to understand the southeastern corner of our country, which I love dearly for what it represents in terms of the endurance required by my ancestors to survive in a region dominated by plantation agriculture. I fear that it is impossible to fully reconcile this history. My feelings today when talking to southerners about history are, "My history is not your history. We're not going to have a conversation where we can bring that together. Let's accept that. It is what it is."

CHAPTER 10

# The Intersection of Race and Higher Education in Georgia

During my years working in Georgia, I learned a lot about issues of race and culture within a specific context—that of public higher education. The first lesson I learned when joining the University System of Georgia in Atlanta was that issues of race can get caught up in a catch-22 from which it is difficult to extricate.

In the mid-1970s, the federal government intervened in Georgia's educational affairs by mandating that the USG develop a desegregation plan. Howard Jordan Jr., a former president of Savannah State College, was the first African American to serve as a vice chancellor for Services in the USG in Atlanta. He helped the system craft the plan that in 1983 was deemed satisfactory. I followed Jordan in the position, with one of my duties being to provide oversight for the desegregation plan.

Under the terms of a consent decree agreement, joint programs were to be established at Georgia's three historically black colleges and universities (HBCUs). Albany State University (historically black) and Darton State College (historically white) were to create jointly a continuing education (CE) center in an office suite of a building in downtown Albany. Two people were assigned to the office, one from each campus. Similar arrangements were to be made in Savannah and Fort Valley among four other institutions, but rather than rent space, new buildings were constructed for their joint programs. The plan was slowly implemented.

In the late 1980s, when we in the USG office felt that the terms of the consent decree were satisfied, I traveled to Washington, D.C., to meet with staff at the U.S. Department of Education (DOE) and presented USG office documentation on all that had been done to comply with the decree. A month or two later, the DOE determined that, since all of the requirements of the consent decree had been met, including the joint CE center, the USG would no longer be under DOE supervision. Not long after, Darton State pulled its staff person out of the office back to its main campus.

Albany State's president went to Atlanta to meet with the chancellor. He said, "I don't know what to do. We're now in this CE office by ourselves." The USG office, however, took no action to enforce the joint relationship. No one had the stomach to demand that Darton uphold its end of the consent decree order, which was supposed to be a permanent change. Nobody talked about it, but they all knew it was a problem about race.

Darton State did not want to collaborate with Albany State, and Albany State was reluctant, too. Neither one was proactive about maintaining the relationship, and so the partnership ended. It was an unsolvable dilemma. Neither side liked or trusted the other. Each group bought into stereotypes about the other. And each side, at times, acted out some of those stereotypes, thereby hardening those stereotypes further.

In the end, what was supposed to be a permanent change fell apart as soon as federal supervision ended. Albany's joint CE center was eventually completely closed.

The way the USG office handled the derailment of the consent decree terms gave me a preview of a second lesson I learned while working there: inaction or benign neglect can take over when an organization is risk averse. Up until the late 1990s, that was how the USG office dealt with its three public, historically black universities. They simply left them alone. My definition of what it meant to be black, cultivated as a teenager, came from the strength I saw in the people around me—at that time, my neighbors. My definition of authenticity came from endurance, perseverance, innovation, creativity, and hard work. Those values that I carried ran counter—in fact, almost completely opposite—to perceptions by USG staff about the nature of the HBCU campuses. In other words, many of the system staff held a low opinion of the efficiency and effectiveness of the HBCUs. Yet they lacked the political will to tackle any processes that would likely precipitate a huge backlash and possibly litigation.

My USG office colleagues in policy-making roles saw the intensity of anger in members of those at the three historically black universities, an anger that was so intense that it was almost dysfunctional. What the white system office staff did not realize was that many at the historically black institutions carried with them the almost unbearable weight of all the slights and omissions that had accumulated and remained unresolved over the years. Whites saw the angry behaviors, but they could not appreciate that the pain ran deep into the core of blacks' beings. As a result, both sides acted in ways that failed to serve the long-term interests of the state, the individual universities, and students.

Because of the complexity of their operations and the impact they had on the state and the nation, the system staff and the USG Board of Regents focused the majority of their time and energy on the University of Georgia and Georgia Tech (Georgia Institute of Technology). When discussion finally came around to the three historically black schools, there was an unspoken understanding: "You touch those at risk. They want to be left alone; they don't want to change." And, as can happen in any circumstances, the result of long-term inattention is that people are no longer interacting, which can lead them to fall back into negative stereotypes about one another, particularly when there is a racial dimension.

I spent most of my time in the USG office looking at how to get all the institutions in the system involved in economic development. During that time, I was also able to watch the racial dynamics between schools and the USG office, and among the schools themselves. During those observations, I discovered a third lesson: in trying to protect their universities, some supporters of historically black schools became their own worst enemy with the strategies they used to influence decision-making.

In my interactions with the various leaders of the system's HBCUs, some seemed incapable of advocating for their institutions without bringing up historical and current unfairness. In fact, a few had learned over the years that they could protect their control over their institutions by using the language of victimization and grievance with the USG office staff. They understood that most people do not have the stomach to be called bigots and racists. The strategy employed, therefore, was "play being the victim of entrenched racism a few times, and the system office will leave us alone."

Sadly, much of what these few leaders said about unfair treatment in the past was not untrue. The historically black campuses *had been* being wrongly and unfairly treated. Up until around the 1990s, there was little political will to address and correct that unfairness. I would hear that from both sides. For their part, system staff would say things like, "We had nothing to do with the injustices of the past. We can't change what was done forty or fifty years ago. These HBCU administrators just need to get over it."

From some of the schools' administrators, the attitude was, "We're not *ever* going to get over these injustices!" I witnessed in more than one system budget-request meeting HBCU administrators, in their opening remarks, saying in veiled terms something to the effect of, "You know, we've never been treated fairly," or "Well, we've always been taken advantage of. We're used to it." System staff left those meetings shaking their heads and saying, "We just can't take this every year. We're tired of hearing complaint after complaint. We know in 1950 and even later things weren't fair in Georgia, but by God we can't play it out at every meeting."

Since I was one of the few African Americans in a senior leadership position at the USG office, after these budget meetings I would get calls from some of the HBCU administrators who turned to me as an off-line, informal channel of communication. Not knowing how the other schools in the system made their budget requests, they sought my opinion on how the chancellor received their budget or program proposals. My advice was always the same: "A budget hearing is not the time to come in with grievances about how your school has been treated unfairly in the past. I suggest you come to the meetings with a plan about how you want to move forward given your institutional assets and identified strategic directions. Do like some of the other schools and come in saying 'We've looked at our peer and aspirational institutions, and we have developed an ambitious strategic plan. We'd like the system office to help us on our journey to reach our potential.' In other words, have a blueprint for moving forward instead of making everyone feel badly about past wrongs."

After one meeting, I pulled aside one HBCU president who was gifted at playing the victimization card, and said, "You keep talking about how the school was funded in the 1950s. Do you think there is the will or capacity to go back and correct all that? One of the things that we perhaps have trouble coming to grips with is that there's not likely to be an apology or reparations. The only thing we have left is the development of these institutions with the resources that we have. Making a case every time for correcting historical unfairness—that just aggravates the whole process." This particular president, and a few of the others I worked with, could not, or would not, hear what I was saying. Or, they did not agree.

Another example of how supporters of the historically black campuses proved to be their own worst enemies was their approach to expressing disapproval of their leaders. I had worked in the USG office for about a month when I received a letter from an HBCU alumnus alleging all sorts of misbehavior at their alma mater. The person writing identified himself or herself only as "a loyal graduate."

Alarmed, I thought to myself, "This sounds egregious! Do we need to call the Georgia Bureau of Investigation or the state attorney general?" I took the letter to one of my colleagues who had been in the system office for a long time. He said, "Art, throw that stuff in the trash. We get those kinds of letters from the HBCUs all the time."

Unhappy HBCU supporters, alumni, and other interested parties would vent their frustrations with campus leadership by going over their heads with letters to the USG office staff, the chancellor, or the governor, or all of them. These letters were rarely about serious academic matters but rather dealt with petty grievances and complaints. Many of the letters we received in the USG office were anonymous, leaving doubt as to their authenticity. Other letters were completely off-the-wall, making it even easier for the recipient to drop it into the trash.

The periodic flood of such letters contributed mightily to the USG office staff's view of the historically black campuses as rampant with unresolvable discord. I doubt the letter writers realized how damaging their actions were to their beloved institutions.

More than anything else, the letters suggested to me that many at Georgia's historically black public universities did not manage conflict in a productive way. The resulting barrage of letters to higher-ups in the state system, all the way up to the governor, fed into existing stereotypes about African Americans and unfortunately led to the devaluation of the HBCUs by the people in positions to help those same HBCUs. I left the USG office for a position at the University of Georgia in the summer of 2000, pondering an unanswered question: could Georgia's higher education governing body and its three historically black universities ever reconcile their differences regarding race, history, and culture?

# PART THREE

# A Region Paralyzed by Its Past

After a decade working at the University of Georgia, I decided to test a semiretirement by moving back to my home state and working at my alma mater. As vice chancellor for International Programs and Outreach, I advised the chancellor on opportunities to further build international programs, strengthen the base of academic and research partnerships, and expand economic development initiatives for a three-campus system, including the University of Alabama, Alabama-Birmingham, and Alabama-Huntsville. I also taught graduate seminars on the challenges of higher education in the twenty-first century and served on doctoral student dissertation committees. Three years later, I accepted the call to serve as interim president of Albany State University in Albany, Georgia.

To gain some perspective on the community and region of what would become my home for the next five years, I did what I always do. I studied the history of the region to understand the context I would find myself working in. Learning about Southwest Georgia's five hundred years of growth and development helped me become socialized there, especially around issues of race.

CHAPTER 11

# Albany, the Egypt of the Confederacy

The nature of the land and a navigable river flowing through the region determined where the city of Albany would be sited. Just north of, and flowing somewhere under, the Hartsfield-Jackson Atlanta International Airport is the source of the Flint River.[1] The river meanders south more than two hundred miles to Albany, then through the Gulf Coastal Plain of Southwest Georgia and into Lake Seminole. From there the waters eventually make their way through the panhandle of Florida and into the Gulf of Mexico.

The original inhabitants along the river were Native Americans of the Southeastern Woodlands. They named the river Thronateeska—"flint picking-up place"—for the abundant flint, a hard sedimentary form of the mineral quartz found in limestone, which was used for making tools.[2] Subsequent peoples living (the Muskogee) or exploring (Hernando de Soto and other Spaniards in the 1500s) gave the river the same name in their own languages.[3]

From de Soto's arrival up until the early 1800s, there would be jockeying and skirmishes for control of land in Southwest Georgia among several groups of Native Americans, and between those groups and Spanish, English, and French missionaries, traders, and military forces.[4]

W. E. B. Du Bois, who studied the area in great depth, recounts that in 1814, "Andrew Jackson knew the Flint well, and marched across it once to avenge the Indian Massacre at Fort Mims . . . not long before the battle of New Orleans [at the end of the War of 1812]."[5] While the United States was fighting the British, it was also engaged in the Creek War, which ended with a treaty in 1814. Part of the terms of the agreement ceded to

Georgia what would, twenty-four years later, include Albany and much of the surrounding land. In the early 1830s, the Native Americans living in the area were forcibly moved west.[6]

Later that decade, the United States entered a recession. It, together with other factors, prompted slave-owning planters from Virginia, North and South Carolina, and eastern Georgia to move into Southwest Georgia to grow their labor-intensive tobacco, Carolina rice, sugarcane, and cotton. The last, however, would be the dominant cash crop in Southwest Georgia.[7]

A confluence of events set the course for cotton to take over as the most lucrative commodity and to increase the demand for slave labor. The invention of the cotton gin in the late 1700s created even greater demand for slaves because planters could push their slaves to plant and harvest more. The thirst for more land grew, too. In 1803, the U.S. purchase of the Louisiana Territory from France vastly increased the availability of land for these land-hungry cotton planters. In the 1820s, the Petit Gulf cotton was discovered to grow well inland, was thought to move more smoothly through the cotton gin than other varieties, and produced a more usable cotton.[8] These factors set up Southwest Georgia, from the time of its earliest white settlers, for a plantation economy of white landowners, white overseers, and black slave labor.

What became the city of Albany started in 1836 as a trading post on the banks of the Flint River, eventually becoming the seat of the newly formed Dougherty County in 1853. As the numbers of white planters grew, more and more slaves were brought in to produce cotton. Du Bois observed that "there had risen in West Dougherty perhaps the richest slave kingdom the modern world ever knew. A hundred and fifty barons commanded the labor of nearly six thousand Negroes."[9]

During the Civil War, Albany provided men to fight, and food and supplies, for the Confederate Army. Du Bois writes that "this was indeed the Egypt of the Confederacy,—the rich granary whence potatoes and corn and cotton poured out to the famished and ragged Confederate troops as they battled for a cause lost."[10]

The superior-subordinate social structure of the region changed little after the war. Many freed slaves left the region to find work. Those who stayed, struggled. As in the Alabama Black Belt, many Dougherty County families became sharecroppers or tenant farmers to white landowners.[11]

Incarcerating blacks for minor transgressions, real or fabricated, had the benefit of providing what was in essence slave labor for the state and for local enterprises. By the late 1880s, the town had the three private contractor-run prisons in Albany filled mostly with African American men. Du Bois writes of one "'stockade,' as the county prison was called; the white folks say it is ever full of black criminals,—the black folks say that only colored boys are sent to jail, and they not because they are guilty, but because the State needs criminals to eke out its income by their forced labor."[12]

Still, slowly, a segregated African American community grew. First, a church was established. In the late 1800s a "Negro school" was started near Albany, "where children go after crops are laid by."[13] Du Bois reported that in 1890, the population of Dougherty County consisted of "ten thousand Negroes and two thousand whites."[14] In the late 1890s, there were about fifteen hundred black families living mostly in one- or two-room cabins built of boards without plastering; light and ventilation came from a single door and windows with no glass panes. Heat was provided by a fireplace.[15]

In 1900, Walter Walker opened the town's first African American business, a grocery, in Albany's "Harlem district." The first black-owned drugstore opened in 1912 and the first African American high school in 1928.[16]

In the early 1900s, Dr. Joseph Winthrop Holley founded the Albany Bible and Manual Training Institute for African American youths. Construction of permanent buildings began on fifty acres on the floodplain of the east bank of the Flint River. The school would eventually become Albany State University.

In the thirty years leading up to the Great Depression, the Phoebe Putney Hospital and Flint River Cotton Mill were opened, a Carnegie library was built, and cars and an electric trolley were introduced.[17]

Farming in the region suffered from soil deprivation and erosion, an invasion of the boll weevil in the mid-1870s, a "Great Flood" in 1925, and the Great Depression in the 1930s. Still, the region remained an agrarian economy. Slowly, farmers began to diversify their crops to include peanuts, soybeans, and pecans. A cattle industry was started in the 1930s on land that had been worn out by cotton production.[18]

The demeaning and abusive arrangement that characterizes sharecropping remained unchanged, driving away hardworking people in search of a better life. The road between Albany and Dothan, Alabama, and on to my hometown of Sweet Water, is still dotted with abandoned, old sharecropper shacks. As I've noted earlier, many sharecroppers left in the middle of the night for the North.

In the 1940s, a tornado cut a swath of destruction through Albany, and an air force training base was built and trained pilots during World War II.[19] In the 1950s, a marine supply base was sited in the area. The location was selected because of its distance from the coast (to avoid corrosion issues) and its accessibility by rail and road.[20] Passenger train business was robust through the 1950s but ended in the late 1970s.[21]

By 1960, Albany's population had grown from almost twenty thousand in 1940 to almost sixty thousand. The city was segregated in all facets of life. It was reported that the city had "a history of generally peaceful if unequal relations between the black minority, representing about 40 percent of the population, and the white majority." In early 1961, however, a "modest petition for reforms by a small group of blacks . . . was condemned by the staunchly segregationist *Albany Herald* and was subsequently rejected."[22]

In the fall of that year, with the encouragement of members of the Student Nonviolent Coordinating Committee (SNCC), Albany's black community groups united in a grassroots civil rights campaign to desegregate the city. It would come to be known as the Albany Movement. Martin Luther King Jr. twice visited Albany to support the movement, but with little success. One difficulty he encountered was infighting among the city's African American community. Another was a formidable opponent: the Albany police chief, who quickly filled Albany area jails and beyond with the nonviolent protesters.[23]

King would later reflect that he miscalculated in his approach to protest segregation in Albany.[24] Even when I was in Albany in the 2010s, locals would shake their heads, saying, "Dr. King had some success in Birmingham and Selma, but he came down here and he couldn't crack this nut." People would explain why they thought they had trouble working with others: "We're out here, where we had plantations and slavery. It infects our politics and our culture."

One of those students who helped start the Albany Movement, Charles Sherrod, still resides in Albany. After his work with SNCC, he went on to become a preacher and continued his activism through work with nonprofit organizations and as an Albany City Council member. My admiration and respect for his and others' efforts grew, as I found throughout my time in Albany the most deeply entrenched feelings about race, history, and culture of almost any place I have ever encountered.

CHAPTER 12

# A City Held Hostage by Its Past

Since the late 1970s, Albany has called itself "The good life city."[1] Demographic and economic data, however, indicate otherwise. Albany ranks as one of the poorest cities in the nation. It is seat to Dougherty County, which has been deemed to be in poverty for at least three census periods, making it one of Georgia's "persistent poverty counties."[2]

During the 2010s, Albany was ranked as being one of the worst cities to live in, as having one of the widest gaps between rich and poor, and as being one of the most segregated. As a result, people in their prime working years left. Albany and Dougherty County are extreme examples of how race, history, and culture correlate with low rates of educational attainment, a low-skilled labor force, unemployment, and high out-migration.

Near the end of the decade, just as Albany's economy started to grow—albeit at one of the slowest rates in the state—Hurricane Michael tore through the area in October 2018, devastating the region's agriculture. One analyst reported that the hurricane "left a snowy landscape of ruined white cotton on Georgia's red clay, destroying a crop and likely bringing hard times to the region's many small communities built on agriculture."[3] Other ruined crops included pecans, corn, and vegetables.

I arrived in Albany in the late fall of 2013. As I crossed from Alabama into Georgia on U.S. Route 280, I noticed again that the landscape, the small communities, and the agricultural structures like silos on large farms, mirrored Southwest Alabama. Here was another cotton culture, though with peanuts added in.

The scene suggested to me that politically, culturally, and socially the two regions would be very similar. Some in Albany, especially some of the African American residents, would tell me "If you think it's bad in Alabama, that's child's play compared to here." Later, I would agree that Albany was an extreme example of both resource deprivation and racial polarization.

The Flint River was a visible representation of the economic, social, and cultural divide of blacks and whites. East versus west, black versus white, poor versus not poor. A hodgepodge of fast-food restaurants and mom-and-pop shops were sprinkled along the east side. Albany State University lay on the flood-prone east riverbank. On the west side lay Darton State College and the Phoebe Putney Memorial Hospital. On the northwest corner of town were large chain stores like Publix and Walmart. The wealth gap was obvious just driving from east to west through Albany. Not so obvious was just how wide that gap was. Simmering under the surface of these divides was an almost adversarial feel. I would find that things were never what they seemed to be in Albany.

One fall, I got to see close up the side that most people would say reflects extreme wealth. I was among a small group of people who, because of our positions, were invited to a high-end event that wealthy people of Albany had organized at a large quail plantation to attract investment in the local area, in particular, and in the state, as a whole. The Red Hills region of Southwest Georgia is famous for its quail hunting. Individuals and corporations buy vast plantations for private and business use. Two that serve the public include Wynfield Plantation (two thousand acres) in Albany, which is down the road from one owned by Ted Turner (founder of CNN), and Pine Hill Plantation (six thousand acres), about an hour southwest of Albany in Donalsonville.[4]

For this recruitment event, wealthy corporate people from all over the country flew in on private jets. Local and state elected officials attended—all the way up to the governor's office—as well as the two-star general of the Marine Corps Logistics Base. Ninety-nine percent of the guests were white. A hundred percent of the helpers and servers at the event were African American, likely descendants of slaves in the region. It was like walking onto the set of a modern remake of *Gone with the Wind*.

When I heard that Albany calls itself "the good life city," I thought about the reports on poverty and education levels in the region that I had been studying in preparation for our new life in Albany, and what I was now seeing, and wondered about the human capacity to ignore reality. What were people thinking when they boasted about being "the good life city" when it was deemed one of the country's worst cities to live in? It reminded me that when I was growing up in Alabama, some politicians tried to sell to voters the notion that "We're poor but we're proud." It disavowed the reality of our economic existence. Today a similar disavowal is playing out across the nation when people dismiss factual information they don't agree with.

Earlier in my career, for more than twenty years I had lived in two of the wealthiest counties in Georgia, Cobb and Gwinnett. Comparing those two counties to Dougherty County is inconceivable because of the cultural chasm that separates them. Wealth in Dougherty is concentrated in a small number of people in contrast to the vast wealth of many more people in Cobb and Gwinnett. Analyzing the data showed that Dougherty faced challenges related to persistent poverty that Cobb and Gwinnett did not, including low educational attainment rates, a huge skills deficit, and high rates of health issues (e.g., cancer, stroke, diabetes) tied to obesity.

In my study of the data, I thought, "You don't have to normalize that!" The data point that really struck a nerve was the low percentage of Albany adults who held bachelor's degrees. It was hard to reconcile these data with the educational assets of the community. In 2013, the city offered at least four educational paths after high school: Albany Technical College, a public community college offering vocational and occupational training programs for little or no cost; Darton State College, a two-year, associate's degree college; Troy University, a public university with a branch campus in Albany; and Albany State University, with undergraduate and graduate programs.

With such educational avenues available, what could explain the low levels of educational attainment and high rates of poverty? I thought that something about the culture, and the choices Albany's citizens were making in relation to that culture, must be the cause. It did not take me long to conclude that the root cause was racial distrust.

Albany's racial distrust was fueled by its history and by stereotypes on both sides. Historic racism by the white community against African Americans collided with the black community's pent-up anger and frustration about the pervasive superior-subordinate social structure that had dominated there for the past four hundred years. I also had confirmed what I had seen many times before: people can move through phases. It starts with distrust, which can turn into fanaticism, and then fanaticism turns into tribalism.

In poor communities like Albany, it was a zero-sum game. Slash and burn. "You denigrate me; I denigrate you." It was adversarial about the worst things imaginable. People were so hung up on race and culture that I could not nudge them forward. It was a difficult lesson for me to learn not to underestimate how attached people can become to their tribal identity.

I had not been on campus long when one USG official made an observation to me over the phone: "Southwest Georgia has been the ball and chain around the state of Georgia's ankle. Do they know how bad off they are down there?" No human society can thrive under the conditions brought on by persistent poverty. The Albany African American community knew it was in their best interest to have a vital and strong community, but they did not know how to reconcile their history so that they were free to harness logic, reason, hard data, and a strategic outlook to shape a future where everybody could be lifted up.

Chuck Knapp, an economist by training and a former president of the University of Georgia, once said that two things dramatically changed the South: air-conditioning and better race relations. Air-conditioning changed almost everything about how people lived in the South from architecture to neighborliness. It spurred industrialization.

Atlanta and Birmingham provide contrasting examples from neighboring states of how to deal with race relations. In the 1950s, both cities were roughly the same size. Atlanta had the Coca-Cola Company; Birmingham had a steel industry. In the 1960s, Atlanta chose to transition to something called "the New South." Atlanta mayor Ivan Allen Jr., together with business leaders like Coca-Cola's Robert Woodruff, started promoting Atlanta as "a city too busy to hate."[5] It is said that Woodruff rationalized the slogan by explaining, "I have difficulty explaining to my Brazilian bottler why he can't stay in the same hotel as my Chattanooga bottler." On the other end of the spectrum was Birmingham, which could not say that it was "too busy to hate." In the same period that Atlanta was trying to break racial barriers, Birmingham created an atmosphere of hate where officials turned dogs and fire hoses on children, and where children were the targets of bombs, earning the city the moniker Bombingham.

As a consequence of their divergent approaches, Atlanta was able to move forward, whereas Birmingham struggled.

Atlanta diversified its economy, using air transportation as arteries of commerce, the way earlier periods had used railroads and rivers. Today, Atlanta's airport is a robust economic engine not just for Atlanta but for all of Georgia.

Although Birmingham had an advantage because of its geographic centrality in the South, it lacked visionary leadership to capitalize on that advantage. Atlanta's leaders looked past the intense social change that was going on, to the future. Birmingham's leaders had an entrenched view of the past, as reflected in their public policy, their practices, and their behavior. It was as if Birmingham was saying, "Our glory is in the past, not the future." This process has been years in the making and is difficult to alter. The residents of both these cities live today with the consequences, for good or ill. These two approaches show that long-term economic benefits and costs depend on the approach taken by a community's leaders.

While Albany didn't experience the level of violence that Birmingham had, its residents live with the consequences of de facto racial segregation in all facets of life. Even as the city might try to break the status quo, it cannot seem to move beyond its history. When I talked to African Americans in Albany, it seemed to me that they had normalized deprivation. I couldn't help thinking about those lines from Albert King's song "Down Don't Bother Me" on his 1967 *Born Under a Bad Sign* album, "I've been down so long, you know, down don't bother me." The normalization of scarcity, deprivation, discord, and distrust had paralyzed the African American community in Albany, and the entire community, black and white, had normalized the divergent racial conditions of extreme poverty and degradation alongside extreme wealth and privilege—a modernized version of segregation.

My grasp of the local history and culture drew me to accept the position of interim president at Albany State University. The setting was almost identical to the one I had grown up in 250 miles to the west. I had lived some of the same history of segregation in a rural community; I knew the culture.

As I've traveled the world, I have found that there is a broad distribution of intellect, but not of opportunity. While my hometown area was poor in material wealth, it was not poor in intellect. It was poor only in opportunity. Where I grew up, almost every family I knew lacked money as well as most other resources. They were subsistence farmers, not wealthy planters with 2,000-acre farms.

The bright youth of Marengo, however, didn't use poverty as an excuse not to learn. In my own family, my parents rejected some of the trappings of what many people would consider success, like fancy cars and large houses, instead prioritizing things of the mind.

That attitude helped me form my mantra that education is the path to economic development. I thought that leading Albany State would be an intellectual challenge for the singular purpose of creating a platform of opportunity for the talented young people of Southwest Georgia, which would thereby help the economy of the region.

CHAPTER 13

# A University with Unsinkable Determination

Joseph Winthrop Holley, the son of former slaves in South Carolina, was educated in Presbyterian freedmen schools before becoming an educator and an author. Moved by Du Bois's reports about conditions in Albany, and encouraged by Booker T. Washington, Holley moved to Albany, where he founded the Albany Bible and Manual Training Institute in 1903. The school provided basic education and teacher training to the area's African American community.[1]

The state of Georgia began assisting the school, financially, in 1917, transitioning it to a two-year college. The name was changed to the Georgia Normal and Agricultural College. In the 1940s, the USG designated the school a four-year college, expanding program offerings, and renaming the school Albany State College. In the 1950s and 1960s, secondary education and nursing programs were added.

After the 1954 U.S. Supreme Court ruling desegregating education, many southern communities looked for ways to circumvent the ruling. At the K–12 level, whites established private segregation academies as a way to avoid desegregation. At the postsecondary level, in Dougherty County, the predominantly white voters approved a $1.6 million bond to finance the purchase of one hundred acres of land on the west side of the Flint River on which to establish a junior college in 1963. Held in 1966, the first classes had more than six hundred students enrolled.

The previous year had been a watershed for higher education nationally. Congress and the president passed several acts to strengthen the country's higher education system. In November, when President Johnson signed the Higher Education Act of 1965, he declared that the

123

act would "swing open a new door for the young people of America." He explained that the bill was "one of more than two dozen education measures enacted by the first session of the 89th Congress. And history will forever record that this session—the first session of the 89th Congress—did more for the wonderful cause of education in America than all the previous 176 regular sessions of Congress did, put together."[2]

The act did a number of things including providing grants and loans to students, assistance for small colleges, and improved library resources to colleges and universities. Title 3 of the act created a special designation for historically black colleges and universities in order to provide them with federal funding. A college or university would be designated as historically black (an HBCU) if it was established prior to 1964 and if its "principal mission was, and is, the education of black Americans, and that is accredited by a nationally recognized accrediting agency or association determined by the Secretary [of Education]."[3] Many have said the Title 3 funding was to make up for past wrongs. It was to be a dedicated income stream specifically to help HBCUs.

Albany State College was one of about a hundred institutions designated as HBCUs.[4] Over the next thirty years, Albany State College and Albany Junior College (renamed Darton College in 1987) solidified their reputations as the "black school," and the "white school," of Albany, respectively. There was just the brief forced continuing education program partnership in the mid-1980s.

I caught a glimpse of the racial animus in Albany when I worked in the USG headquarters as acting executive vice chancellor. In that capacity, in 1994 I joined a delegation to survey the extensive damage to the Albany State College campus by an historic flood caused by Tropical Storm Alberto, which over a number of days in July dumped some twenty inches of rain and lashed the region with high winds. Downtown Albany was underwater, more than twenty thousand residents were forced from their homes, and the Oglethorpe Bridge over the Flint River was impassable.

We verified that our tetanus shots were up to date and donned full-body hazmat suits before conducting the damage assessment. The whole bottom section, almost two-thirds of the campus, had been flooded, with all the buildings under water up to their roofs. Inside the buildings we sloshed through mud and debris, dodging any lingering snakes and turtles.

The devastation was heartbreaking. Even more so were the suspicions voiced by Albany State staff as we made our tour. One senior administrator pulled me aside, angry, "Dr. Dunning, I know you're part of this delegation. Do you think those goddamn crackers are serious about rebuilding, or are they going to take the opportunity, right now, since we are destroyed, to close us down? Do you honestly think they really will rebuild?"

"I've heard nothing to suggest that there will not be a rebuilding effort," I responded in all honesty. There was no way I could know if what I had just said would be held up over time. But I was direct and candid with him: "I've not been in any conversation or meeting where it was even hinted that the school might be closed."

As the community was still reeling from the flood damage, and the chancellor and the governor were promising to rebuild the school, a rumor spread among the community that one of the USG regents was plotting to have the school shut down. The rumor went that this regent and a group of white Albany businessmen were meeting in secret to ensure that the HBCU would never reopen.

Although this sub rosa effort failed, and regardless of whether the rumor was true or not, it was widely believed in Albany. It fueled a legitimate paranoia by the black community and seriously damaged any hope for trust between the blacks and whites of Albany. Were it not for the leadership of the sitting chancellor Stephen Portch and Governor Zell Miller, Albany State might never have recovered sufficiently to continue. Together, these two chose to rebuild the campus and enthusiastically started promoting it to be a "bigger and better" school.

Albany State was indeed rebuilt under the slogan "Unsinkable Albany State—Bigger, Stronger, and Better."[5] With a $153 million flood-recovery program, the school renovated some of the existing buildings. Land outside of the floodplain was purchased and laid out for new construction. Over several years, five student housing buildings, a dining hall, an academic building, a gymnasium, and a student center were built.[6]

In my USG capacity I returned to Albany State at the opening ceremony for some of the buildings. I spoke with several elderly Albany State graduates from the 1950s who, through tears, expressed their joy and surprise at seeing the impressive new buildings of their alma mater. One said to me, "We did not think that we would ever see Albany State look this good. We can't believe what we're seeing."

What I had taken away from surveying the damage was how important an educational institution could be to a region. I began to consider how much more could be done to raise the school to an academically higher level. I had grown weary over the years of hearing people in the circles that I operated in talk either overtly or obliquely about Albany State and the other USG HBCUs as "less than," as lacking the rigor that is necessary for a quality college.

I rejected that view. I had been around so many people who clearly viewed the HBCUs as quaint places unwilling to change, unwilling to address some of their challenges, and holding on to old ways to the point of strangling what could be rich and bright futures. I thought that Albany State was well positioned after the flood and the rebuilding to raise the level of education for the twenty or so counties in its service area. It could reinvigorate and reinvent itself by doing what all universities have to do to keep up with a rapidly changing world.

Prior to the flood, Albany State had been growing its graduate programs slowly. As the school was being physically rebuilt, the USG Board of Regents gave the institution university status in 1996. Despite the elevated status and all the renovation and expansion of the late 1990s, however, the institution remained on the east side of the Flint River. The river represented not only a physical divide, but also a cultural divide from the wealthier districts on the west bank. With the river between them, Darton State College would continue to be viewed as the white school and Albany State University would be viewed as "the HBCU."

What the Albany community didn't seem to realize was that, in a race-neutral setting, the two institutions were not even remotely comparable. Albany State was a university offering undergraduate and graduate degrees; Darton State was a two-year college. In 1958, the Georgia General Assembly passed legislation to create local, two-year colleges to help students access college educations. The idea was that every student should be able to find a place in the state's postsecondary education system. Some could meet the requirements to go straight into a four-year degree program. Others could start at a junior college, and if they did well, could earn associate degrees, and then move on to a college or university. It was not until 2012 that the USG approved Darton College's first four-year degree program and changed the name to Darton State College. That the two schools were viewed as equivalent institutions was a holdover from the South's superior-subordinate social structure based on race.

When I arrived in Albany as interim president some twenty years after the postflood rebuilding, I was reminded that reconciliation and working together for the common good are difficult when feelings about race are so deeply entrenched. It is challenging when some people persist in harboring, even subconsciously, feelings of superiority and fears of losing their advantageous position. It is also hard when others cling to memories of being wronged long ago, whether from resistance to calls for desegregation and civil rights, or from efforts to close a university. As I discovered almost as soon as I arrived in Albany, those who want to work together must be prepared to encounter resistance from both groups.

CHAPTER 14

# The Calm before the Storm?

My first thoughts after I accepted the position of interim president of Albany State were about the flood of 1994 and the symbolic and real racial divide that the Flint River represented for Albany. I knew going into the position that race, history, culture, and exaggerated stereotypes added an extraordinary complexity to the task. I had no way of knowing that before I was there two years, a consolidation with Darton State College would be announced, adding a whole new dimension to an already strained environment.

On day one, in December 2013, I was confronted with a number of issues that posed four specific risks to the university. My first step in facing a problem is always to mentally enumerate and categorize those risks. I would ask myself, "Does this problem cause a reputational, strategic, operational, or financial risk to the school? Or a combination?" I knew that at Albany State any problem would pose "a risk on steroids," as it would be exaggerated by the stereotypes associated with race and with HBCU institutions.

Organizational reputations take years to build. They can be lost overnight by any one of innumerable policies, practices, or events. Reputational risks can include negative publicity (warranted or not), illegal activities, litigation, poor operational practices, and negligence. Any one of these can accumulate to damage a reputation.

The reputational challenges I found at Albany State centered on a reluctance to acknowledge and deal with the wider community's negative perceptions and deeply held stereotypes about the university. The stereotypes were so embedded so as to go undisputed among some. For example, some whites openly challenged that faculty members held the proper qualifications, despite the fact that Albany State was fully accredited by the Southern Association of Colleges and Schools (SACS), which monitors faculty credentials as part of its accreditation process.

Pointing this out did not satisfy them. "Are you sure about that?," they would ask me. "We hear most of them have mail-order degrees." They would say this in all seriousness, as if Albany State functioned in an alternative universe in which accreditation was issued without any requirements being met. One white businessman went so far as to say to me, "We hear that you can drive by the campus, slow down, and they'll just throw you a degree in the window." This was a patently false claim, but that didn't stop him from saying it. The perception was that Albany State was there solely to provide African American students with a social experience. "No serious education happens there. They'll let anybody in," was a common refrain.

People at Albany State knew about these perceptions. Rather than try to understand what was fueling the views, however, the perceptions were dismissed as being driven purely by racism: "They're just a bunch of bigots." Discussion about addressing any underlying truths would get shut down almost immediately.

Another reputational risk was student behavior, which is something that all college administrators worry about. Our first concern is the health and well-being of the students. Once student health and safety are assured, we worry about the impact their actions may have on their reputations as individuals. Last, we consider the impact that student behavior may have on the reputation of the institution.

At Albany State, I tried to address these risks proactively by meeting with students in small groups. My wife and I often invited students to join us for a meal at our home. We let the community know we were doing this, not to pat ourselves on the back, but to set an example for how a university community can support its students. One press release, for example, read, "The Dunnings are continuously demonstrating their support of students and engaging them on campus and at their home. On Thursday, they opened their home to more than a dozen student leaders. The agenda: dinner and conversation about student perspectives on how to strengthen the collegiate experience at ASU. It was a scene that has played out several times ... with ... many other constituent groups."[1]

Other times, I met with students after they had gotten in trouble—fighting in a residence hall, stealing a computer, or being charged with a DUI at 3:00 a.m. I would start a conversation by saying something like, "You were listed in the police blotter of the *Albany Herald* as Albany State University students."

"Well, Dr. Dunning, I don't know why they would do that!"

"If I were out at 3:00 a.m. and the police stopped me and charged me with some kind of mischief, don't you think that when the paper reports it, they will also say that I am the president of Albany State University?"

"Oh, yes, sir," they would say.

I would continue: "Well, the thought of such a headline helps me understand that I have a bigger responsibility than just myself. We all have a hand in enhancing the reputation of this institution. I would embarrass and shame this university by getting in the streets of Albany, Georgia, doing things that no one expects of a university president. So, I have an obligation to you as students—to hold this job in trust in ways that are beyond just fiduciary. It's also ethical. Do you not understand that?"

"Well, yeah, we do," they invariably would admit.

My parents used this approach with me when I was growing up. They lived in a community of hardworking people striving for respectability, accountability, and dignity. That was what I grew up around. I tried to impress on students the value that my mom taught me about representing oneself and one's family and community.

An experience when I was in middle school has always stuck with me. I was out one night with a friend throwing rocks at things in the dark. One of the rocks hit me on the forehead, cutting me. I went inside to find my mom so she could put a bandage on it. I was probably also looking for some sympathy. Instead, she said, "Well, it's nine o'clock. Your bedtime is at eight o'clock. What were you doing out there so late?" I had no answer.

"Well, you set this in motion by not being inside." She traced the sequence of events from my bleeding forehead all the way back to my choice to buck my bedtime by going outside to play. By the time she got all the way back to "What decisions set all this in motion?," I was completely worn down. Her bottom line was, "You have to be accountable for your behavior." That was what I tried to impress on these young college students. At the same time, I had to be practical. I would say, "I'm not going to tell you not to go out to clubs because that's unrealistic. But can you find ways to get in and out of these places without having handcuffs put on you? If you have to be fingerprinted, it needs to be because you've just accepted a position working for a federal agency like the National Security Agency, not because you got a DUI. You have choices about these things."

I was saying to these students what my dad had said to me when I thought I should be able to drive home from college at eleven or twelve o'clock at night because I was a veteran and twenty-two years of age. He would say, "That may be true, but that's not the place to try and assert your manhood or your freedom. That's inviting an arrest. You can manage to get home at a different time. Go on to bed and then get up early and drive here at eight in the morning. That's a very different timeframe than midnight." That was what African American parents had had to do for generations to keep their children safe. Now, I was trying to keep our Albany State students safe.

The reputational risk of student behavior to the institution was augmented because the school was an HBCU. College students being college students, some will do things that wind up in the paper, whether it's drinking, fraternity and sorority shenanigans, or fights on Main Street. But when normal college behaviors happen to students at an historically black campus, they feed right into the stereotypes of African Americans. The reaction is not "boys will be boys, and girls will be girls." No. Instead, a racial slant is added to it. People are quicker to judge and criticize behavior at an HBCU than at an historically white school. This tendency exacerbated the strategic, operational, and financial risks dealing a double blow to the school's reputation in each instance.

---

The biggest strategic risk to Albany State was decision-making not based on hard data. Strategic thinking seemed to challenge the status quo in ways that caused discomfort. Over and over again, I encountered emotion and passion about the past. There was intense nostalgia about the days of struggle and deprivation. People acted in ways that said to me, "If you change things, you're changing our identity—you're doing away with the symbols of what we consider important." This symbolic connectivity that many people held for past wrongs made it difficult to think and then act strategically.

One of the most detrimental data points for the university was the trend for the young people of Albany State's service area to out-migrate.

Groups probably got tired of hearing me harp on this issue: "We lag on almost every measure whether its education or housing. No state or city can survive when it loses its best and brightest."

What was happening in Albany was similar to what had happened in Sweet Water in my youth. Every bright young African American could not wait to graduate from high school and get out of Marengo County. They left their parents, taking their energy and skills north or west. What little Alabama had invested in those young people from birth to eighteen, was lost to Chicago, New York, or San Diego.

I remember asking a school friend, "When did you decide to leave the Alabama Black Belt?"

"As soon as I realized where I was," he responded. He was talking about the lack of jobs and social freedom in the environment we grew up in. Alabama sustained a devastating loss of human capital, just as we were entering our most productive working years at about age twenty-five. The receiving cities benefited for the next forty years, not Alabama.

I would use this example when I spoke to various groups in Albany. I would try to push the notion that—although I did not use these words—"We're in the ditch down here on every sort of measure of quality of life. Albany lags, and so our young people are leaving."

What did this mean for Albany State? Despite my efforts, I could not get university staff to look at the types of businesses and organizations in our service area, and then to brainstorm programs that would help our students get local jobs. When people at Albany State became really exasperated with me, some would come to me and say, "Dr. Dunning, I don't mean any disrespect, but we're an HBCU," as if that had anything to do with designing curricula. I must have heard that refrain a hundred times.

When I would suggest that we needed majors in high-demand areas, if I said that to faculty in, say, the humanities, the response would be "Are you saying we're not good enough?" I would get similar responses when I would suggest, "If we're living in an area with one of the two largest U.S. Marine Corps logistics bases in the nation within five miles of us, shouldn't we be emphasizing programs in supply chain logistics? Not at the expense of English literature, but in *addition* to. Let's be thoughtful about the STEM disciplines. Let's be nimble and agile in adjusting to a changing environment for the students. Our thinking should be student focused. Student driven. How can we enhance their academic experience? The curriculum is not for our pleasure; it's to serve the students."

Whenever I suggested we ought to be looking at data, trends, and information, however, I was perceived as being harsh. When I asked members of Albany State to look at the reality of what they were doing compared to what they could be doing, it was uncomfortable for many.

But, I persisted. Thinking strategically, I wondered, "How can we make sure that the majors we offer reflect the needs of the local economy?" Dougherty County has primarily an agricultural economy. So, could Albany State connect to this historical piece of Southwest Georgia? The agricultural sciences were primarily in the purview of the University of Georgia and Fort Valley State University, but I wondered if we could look at intersections of various disciplines to carve out a niche major at Albany State.

One of the ideas I thought had great potential was developing a program for drone technology, which could help improve farming techniques on the vast farms in the area. To explore the possibility and to pique the interest of faculty and students, I invited an expert in drone technology to the campus to demonstrate how farmers could be more efficient and get higher yields by having the drones fly over fields taking photos to identify problems like erosion and uneven crop growth. Farmers would need people familiar with drone technology and people to analyze the photos. Allied businesses would then sprout up to support the technology. Developing a drone technology major for our students would benefit other disciplines and majors, as well. The program would produce marketable graduates and ultimately would contribute to the local economy, binding together the university and the community in a mutually beneficial endeavor.

Although I invited white farmers in the area to attend the session, only a few attended because most didn't consider Albany State to be a local resource. If they sought advice, it was more likely to be from Darton State, the University of Georgia, or Georgia Tech. The students, however, seemed excited. During the lunch session, they got to fly the drones around the room using handheld devices. Still, I struggled to get those at Albany State to think about scholarship in a new way, or to embrace ways to integrate students into the local economy.

Even though the students were enthused about drones, I got the message that the staff were not onboard. Their response seemed to be, "We're an HBCU; this is our school." My drone dream also ran up against a cultural barrier in the African American community. Many of our students' parents and grandparents had painful memories of what their ancestors had had to endure as slaves on farms and plantations, and so they didn't want their children to consider anything related to agriculture as a major. They failed to recognize that the intersection of technology and agriculture today had changed farming dramatically from the farming their parents did. So, in this instance, there was almost a mutually agreed-upon distance between whites and blacks.

Three trends posing strategic risk to the university were technology, globalization, and climate change.[2] Individuals, communities, states, and nations need sophisticated skills to face challenges brought on by these three rapidly changing forces. The gap between those compelling challenges and where Albany was with its huge skills deficit was so wide that even I had difficulty imagining it would be possible to close the gap merely by changing the academic offerings.

The deficit in skills in Southwest Georgia was staggering. Taking into consideration all the things that impact companies, plus the knowledge and skills that their employees would need to cope with change was almost too great a task. Still, universities have to change if they want their graduates to be successful in this environment. At Albany State, however, there was an entrenched mentality: "the environment can change fifty times, but we're going to stay the same."

One way I thought that Albany State could meet these three trends was by being a regional leader in the scholarship of engagement. That would mean that the university would listen to the needs of the region, conduct research to inform those needs, and apply knowledge learned via outreach programs and activities by faculty, students, and staff. Could we do that? To every campus group I spoke to, I pressed the idea that we should not merely meet expectations but exceed them: "Let's get out in front of the trends. If we are in an area with poor health and education, we should be one of the leading universities in the country talking about the scholarship of engagement on the issues of health and education." I would then challenge the group: "How can we channel our research, teaching, and outreach efforts to tackle the tough issues in the environment that we exist in?"

This frequently got me into trouble. Some people would turn to me in exasperation. "Dr. Dunning, We're not a white university. We're an HBCU," as if somehow it were mutually exclusive to engage with our community while being an historically black institution at the same time.

Despite the resistance, I remained adamant that we had to create a twenty-first-century platform for Albany State to function. The market forces would be unforgiving if we failed to think with vision. Thus, another strategic risk was whether Albany State was giving its graduates the skills and knowledge to be successful. We needed to be asking, and then answering, these questions: What are the current and future skills needs of the region? Are Albany State's programs and majors meeting and anticipating trends? What do employers think about our graduates?

A trend that could mean life or death for any university is enrollment. Since 2011, Albany State's undergraduate enrollment had been declining. It's a troubling but inevitable fact that when enrollment goes down, the budget also goes down. To meet a several-million-dollar budget reduction, we had to eliminate vacant and even some filled positions, and also reduce our operating budget.

Declining enrollment at Albany State was caused by a confluence of factors. Although the long-term national trend for enrollment was generally upward, in the first half of the 2010s some schools saw enrollment declines. Albany State had historically drawn a substantial number of students from Atlanta area high schools. However, the economic recession of the late 2000s and early 2010s meant that many students from Atlanta enrolled in local colleges so they could live at home and save on room and board fees. Georgia State University also began to recruit African American students intensively. Finally, we had been doing OK enrolling students, but we had a low retention rate.

To my mind, the strategic risks facing Albany State resulted from the leadership team not always thinking in nimble and agile ways about the future of the institution. I hoped that, over time, we could examine and confront issues and trends using data and information. From there, I wanted us to get out in front of trends, to think strategically about relationships and alliances so as to strengthen the university's mission and improve its reputation.

---

My third concern was the operational risks associated with ineffective and inefficient policies and procedures. It was evident soon after my arrival that operational risks were rampant. We had some impossibly ineffectual business processes, whether it was financial aid or admissions. In the first year, my leadership team and I looked at those operational areas where we could audit, evaluate, and assess with an eye toward improvement.

I devoted a lot of time to improving back-office operations (e.g., accounting, technology support, regulatory compliance, records). We discovered academic programs that marched on despite insufficient students majoring in that field; some departments that essentially worked in silos from which they pointed blame at other departments and units; outdated and inefficient processes and technologies; a tendency to overlook unethical and unprofessional behavior; and a resistance to collaborating with other local and regional higher-education institutions.

---

Finally, strategic, reputational, and operational risks could all be tied in some way to the fourth concern: financial risk. Sound fiscal stewardship is crucial to the survival of any institution. Sadly, in my first years at Albany State, we had to deal with several instances of financial malfeasance that put the entire institution at risk. One instance involved four staff members in the financial aid office who had over several decades misappropriated student aid funds. This discovery and the resulting press coverage were devastating, feeding into some of the ugliest stereotypes about African Americans.[3] "You can't put 'those people' in charge of money—they'll steal it."

My own history, heritage, and understanding of the destructive nature of stereotypes had taught me that people reading about this would form their opinions based on race, rather than on the acts themselves. The situation hit all the risk categories, which was one reason why it caused me so much anguish and pain. I was especially disappointed in the four involved. They were supposed to be the fiscal stewards of the school's money but, instead, acted out of greed and dishonesty. They seemed not to have cared at all about the institution. I wondered what values led people to behave in that way, and what would make them think they wouldn't be caught. As it was, their actions endangered Albany State's eligibility to receive further federal financial aid funding. Losing that funding would have had devastating consequences for the high percentage of our student body who qualified for and received federal aid and probably would have spelled the end of the university. Luckily, the audit that revealed the long-time malfeasance, the subsequent firing of the four individuals, and turning the case over to the state's attorney general were exactly the right actions for the university to take in order to preserve its eligibility.

Some in the community criticized the university for firing the four. "The university is being unfair to these poor people." They perceived the firings as mistreatment, rather than as an appropriate response. In their minds, the four staff members were victims, not perpetrators of fraud and theft. Over the years, Albany State had been so marginalized by the larger community that some African American community members automatically concluded that the whole incident was a result of a conspiracy against the institution. It was almost as if the community had lost its ability to say "Wrong is wrong."

The whole situation contributed to the institution's inferior reputation. Anything negative said about Albany State suddenly looked entirely plausible.

We faced other financial challenges as well. I used to wince when off campus I would run into a vendor or supplier who would tell me, "Dr. Dunning, I work with Albany State, but I can't get paid. They won't pay me." Our business operations were hampered by inefficient practices.

In another headline-grabbing case, shortly before I arrived at Albany State, two former employees of the school's foundation office were indicted by a grand jury for allegedly stealing funds from the office some years earlier. The acting head I appointed to put the office on the road toward operational efficiency came to my office one day. "In one of the office's desk drawers I just found several checks that donors have written to the campus—they've never been deposited!"

Not long after that revelation, I was in the grocery store. An elderly woman came up to me and said, "I'm a graduate of Albany State. I'm on a fixed income, but I like to write a little check to the university every month. When I balance my checkbook, I can see that they aren't depositing my checks. Won't you just see what's going on out there?"

A process was put in place to begin to correct the long-standing multiple challenges facing the foundation office. A much longer-term problem was the historically low number of alumni making donations to the institution. Always driven by data, I looked at alumni giving rates to HBCUS in general. Claflin University, a private HBCU in South Carolina, ranked among the top in the country for support from alumni.

In contrast, while we had some generous givers, overall our private giving rate was among the lowest. When I conducted a casual survey of alumni who I could count on for their strong and candid opinions, I heard from each, "I'll give money to our church. I'm not giving to Albany State. It's a state university. The state provides all the money that's necessary to run the place."

I explained that the difference between a good university and a great one is its culture of giving. We needed to figure out ways to encourage alumni to make private giving a regular routine, rather than just at annual events and galas. Could we get to a place where donors would do their giving through payroll deduction, maybe twenty or thirty dollars per month? How could we normalize an alumni mindset along the lines of, "The three places I'm going to give to are my church, my alma mater, and my child's school."

While there were some faithful alumni who gave to the school, like the elderly woman who had stopped me in the grocery, we needed to implement steps to encourage giving from more people we knew to have a passion for the institution. I knew that an endowment would give the institution flexibility. Unlike state or federal funds, private giving could be directed to help students participate in study-abroad programs and internships, engage in research projects with faculty members, and to connect with communities through service-learning activities, all of which I think are crucial in improving the student experience and expanding their horizons. My goal was for us to match or exceed what other schools were doing to support their students.

For reasons that still escape me, I just could not get some in the Albany State community, including some alumni, faculty, and administrators, to see the long-term consequences of not having foundation funds available to help students beyond what state and federal funds could do. One such consequence was students choosing to matriculate elsewhere. Students who were able to choose among regional universities and were interested in study abroad were far more likely to choose, for example, Kennesaw State, which has a permanent international facility in Montepulciano, Italy, where students can study. But the lack of foundation funds at Albany State made it difficult to arrange for any kind of off-campus student experience. Plus, with a high percentage of the students on financial aid, they had to work during the summer.

That the school had neither striven in the past to reduce its dependence on state and federal support nor built an endowment ran counter to my values about self-reliance. When talking to groups about this, I would say, "OK, here are our sources of money: We get a subsidy from the state of Georgia based on the number of students enrolled. We get money from the federal government, federal Title 3 funds that are tied to enrollment and student financial aid. A majority of our students are on federal financial aid. Yet, our Albany State community gives almost nothing. Private giving is almost zero—we get some, but not much. The Albany State community doesn't have any skin in the game."

I would point out that the ability for an institution to engage in intense fund-raising activities in order to provide rich experiences for its students (e.g., Foundation Fellowships at the University of Georgia or the Morehead Scholarship at the University of North Carolina–Chapel Hill) sets institutions apart from those that are just sitting and waiting for dollars to arrive from the federal or state funding source. I would conclude my remarks with a rousing call to "Help our students have an experience equal to or that exceeds what other schools are doing!"

To show that *I* had skin in the game, my wife and I made a financial challenge gift of $25,000 to the institution, hoping to foster support from the community. The Dunning Matching Fund was to be used for need-based scholarships and to help the school's marching band travel to Pasadena, California, to perform in the 2016 Tournament of Roses Parade. We hoped this would be something that the community could rally around.[4]

Employee theft-fraud and low rates of private giving presented institutional problems that needed to be solved, they presented real financial risks to the institution, and on top of all that they damaged the institution's reputation in the community and beyond. The only solution was for the institution to become fully accountable. If a department couldn't pass an audit because staff had done something inappropriate, there had to be a sanction for that. I stressed to my leadership team: "Please don't you or the staff in your units damage our institution by giving poor customer service or by mishandling funds."

---

Each of the challenges and decisions needed at Albany State, which represented strategic, reputational, operational, and financial risks to the institution, intersected with issues of race, history, and culture. In that same meeting where I challenged my leadership team to improve customer service and money management, I ended my remarks with "Every time someone asks you about such incidents, you can't claim it is racism." It had gotten back to me that a member of my leadership team had said, "Dr. Dunning is trying to get us to be like the University of Georgia." The implication was that I wanted Albany State to be more like a white university. I pushed back against this mischaracterization: "I would like us to be *better* than the University of Georgia. I'd like there to be better predictability of what our systems can do—and should do. We have to have predictable retention and graduation rates. We have to have good programs that directly result in good outcomes. That's not a black or a white issue. That is an issue of good leadership, good management, and good operations." I closed with, "How has everything become a race issue?"

"We're an HBCU. This is how we do it," someone actually replied.

"That's wrong then. It's just wrong," was all I could say in response.

This mentality only succeeded in perpetuating stereotypes. While there were certainly inefficient and ineffective practices at Albany State, rather than acknowledge that and move on, or even attribute the failures to mismanagement, the white community used those examples to reinforce stereotypes about African Americans. They would say, "They're shiftless, irresponsible, and lazy with low intelligence."

People were used to seeing this particular stereotype on stage and in film since the 1930s and 1940s by Stepin Fetchit, Mantan Moreland, and other actors. Fetchit routinely played "the Laziest Man in the World."[5] Moreland was the "scared, wide-eyed manservant" in Charlie Chan films.[6] The entertainment industry created cultural icons that stood in for the entire race.

It's especially disappointing when national leaders fuel such stereotypes. One example that sticks with me were comments made by Earl Butz that ultimately, and quite rightly, cost him his job as Secretary of Agriculture for President Gerald Ford. In his obituary, the *New York Times* recounted, "On a plane trip following the Republican National Convention in August [1976], . . . Mr. Butz made a remark in which he described blacks as 'coloreds' who wanted only three things—satisfying sex, loose shoes and a warm bathroom—desires that Mr. Butz listed in obscene and scatological terms. . . . Prominent figures from both parties called on Mr. Butz to quit. . . . Mr. Butz resigned within days."[7]

Such comments as those by Butz, and Hollywood representations by actors like Fetchit and Moreland solidified stereotypes, especially in the South, that persist even today. These and other stereotypes, as well as pure animus between the races, were strong in Albany and would surface in ugly ways throughout my time there.

After almost two years at Albany State, I found myself part of an extreme conundrum. The African American community harbored deep-seated hurt and distrust from centuries of wrongs by whites. Some whites still harbored feelings of superiority, while others held on to ugly stereotypes. When anyone in the African American community succumbed to human frailties, some whites were bound to see justification for those stereotypes. Somehow, we had to find a way to break what seemed like a vicious cycle.

In an effort to move forward, I sent out a communication to the university community in late October 2015. I wanted my message to be loud and clear that we at Albany State were closing one chapter and opening a new one. These days were over: not committing ourselves to recruiting, retaining, and graduating students; ignoring perceptions, whether false or justified, regarding our image and brand; ignoring people who provided fiscal resources and thinking we could continue to grow without private donations; and fueling the rumor mill, as opposed to operating with facts and data when making decisions.

In our new chapter, we would be student centered in every aspect, from defining core values; to elevating and engaging scholarly discussions about image, respect, and reputation; to conducting research that improves the human condition; to leveraging resources and economic impact to provide the best opportunities for students. All jobs—from teachers in the classroom to groundskeepers—would be student centered.

We were assessing how to streamline our operations. We would improve business processes and make better use of technology. We were in the process of increasing fund-raising efforts focused on student scholarship and need. We were working to reinvigorate institutional research and to create an institutional effectiveness function, which would be key in advancing data-driven decision-making. From this point forward we would set a high bar of accountability.

As part of being more student-centered, we would work to increase enrollment. For already enrolled students we would look for ways to more effectively monitor their progress and success. Helping students succeed would also help improve the institution's retention and graduation rates. Part of our strategy would include improving technology in the classroom. Another would be to get faculty members more involved in student success beyond the classroom. I would work very hard to secure funding for a new fine arts center to create an up-to-date facility that would be more conducive to learning for students in the fine arts. I closed my message with these words: "During the next three years, you will see transformational change at Albany State University, and we need every employee to embrace the process as well as the change. We need employees who are constantly seeking ways to be more efficient, more customer friendly and more committed to the success of our students, our university and our community. I look forward to working with all of our employees who have the capacity and commitment to raise the academic reputation of this institution to one of excellence."

This message in itself, I know, made some on campus uncomfortable. An announcement a few weeks later would greatly add to their discomfort.

My paternal grandfather, Willis Dunning (1858–1948), and paternal grandmother, Delia Dunning, née O'Neal (1867–1940), circa 1888.

My mother, J. L. (short for Johnnie Livingston) Dunning, circa 1931. A first-grade teacher, she dedicated over forty years to teaching in Marengo County, Alabama. She first introduced me to the value of social and ethical responsibility to community.

My father, Arthur Dunning Sr. He and many of his brothers went to college in the 1920s and 1930s, at a time when most families kept men home to work the farm. He became the principal of our high school and always celebrated achievement.

My parents, sister Jean, and me in the late 1940s. My expression suggests that this photo was taken after a long day at church.

My sister, Jean, and me in the late 1940s.
Our home was full of educators, including
Jean, who taught high school for over
thirty years.

My church community in the late 1940s. This church community helped shape my values, especially those of respect and intellectual curiosity.

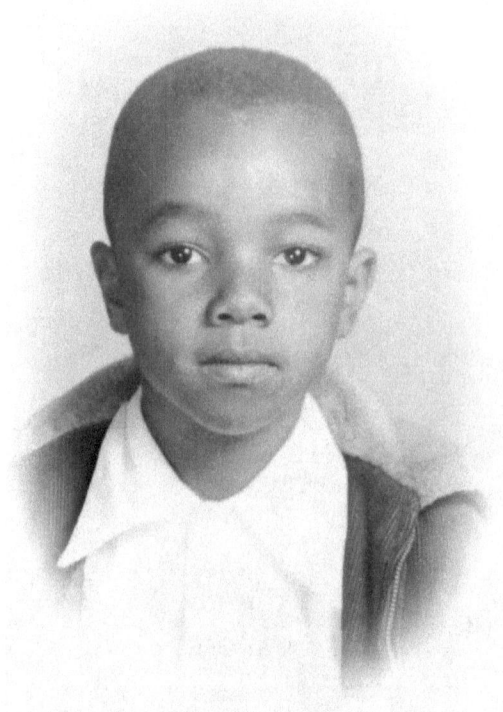

My earliest school photograph (early 1950s). I came of age in the heart of the Alabama Black Belt during Jim Crow.

**MEMORANDA**
Take Simmons Liver Regulator for Dyspepsia.

*Received of Willis Dunning $10.50 for Ginsh 7 bales of cotton N L Bates Sept 22 1896*

This receipt of sale for seven bales of cotton dated September 22, 1896, is significant because it shows that my grandfather owned his land and that he could provide for his family by the sale of his harvests. This was in contrast to the fate of many sharecroppers, who did not own land and were paid poorly, or not at all, for their labor.

**School Improvement Association**
Mrs. G. M. Watson, Pres., Linden, Ala.
Miss Emma Norwood, Sec'y.-Treas., Shiloh, Ala.
**Teachers Reading Circle**
Mrs. W. S. Lewis, Sec'y., Linden, Ala.
**County Teachers Association**
J. F. Gibson, Pres., Thomaston, Ala.
Mrs. G. W. Cuninghame, Sec'y.-Treas., Linden, Ala.

**Marengo County Department of Education**

GEORGE M. WATSON,
SUPERINTENDENT

**County Board of Education**
W. W. Barr, Chairman; Nanafalia, Ala.
T. W. Shields, Pine Hill, Ala.
E. M. Moseley, Thomaston, Ala.
J. C. Dunn, Linden, Ala.
R. P. Allen, Old Spring Hill, Ala.

LINDEN, ALA.

November 21, 1918.

Willis Dunning, Vangale, Alabama.

Dear Sir:

A letter has been referred to me relative to a project to erect a colored school house in your community.

Inasmuch as the war is over the the War Industries Board has agreed for the erection of school houses to be resumed. Therefore you may go ahead with your plans for a State aid building.

I understand that if you will raise locally $300 the Rosenwald Committe will contribute $400 and the State will appropriate $300, which would make $1000. The State Department of Education believes that you could build a one-room school house with this amount.

I hope that you will take steps immediately to carry out this plan. You get a modern, well built, painted school building for an outlay of three hundred dollars.

Very truly yours,

George M. Watson

This letter from the superintendent of the Marengo County Department of Education to my grandfather documents the plans for the county's first Rosenwald school (November 21, 1918). It represented a joint venture between the Rosenwald Foundation, Marengo County Board of Education, and three community leaders—including my grandfather. It was an extraordinary example of cooperation, collaboration, and leveraging of resources to educate young African American students in the twentieth-century Alabama Black Belt.

My parents first worked together as teacher and principal in the 1930s and I attended first grade in this two-room school in Putman, Alabama (still standing in the 2010s). Constructed by local carpenters, the schoolhouse was funded by community members, as the state of Alabama invested very little in education at that time.

This is me with fellow airmen in October 1962 at Lackland AFB, Texas.

Here I am as a newly minted airman, circa 1962. The photo was taken just before I left the black and white world of the United States for Taiwan and a global world of rich diversity of race and culture.

The Albany State campus was submerged in the flood of the Flint River in 1994. (Albany State University)

I was invested as the ninth president of
Albany State University on September 30, 2016.
(Albany State University)

I am flanked by my sister, Jean, and my wife, Karen, at the investiture. (Albany State University)

Karen and I are surrounded by the Albany State women's basketball team after the Southern Intercollegiate Athletic Conference tournament, March 2015. (Albany State University)

Darton interim president Richard Carvajal and I answer questions about the school merger at a town hall meeting at Shiloh Baptist Church, March 2016. (*Albany Herald*)

PART FOUR

# Never before in Our Nation's History

In 2011 the chancellor of Georgia's higher education governing board initiated a study of the thirty-five institutions then in the USG to determine if consolidating some of them would make educational and financial sense. The study committee devised a six-point test for assessing potential consolidations: would consolidating two institutions enhance educational attainment, improve access, avoid duplication of programs, create economies of scale, help regional economic development, and streamline a quality administration?[1] By January 2015, ten system institutions had been consolidated to five. The ultimate purpose of any of the consolidations was to "increase the system's overall effectiveness in creating a more educated Georgia."[2]

In November 2015, a sixth consolidation was proposed and approved by the USG Board of Regents—that of Albany State University and Darton State College. The chancellor outlined his rationale for the decision to the board: "The University System of Georgia is preparing students for the 21st century economy and citizenship. Today the System must look internally to ensure that it has a 21st century structure, providing a network of institutions offering the proper range of degrees and opportunities in research and service to students and faculty."[3]

The consolidation of Albany State, an historically black university, and Darton State, an historically white two-year college, would be the first such consolidation in U.S. history. The only prior consolidation of an HBCU and an historically white university had been a court-ordered one in Tennessee. A case, *Geier v. Tennessee*, had challenged the dual system of higher education in the state based on race. The case was settled in

1979 with the mandate to merge the University of Tennessee at Nashville with Tennessee State University, an HBCU.[4]

Having worked in the USG headquarters, I felt confident that the staff was aware of the national dialogue about the role of HBCUs in a desegregated era. I assumed that all aspects of HBCUs would have been investigated from the original federal designation in the 1965 Higher Education Act, with its many subsequent reauthorizations, to consultations with the federal Office for Civil Rights to make sure that putting Darton State in with Albany State would not do anything to jeopardize the latter's HBCU status and the federal funding that flowed from that designation. Their research would confirm that neither the chancellor, nor the governor, nor the state legislature, could do anything to alter the federal designation.

Thus, the chancellor stood on firm ground about the USG decision: "We recognize this is a historic milestone for Albany State. We are committed to continuing to serve the HBCU mission and building upon the mission to serve an increasingly diverse student population and community. We also recognize the key role Darton has played in meeting the access mission and offering workforce related associate degrees. We will maintain both missions under the consolidated institution and believe this strengthens public higher education in Southwest Georgia."[5] One thing that the USG did not anticipate, however, was just how strongly people would cling to historic designations—not the university-state college designations, but the black-white ones.

CHAPTER 15

# Pushback in Black and White

Several USG chancellors and many others had asked me over the years, "Could Georgia be a different state if we could pull the southwest region up to the level of the state as a whole?" When I got to Albany, I would be asked, "Do people think and talk about how to lift the region up? Are they bringing all their human capital and political will to address the issues holding them back? Do they have a grasp of just how far behind they are from the rest of the state?"

What these people were alluding to was the long-held belief that there were two Georgias. One was made up of the up-and-coming, forward-thinking, comparatively better-off urban parts of the state, and the other was made up of the stereotypical poor, backwater, uneducated, mostly rural parts.

By mandating the consolidation, the USG was giving Southwest Georgia the gift of a single public university. If state and local leaders could work together to rally resources and energy in support of this university, it should be possible to raise education levels across the region. It gave Albany a chance to break with some fifty years of an adversarial, destructive educational relationship between Darton and Albany State.

I am certain that the sitting chancellor sincerely believed that the USG could lift that section of the state up by creating the largest institution of higher education in that southwest corner, enrolling nearly ten thousand students. It could help overcome the enrollment challenges that each institution had experienced over recent years by focusing recruitment and retention resources in a single university. It would establish a direct path for students from associate degrees to bachelor's degrees.[1]

As I've already mentioned, it was a problem that people in the community did not talk about the two institutions as "the university" and the "state college"; they talked about them as the "black school" and the "white school," a "bad school" and a "good school," "their school" and "our school." It solidified in people's minds the notions that "if you want a real *education*, go to the white school; if you want a cultural *experience*, enroll at the HBCU." These attitudes had persisted so long that they became fossilized.

Academically, the perceptions were misinformed. Albany State offered a liberal arts education with bachelor's and master's degrees, as well as education specialist degrees. Darton State offered access to higher education with associate-level degrees, and some bachelor's degrees. Its programs were designed to meet the economic development and workforce needs of Southwest Georgia. Its curriculum offered courses in humanities, social sciences, business, math, computing, nursing, and health sciences.

The chancellor's and the USG board's hopes addressed what I worried about daily: enrollment, retention, and graduation rates. Like many colleges and universities, Albany State's survival was tied to enrollment. Enrollment was tied to the budget; the budget was tied to growth and development. If enrollment went down, we lost money; if it went up, we got more and could enhance program offerings.

Once students were enrolled, retaining them for all four years gave us an advantage, because we didn't have to keep recruiting students to fill those places. At the most basic level, enrollment, retention, and graduation rates would dictate many of the decisions we would have to make during the consolidation process.

The chancellor presented the consolidation plan to the Board of Regents of the USG, which approved it in November 2015, noting that the decision would strengthen "the long-term health of public higher education in Southwest Georgia and our partnership with the Albany community."[2] As a consolidation rather than a merger, the missions, leadership, faculty, and staff of both institutions would be integrated. The best from both institutions would be joined on an equal footing in the new institution.

The minute it was announced, however, the entire Albany community was in an uproar, expressing indignation and confusion. Some did not believe that the board of regents had the authority to do this without consulting anyone in the community.

I tried to explain: "The Board of Regents provides leadership for higher education in the state. Let me tell you four of the main things they do. One, they hire and fire presidents. Two, they approve budgets. Three, they set policies and procedures, and four, they approve academic programs. That gives them a great deal of influence over the system's campuses."

People had never heard about the board of regents "interfering" with the University of Georgia or Georgia Tech's operations, so they couldn't understand how the board could make such a monumental decision about Albany State and Darton. But they also didn't understand that the reputation of the entire USG is in many ways driven by those two institutions. They had earned national reputations as excellent universities, which also meant that it generally wasn't necessary for the board of regents to step in. In this consolidation case, I think the board felt badly that the decision hadn't come sooner, so that it could have benefited the region sooner.

Still, people went crazy about the mandate. Perhaps more to the point, it was hard for them to acknowledge that what they thought of as "their" local institution was actually part of a statewide system that was governed by state law, which put the Board of Regents of the USG in charge.

Again, I tried to explain: "The decision by the system leadership is for the well-being of Georgia—not for my pleasure or your pleasure, but for the citizens of this state." That was hard for people to hear. It was difficult to have the same conversations over and over with people and not feel as if they refused to understand the bureaucratic realities, never mind the enormous potential benefits. When I got really frustrated, sometimes I ended the conversation by saying, "I don't get the chance to make that decision, nor do you. It's the chancellor's decision. Sometimes that's difficult to hear those words—that it's not your decision to make."

On one level, the Albany community understood what the board was telling them. They understood that infrastructure and business processes would be blended, and that we would build a new leadership team with people from both Darton State and the old Albany State. On another level —a cultural, racial level—they just could not comprehend. In hindsight, I see that some groundwork would have been helpful in preparing people for the consolidation, but that's not what happened.

Over the next two years, I would have to lean on all the values I learned as a child to sustain me, as well as to sustain the decisions I had to make that often brought me in direct conflict with people who viewed the consolidation as a threat. I grew up with a sense of my place in the family unit and knowing that I had a duty to do my best and to make decisions in the interests of not just me, but of my family. Not only did I have that responsibility, but the families around me had the same—to make sure that I did the right thing. That was part of what it meant to be an upstanding member of a community.

This value applies not only to the individual, but also to organizations. Each member of a university community has an implicit duty to do what is in the best interest of the institution and to make decisions that are in the best interest of the school and the school's reputation. That this value was not commonly held at Albany State would be a hard lesson that I would learn over the course of the consolidation. Thus, in the first few weeks after the consolidation announcement, I realized that the challenges I faced in the first two years at Albany State were nothing compared to those that would follow.

One reason the process would be so difficult was that the consolidation was long overdue. Twenty-five years earlier, when I was working in the USG headquarters as vice chancellor for services, it first struck me that consolidating these two schools would greatly benefit the region—and that realization had nothing to do with race but everything to do with helping students. Shortly after the consolidation had been announced, I traveled to Atlanta for a USG meeting. I asked a long-time colleague there, "Why did we avoid consolidation twenty-five years ago? It would have made sense at the time, and may have avoided a lot of the difficulties I foresee us facing as we move forward with consolidation now." My colleague replied, "Well, you can always count on being on the wrong side of everything in fighting. And Darton State and Albany State fought all the time. Every time we did make a decision, both sides would try to calculate who was going to get the benefit from it—the black school or the white school. So, we avoided them. We'd rather go to Macon State, Georgia Southern, or Kennesaw to try new initiatives or innovations. Feelings are hard across the nation, but in Albany they're raw!" So for twenty-five years the system office staff, in many ways, avoided making any decisions about Albany State in order to avoid being criticized as having made a racial choice.

It was the same in Albany itself. No one there wanted to shake up the social status quo, which had been calcifying for decades. Albany's blacks and whites were used to the more-or-less segregated social relationship, and they were loath to see it change. People new to Albany were almost forced to pass a litmus test of "Which side are you on? Are you going to support the blacks or the whites here?" These questions had been simmering under the surface, but the consolidation announcement brought all that right to the top.

Over my career, I had talked to people all over the world and become comfortable seeing people for who they were and what they were, rather than just judging them based on their background. It seemed to me that almost no one in Albany could operate in that mindset. Instead, it was clearly all about standing with one or the other tribe. I really struggled with that. I would push for using logic, reason, data, and information when trying to elevate scholarship, but before I would be allowed to talk about student needs or the new university's academic programs, I would invariably be challenged to choose a side, choose a tribe.

Since I was a relative newcomer to Albany, and certainly because of my resistance to choosing sides, many people questioned my motives in leading Albany State through the consolidation. Black members of the community thought I was "too cozy with whites." White people thought it was impossible that Albany State could have, in me, a leader with the judgment and strength to think in a balanced way about the academic needs of the school's students. More likely, they thought, I would act on race to maintain the HBCU culture of the institution. "This won't be a new Albany State University—it'll just be an HBCU warmed over." Maybe some people thought that, because I was an African American, I needed the job and wouldn't do anything to jeopardize it. Obviously, if they thought that, they didn't know me. I am fiercely independent, particularly about my own thinking processes. I knew that the decision to consolidate the two institutions was the right one.

Early in the consolidation process, I attended a small conference of about a dozen or so HBCU presidents on the topic of strategic planning. At one session, we were going around the table to talk about what we were working on at our institutions. When my turn came and I described the steps being taken during the consolidation, as well as some of the reactions, the whole room got quiet. One of the other presidents asked if he could take the microphone and make a comment. He chuckled, saying, "I sure hope you have some 'go-to-hell' money to take on that assignment! You're going to get it from all sides."

"I think I'll be OK," I replied. I was in a fortunate position. Not only was I fiercely independent, but I had retired once already, with my finances well in hand. I put my name in the applicant pool for the position of interim president because I was interested in the post intellectually and I felt that the combination of my experience in the military, in living abroad, in helping to diversify the University of Alabama, and in working in higher education for many years were particularly well suited to the needs of the institution at that time. I had a context and a body of knowledge that I thought I could bring to bear on the school's many challenges.

I accepted the position for two reasons. First, I was drawn to the Albany region because it was almost identical to the Alabama Black Belt, where I grew up and still had strong ties. I knew the kind of people who lived in those communities. I saw my teenage self in the students of Albany State.

Second, I thought I could add value to the institution by helping to create a first-rate experience for students after high school. My motives were equally "This would be interesting to do" and "I think I can be an asset to the institution." I had no other motivations than to be ethical, honest, and fair. My goals were straight down the line for a better experience for Albany State students. I was driven not by a crass lack of values but rather by those core values that were deep inside me.

---

As I've noted, the reaction to the consolidation announcement was swift. Much of the response traded in conspiracy, rumor, innuendo, lack of telling the truth, and lack of racial trust. Everything seemed suspect. Anytime one tries to move away from racial orthodoxy, both sides will push back, hard, and engage in name-calling.

Black and white members of the two institutions, as well as those in the greater community, would not talk to one another about their concerns. Instead, they came to me because of my position. It seemed that, everywhere I went, I was a lightning rod for people who wanted to report, or repeat, the rumors and complaints. I heard it all, from both races. They off-loaded their perspectives, pains, concerns, and anger and then either tried to steer me in a direction or censored me for not trying to stop the consolidation.

They often seemed to think that they were telling me something I didn't already know, or that they could get me to tell them some secret that was being kept from them, or that what they were telling me was a secret—"don't tell anyone, but . . ." Regardless of the venue, public or private, however, I never said anything that I couldn't repeat. I used to say, "Please understand that what I'm saying, I'll say to anybody. I won't be having two discussions—one behind closed doors with the chancellor and then one where I come out and present another face." My private and the public faces were consistent.

That was hard for a lot of people to accept. They wanted to pull me into the fray. They would say things like, "Dr. Dunning, what do you think about this? Let me tell you what I think . . ." I always tried to come down straight and squarely on the fairness of a decision. When I did that, it got people's backs up. The consequences of not choosing sides meant that for the first six months of 2016, I caught hell from both sides.

One white businessman in Albany who seemed to know everybody up in Atlanta, including the chancellor and the governor, approached me after he heard the consolidation announcement, asking, "Why in the hell did the chancellor do this to us? Nobody told me about this! He's done this as an edict."

"Had he told you, you'd have gone to Atlanta trying to reverse the decision," I replied matter-of-factly.

"By God, Art, you've got that right!"

I continued, "If they'd given you a month's notice, instead of just a couple of days, you would have been doing everything in the world to try to unravel it. You'd have been driving to Atlanta every day to change the chancellor's mind."

"Well you know, this is going to be a mess down here for us," he replied. "Do you think they know what they've done? Do they understand where we are as a community? We're a hundred years behind other people in this state, and we thought we had a good thing going. We had a black school and a white school, and we were all happy about things the way they were."

"That hasn't helped Albany. Look at the demographics. Look at the data," I said.

"Yeah, well, I know. But this is going to unleash a whole lotta trouble for us."

Less than two weeks after the chancellor's plan was made public, a prominent Albany attorney asked me to meet with him and a dozen or so of Albany's leaders at his law office—lawyers, businesspeople, and civic leaders. All were white; all but one were men. After a few polite comments, one came right to the point: "This is not going to go over well! Doesn't the board of regents know this'll tear up this community?" He continued, "At least, give the merged school a whole new name! Some kids will never go to a place named Albany State! Rename it something like the University of Southwest Georgia." What he meant was, "*white* kids" wouldn't go to Albany State because it had always been the "black school." He closed his outburst with, "And, Art, what the hell is an 'HBCU,' anyway?"

"How much time do we have?," I asked.

We had the whole morning. So, over the course of three hours, I briefed them on the history of historically black colleges and universities since the mid-1800s, and their connection to changes in the South over time. I had gotten to know all of these people very well. They asked pointed and direct questions. I, in turn, asked them, "Have you looked hard at the twenty counties around Dougherty County? Albany State and Darton have been fighting for almost fifty years, forcing the community to choose sides about race. You can't tell me that it's been good public policy all these years to have two separate institutions." At the end of the session, the group acknowledged that I was right. Still, a perception persisted among other community leaders that Albany State was second rate. And so, whites did not want any part of the consolidation. They perceived Albany State as setting low expectations for students and of lacking academic rigor. They also could not abide the black culture of the school.

Later during the consolidation process, it got back to me that someone was overheard saying about me that "This guy hasn't done anything to change the image of the school. There's no 'Darton' in the school's name. He's keeping the Albany State mascot, the music—all that culture stuff they do there." Another white acquaintance said to me, "Our opposition isn't all about race. Some of it's about economics. If some of our students—white or black—don't want to go to Albany State, they're going to try to go to another school farther away. They'll have to pay more to go elsewhere, and they just won't have the funding to do it."

The white reaction to the consolidation fit every aspect of historical racial stereotypes. When I left that meeting with white community leaders, I thought, "Here is a group wanting no part of the consolidation or of Albany State." What I considered as a gift to the people of Southwest Georgia felt—to some of Albany's most privileged and advantaged community members—as oppression. In their minds, Darton State was a superior institution to the inferior Albany State. Thus, to them, a sudden equality of programs housed within a new institution felt like oppression.

Back on the Albany State campus, however, people were convinced that the whites downtown were up in the middle of the night plotting and conniving to take the school away from them. This seemed like fantasy to me, since I thought, "If those people in the meeting I just left were doing that, then they're some of the best actors in Hollywood, because what I heard that group saying was, 'For God's sake, let those folks at Albany State do what they want, but don't pull us into it. We have a legitimate institution in Darton. We're not mad at Albany State, but just don't make us a part of the stuff that's been going on over there.'"

Still, Albany State supporters would not believe that. They thought the school was being stolen from them, which maybe isn't surprising given how used they were to whites generally taking what they want, and blacks having to make due with what's left. No one seemed to be able to answer my question, however: "How do you steal a public institution? What elements would you have to see in place to see the institution as stolen? Even if they put an Asian, Hispanic, or white president in charge, the facts of the school's history would not change. So, what would it look like—a stolen institution?"

These two views, that whites wanted no part of Albany State, a university they considered as "less than," and blacks who thought whites were trying to steal their school, exemplified the distrust, fanaticism, and even tribalism playing out in Albany. The fact that Albany State was an historically black university could not be stolen. It was not mine or the chancellor's to give away.

What I tried to communicate to people on both sides of the issue was that the Board of Regents of the USG by law and by policy could govern Albany State as they deemed appropriate. They would, however, not do anything that might jeopardize the status granted by the 1965 federal Higher Education Act, which supported the institution with federal funding.

What had happened over time since passage of the 1965 act was that "HBCU" had come to signify more than a designation for funding. It had morphed to now also describe a cultural experience at these institutions. Prior to the act, there was no HBCU designation. My sister, Jean, graduated in 1954 from Alabama State College, but she doesn't consider herself as having gone to an HBCU with all that that implies today. HBCUs developed as cultural icons only after the 1965 act creating the designation. For some reason, however, that remains hard for people to grasp.

My fact-based, unemotional perspective only seemed to exacerbate distrust in the Albany State community. Even before the consolidation was announced, my behavior caused what I consider to be racial orthodoxy from the African American community to surface. They would try to insult me by saying I wasn't "black enough" for them. Or they would demand that I put on a performance by showing up "a little mad" at the USG headquarters in Atlanta to try to force some action on a particular matter. These attempts invariably failed, not least because they weren't the first to try. In some previous jobs, I would get static from African Americans because they thought I didn't look or act angry all the time toward the administration. Instead of storming the barricades, I would intentionally choose to help the institution's black students in quiet, targeted ways.

When I worked at the University of Georgia, African Americans criticized my involvement in an initiative to help Latino students because they thought I should be helping African American students instead. To these naysayers, however, I replied, "You guys are too mad all the time. Y'all stay angry; I can't deal with people who are upset all the time." That made them laugh, but my point was that I had a logical demographic reason for where I put my efforts. During the late 1990s and into the 2000s, the Latino population was growing rapidly in Georgia. Latinos in Georgia were going to need postsecondary education, and the university, as a land-grant institution, needed to figure out how it was going to help address that need.

Responding seriously to those who questioned my motives, I said, "I fear that if this university had an African American initiative, it would turn into a grievance and victimization session, and that's not the world I live in anymore. I left that when I came back from Taiwan in '64. I've long since moved away from grievance and victimization and have tried to get in the world of thinking."

It griped people at Albany State that they couldn't detect any grievance or victimization in any statements I made. "You keep talking data and information. You don't seem to be talking passion and grievance," they would complain. Finally, somebody pushed me to explain myself, so I responded: "You know, when I went into the military, I found out that there were people there that said, 'I had nothing to do with what you are so angry about. I had no role in that.' They had a concept of happiness, and they had a smile on their face most of the time. I said to myself, 'I think I'll try that. That looks comfortable. The whole idea of a rich life of comfort with self and with the environment. I'll work to change what I have the capacity to change but being tied up in knots is not how I'm going to live my life.'" The self-esteem and critical thinking that my parents instilled in me at an early age insulated me from being bullied and meant that my strategy would always be to use words to explain, describe, and persuade rather than to bully others myself.

It felt as if the Albany State community had decided that I was supposed to be the keeper of HBCU traditions. Not living up to their expectation meant that I had "sold out to the white folks." What caused further rancor among Albany State supporters was my reaching out to white people in the community. I heard some say, "He's talking to those businesspeople [white people] downtown." I thought, "This is a public university. You have to work with all people, regardless of race, if you expect this school to grow and thrive. This job as president requires me to talk to everybody."

And yet, if a school defines itself narrowly and solely as an HBCU, it is in effect saying that it wants to maintain the status quo culturally, socially, and politically. I would say, "That's fine if you have the money. But if you're getting funding from the state and federal governments, then you have an obligation to do something different: you have to be engaged with *all* members of the public. Moreover, it is not mutually exclusive: you can be an HBCU *and* still be inviting to other people at the same time."

The situation reminded me of my dad's response when I hesitatingly asked him about my enrolling at the University of Alabama. He reminded me that tax monies paid to the state are not segregated but are aggregated, so in effect his and my tax dollars entitled me to go to any public university in Alabama, regardless of what race the majority of students were. So I would tell African Americans in Albany, "I can't ignore a population that you consider hostile and historically against you."

This just elicited the same fearful responses about whites taking over the school. Whites, for their part, continued to recoil from having the "white school" associated with the "black school." Later, when I became president of the consolidated institution, I would learn that Darton had its own deficiencies that were well documented in SACS accreditation reviews. Despite those hard facts, whites clung to their misconception that Darton was superior academically and operationally. But in fact both institutions needed to be challenged to improve.

---

The conspiracy theories about the consolidation raged on, ranging from irrational to sad. At one point, a member of the African American community approached me and said, "I don't mean any disrespect, but why'd they put you in charge of this merger, anyway? Why didn't they put a white man in charge? Then, the white folks would be happy. You know, some of us will work harder for a white man. You grew up in Alabama. You've seen how things get done on the plantation. You put in a white man as boss, and overnight you'd have more efficiency and effectiveness. You know we work harder for whites than we do for each other."

For this person, and for some other blacks, being designated as "Other" and "less than" in the South for so long had worn them down to the point where they accepted those belittling designations. Feelings of self-loathing would sometimes surface because the pain of subordination was so deeply ingrained. Every time I heard something like this, it showed me how deep the fault lines are in U.S. culture, and especially in southern culture, around diversity and race. It also made me appreciate once again my military service to my nation. In the air force, people from all over the country were thrown together under the same conditions and same expectations. It gave me a perspective I couldn't get anywhere else, because in my whole life, I've never had such an experience of extreme diversity.

Still, it's disheartening that one of the strongest propellants of hope for southern African American males of my generation was military service. Yes, it allowed these young men to have the same experience I had, which was to compare and contrast themselves with people from all races and backgrounds. And yes, there were imperfections in the military, but when comparing it to living under Jim Crow, it was great. Black servicemen hadn't ever had that experience in their lives before, and they wouldn't have it afterward, either—unless they stayed in the military. In short, few other societal institutions in our country could mirror the meritocracy of the military.

Several of my friends from my military days share this sentiment. We still talk by phone frequently, and recently one said, "I thought I was a smart guy growing up, but when I got in the military, I *knew* I was. I stacked up pretty well against all the others." Our feelings about serving our country are not tied to militarism, or to patriotism, for that matter. For those of us who lacked status, prestige, and resources, military service gave us a whole new view of what was possible for our futures.

So in Albany, where I saw how people could define good and bad around race, I thought that perhaps I could have ended up with the same worldview had I not had the opportunity to compete fiercely in an open system—physically and mentally—and recognize, "I'm pretty good at this"—among a diverse group of people. That environment, which was the result of the country's public policy at that time, allowed African American young men like me that came from small rural towns and farms across the Deep South to discover that they were bright and talented and could compete at high levels.

---

The ministry in African American culture can be best understood as a continuum ranging from well-educated, well-spoken, sincere ministers to fraudsters. I was fortunate to grow up with the former. Our minister in Sweet Water used Scripture to help us think for ourselves. Grounded in the values of Christianity, ours challenged us to go out into the world with critically thinking minds.

In other churches, poorly educated, self-aggrandizing pastors behave in ways that play directly into an ugly stereotype of a lack of scholarship, and of being shiftless. As part of the stereotype, it has been cynically said of some black preachers that "They don't go to seminary. They get the call to preach when they're broke."

The Albany community had its own share of preachers along the continuum. And those preachers ministered to congregations who, for better or ill, carried into the community the attitudes they heard from the pulpit and saw in the way their pastors conducted themselves in the community.

Albany was also saddled with a street committee, an informal network of relationships in Albany's African American community that had been used over the years to do harm. The attitudes and ideas held by some of Albany's preachers would find their way into the mindset of the street committee. My first inkling of this disruptive element came when an employee stopped me on my walk to the office one day to inform me that my wife and I had joined the wrong church. It dawned on me then how some of the other preachers in Albany operated.

"You're going to have problems. The ministers who think you should have joined their churches are going to get mad at you. So, Dr. Dunning, let me advise you, there are a few preachers, in particular, that you should pay no never mind. They're crooks and womanizers. They don't live what they preach. And yet, if you don't kiss their shoes, they're going to talk about you. I know you say you're joining a church with a minister who is an ethical, dignified man, but you're going to catch hell from the ones who think that if they can't control you, you're going in the wrong direction."

While I was listening, I reflected on what had driven me throughout my adult life. The least of my worries was what some preacher was saying about what I was doing. I did not care what they said or to whom. This employee was advising me to be prepared for some vicious, vile comments from a handful of folks who did not live what they were preaching.

To her, however, I said politely, "Well, we made a choice. We've decided which church we feel comfortable in. It was a personal choice, not a political, economic, or class choice. But I thank you for your concern."

My primary concern was the well-being of the next generation of students who were very much where I was as a young adult. I remain seriously, deeply concerned about the future of students of color in this country, knowing that if there is anything that can come close to giving them an advantaged position, it is a first-rate education.

One way to mitigate some of the challenges students of color face is to help them hone keenly developed minds. It was dismaying that some religious leaders were not at all interested in helping that process and were in fact hindering it. Stoking a class-conscious church bordered on insanity as far as I was concerned. One pastor in particular encouraged victimization, rather than personal development, as a means to exert control and influence over others. I learned that he routinely used the language of victimization, grievance, and distrust in his effort to challenge policy makers and hijack public agendas.

People who know me well would say that I am, like my parents and by nature and development, very measured. So it's saying something that the words and actions of such preachers really struck a nerve with me.

I grew up listening to a preacher with a deep understanding of the Christian faith. I read Martin Luther King Jr.'s letter from the Birmingham jail chiding white Baptist preachers for remaining on the sidelines of the civil rights movement. I think I have not a romanticized notion, but an ethical notion, of preachers. I do not care what they do in their personal life, but they do not dictate to me how to manage and lead a state public university. I felt some of my deepest emotions in Albany around this issue of the sheer lunacy that a preacher of any church would expect me to kowtow to him about decisions I made.

What also struck me was how many of the Albany State employees worried about what some of these preachers would do, as if they were bosses of the black community in Albany. This also did not make sense to me, and it saddened me that people in the community surrendered their autonomy to anyone, never mind those who clearly were advancing their own interests and agendas, rather than seeking to do their utmost to help their congregations and the wider community. Two added factors contributed to the community being vulnerable to this manipulation: the lack of education in Southwest Georgia, and the religion-centric culture. Some pastors acted like they had a right to be unreasonable. They encouraged their congregants to do the same.

Of course my motives were again under attack, from the pulpit, by word of mouth, and even on the internet. Pastors accused me of being an Uncle Tom, of being the chancellor's lackey, of taking the job to line my pockets, and other nefarious purposes. Of course, pastors who were themselves acting purely in self-interest couldn't conceive that there might be someone who didn't do the same, and I was a large, very public target during the consolidation process.

Their strategy was the racial reverse of what I had witnessed as a young man in Alabama. Sergeant Tucker risked being called a "nigger-lover" in order to help me as an African American. I was now being called an Uncle Tom for talking with "those crackers downtown." Each example—Alabama in the 1960s and Albany in the 2010s—was a sad intersection of race, history, and culture.

Looking back, I know that I didn't take any of this well, but I didn't take it lying down, either. This no doubt aggravated the pastors who thought they could get me to back off from the job I was supposed to do, a job I fully believed in.

Some congregants saw through the charade. They would talk to me about it in a cynical way. However, rather than acknowledge head-on that a pastor's actions were wrong, people would attack his character. So, after warning me that a pastor's criticisms of my leadership were dangerous, in the next breath, they would say things like, "Don't worry about these pastors. They have big churches. They have healthcare and retirement, and think women are a fringe benefit too. They're womanizers, and they don't live what they're preaching. They're mean as snakes, but they're nothing but crooks. They're in the pulpit every Sunday, but they don't live what they're professing."

For me, the worst part about this environment was the people it was hurting—the very people that the preachers were supposed to be ministering to. If their churches were sitting in the poorest neighborhoods, could the church help the people there? And we are talking about the poorest of the poor—grandmothers raising grandchildren, the elderly with disabilities, young people with no job skills. Helping would require these church leaders to work with city government officials and businesspeople. It would require pastors to let go of some of their control and allow their congregants to trust whites and to partner with them to improve the community. As it was, those congregants who wanted to collaborate with whites to improve conditions in Albany would have to buck their pastor's authority. The same was true for those who wanted Albany State to succeed as a new, consolidated institution.

And so, one event—the consolidation of two schools—was seen through the lenses of race, history, and culture. Both sides felt they were victims. I thought to myself, "This sounds like the lyrics to the Marvin Gaye song, 'Make me wanna holler and throw up both my hands!'"[3] Everybody had an intensity about being the victim. At the same time, they felt they were innocent in the process. They took no ownership for how the racial polarization had become so extreme.

While all this "noise" was going on, every day I thought about the data about the persistent poverty in the region, and what I could do to help those young people in the community who had the ability and desire to learn and achieve. Two institutions were fighting tooth and nail to stay separate when they could have been figuring out ways to better serve their students. It made me sad to ponder all this as I made the routine drive from Albany in one of the poorest areas of the state, to meetings at the USG headquarters in Atlanta to report on the progress of the consolidation process.

CHAPTER 16

# A Near Derailment at Square One

In January 2016, the consolidation began. The process involved more than two hundred faculty, staff, and students working in seventy-nine operational work groups, and with a forty-member Consolidation Implementation Committee. The chancellor appointed me as the ninth president of Albany State and Richard Carvajal as the interim president of Darton State, and charged us with leading the two institutions through the consolidation process. Since I would be the permanent president of the newly consolidated institution, Richard deferred to me to take the lead as the primary communicator during the process. Twenty members from each institution were selected to serve on the implementation committee, which in turn identified the seventy-nine operational work groups. Those work groups were charged by the USG staff with undertaking some nine hundred consolidation tasks (e.g., admissions, financial aid, business operations, facilities, student affairs). Other tasks were identified by staff at each institution. Each task was assigned to the appropriate work group.

The seventy-nine work groups were cochaired by Albany State and Darton State personnel who were selected for their expertise related to the topic assigned to the work group. These cochairs, in turn, selected members for the groups based on their expertise related to the tasks at hand. For example, for a work group on admissions, we tapped the director of admissions from each campus together with some of their offices' staff; a few people not from admissions were asked to serve to give an outside perspective. Where appropriate, students were included. The groups were organized in twenty-two areas, each headed by an area coordinator who was a member of the implementation committee.

The groups developed plans, monthly status reports, and recommendations, which the cochairs forwarded to their area coordinator. A master tracker circulated recommendations to leaders of functional areas (e.g., academic affairs, legal affairs, the two presidents) in order to ensure compatibility among all the work groups. Once that was done, recommendations were forwarded to the implementation committee for deliberation. Some approved recommendations had to then be approved by the board of regents.

Concomitant with the work of the implementation committee and the work groups, a team was assembled to begin working on a prospectus that was required by the university's accrediting body, the Southern Association of Colleges and Schools—Commission on Colleges (SACS-COC).

A series of deadlines would ensure that everything was in place for students to matriculate at the new Albany State University in the fall of 2017.[1] Of all the deadlines, my greatest concern was for the prospectus, which was due to our accrediting body in nine months. I wanted to make absolutely sure that we made that deadline. Moreover, I wanted us to exceed expectations—not just meet them—on every element we were responsible for.

At the implementation committee's first meeting, almost all the faculty from both institutions convened in one large room. I welcomed the group and tried to set the tone for the process. I wanted to shift the focus from me to the implementation committee as the leadership for the consolidation. I saw my task as nudging the committee to become the voice and the "tellers-of-the-reality" for the process. I needed them to take charge of the many tasks that lay ahead. We had to integrate processes for admissions, financial aid, academic programs, and finance and administration—all the normal operational functions of a complex university campus.

Over the next six months, the implementation committee members deliberated. In their first few meetings, all the members from Darton State sat together on one side of the room, while all the Albany State members sat on the other side. The first meeting was clouded by suspicion. Signs of racial stereotyping appeared as the discussions progressed. After the first few meetings, implementation committee members and other faculty members individually sought me out to illuminate me on various "challenges" they saw. "Challenge" would become the code word for problems one side saw because of the other side's race.

For example, the staff in Darton's nursing program wanted to make sure I knew that, "We [Darton] have one of the top nursing programs in the state. If we merge with Albany State—well! They have challenges with their pass rate. We don't want to diminish our reputation. It just won't work." When I asked the Albany State nursing faculty about the accusation, they replied, "Look at our pass rate for the state and national exams. We've only had one time where there were problems."

The "challenges" all had to do with stereotypes about "rigor" at Albany State by those at Darton State, as well as in the broader Albany community. To the white community, Darton State represented "quality," whereas Albany State represented a "lack of quality." The perception of lack of quality and achievement at Albany State had permeated the whole community to the point where even some African American students at Darton expressed concerns to me that the consolidation might diminish the value of their diplomas: "Can we have Darton State on our diplomas rather than Albany State? We'd rather our diplomas show that we graduated from Darton."

With all the suspicions and accusations on both sides, it might have been something of a miracle that we never had to cancel or shorten a consolidation committee meeting because of acrimony, which was not unheard of in the system during consolidations. Several people involved in consolidation processes elsewhere in the USG related to me that some meetings became so contentious that they would end the meetings early to allow for a cooling-off period before continuing at a later date.

I sought advice from those who had been through the fire elsewhere about how to manage committee meetings. In order to start committee meetings off on the right foot and to corral everyone's thoughts, I opened each meeting by reminding everyone of the larger context. I would say something like, "We have a deep, deep responsibility to the people of this community and this region, as well as to the people that gave us the gift of consolidation to take us to a higher level of performance and achievement. You forty people in this room have to think in ways where you are planning for one or two generations beyond where we are now."

Keeping the larger context in mind helped elevate those assembled above parochial and racial interests. I would continue, giving examples, "If you are an English professor, you have to think broadly, like how technology and English can be merged. Think like a Caltech, a Carnegie Mellon, or a Stanford. They do some fascinating stuff with the liberal arts and technology." When I did that, it almost always kept everyone on their best behavior.

I constantly framed the significance and importance of the consolidation. At some point, I asked people to wear nametags so that I could begin to mix people up. Once consolidation committee members were assigned to the smaller work groups, with members from both schools, that gave more movement around the room. There were some undercurrents from the two camps, but I never felt or sensed overt hostility.

---

The first requirement of the consolidation was to determine the new university's mission statement, which was to be submitted to the board of regents for their approval in March 2016. At the same time, but without the deadline of board approval, work began on a vision statement, guiding principles, and official history of the new Albany State, which would incorporate the history of both the old Albany State and of Darton State.

The USG's only guidance was that each institution should find itself in the new mission statement. My staff and I delved into research and data collection—my typical approach at the start of a major project. In this case, we looked at the top twenty-five HBCUs as identified in *U.S. News and World Report*'s well-known rankings of colleges and universities. While many higher education officials complain about these rankings, most consult, talk about, and use their data.

About half of the top twenty-five HBCUs did not mention "HBCU" in their mission statements. Rather, they said generic things about striving to be world class, their academic programs, or their liberal arts focus. Mention of their historical designation appeared in their second tier of foundational documents—in a core values, goals, guiding principles, or guidelines section.

Our team and I didn't think that mentioning Albany State's historically black designation or Darton State's white history was appropriate for the new mission statement. The institution's HBCU designation was the most secure thing we had. We held no fear that the new institution could lose its HBCU federal designation, which had been set fifty years prior by federal statute. Moreover, the Board of Regents of the USG had already acknowledged that the designation would remain intact. Thus, we hoped that the implementation committee would agree to move wording about HBCU status from the mission statement to one of the other foundational sections, which would allow the mission statement to be robust, vibrant, and focused on the institution's future rather than on its divided past.

Getting the committee to think outside the boxes of self-identity and preconceptions about the two institutions would be critical. I wanted the implementation committee members to deliberate on ideas like, "Can we get language about striving to be the best regional institution in the nation in the statement? Can we emulate some of the top schools in the country? Can we redefine ourselves and aspire in the wording to be elite without being elitist? Can we not just be the best HBCU, but the best public university of all backgrounds?"

So, the committee members persevered in crafting a new mission statement. They reviewed the preconsolidation mission statements of Albany State and Darton State.[2] In the charge to the committee members, my cochair and I asked them to craft a new, single, blended mission statement that stated boldly that the new Albany State University was poised to become one of the best regional universities in America. I told the committee, "We have the ability to consolidate two campuses. The enrollment will make us the largest university in Southwest Georgia. Let's move into a different arena. Let's compete to be one of the best state regional universities in the nation. To accomplish this goal, I ask you to consider moving the federal designation of 'HBCU' from the mission statement to the vision statement or guiding principles. Let's model ourselves after some of the top HBCUs in the country that do not have 'HBCU' in their mission statements."

The members of the implementation committee were decidedly not onboard with this approach. Listening to their reaction, I thought, "Boy, were we wrong thinking we could raise the discussion to a higher level!" As far as the committee members from Albany State were concerned, moving the federal HBCU designation out of the mission statement was tantamount to stealing it. It seemed to me that, although the federal designation was designed to help HBCUs, it also did damage by essentially putting a fence around a set of institutions with a special status. It provided a flow of money to help the schools, with the unintended consequence that it encouraged an insular way of thinking and behaving, at least at Albany State.

Having been at Albany State for two years, I was already aware that staff and faculty identified with other HBCUs, like Florida A&M or Tuskegee, rather than with other regional schools in the USG. In contrast, the Darton State members of the implementation committee identified themselves as being peers with other colleges in the USG.

This self-identification played out in committee meetings. The Darton State two-year college administrators could quote chapter and verse from the regents' policy documents. The Albany State people sat slack-jawed because, having identified their institution more with HBCUs in other states, they hadn't dedicated time and effort to become acquainted with USG policies. Darton had benefited from USG oversight by everyone learning the policies, whereas another disadvantage of the USG ignoring Albany State for so long was that no one on that campus was familiar with the intricacies of protocols and regulations of the system. This scenario in committee meetings further solidified the stereotypes the Albany State people held that the Darton people were arrogant. Moreover, it showed me just how entrenched "HBCU" was as a cultural designation as opposed to just being a federal funding designation.

In hindsight, I probably didn't fully appreciate the angst that the entire Albany State community would experience at the mere suggestion that "HBCU" be shifted out of the mission statement. A lot of backroom and sidebar discussions followed between implementation committee members and the rest of the Albany State community. The reaction was so negative that even people who supported the shift were reluctant to come out and say so without risking a backlash.

The most public display of this angst came at a Founders' Day event at which I was scheduled to speak. Some students arrived at the event dressed in black. While I was addressing the audience, they got up and walked out of the hall in protest. The audience didn't know what to make of this. I said the most honest thing I could: "You know, one thing I dearly love about this nation is the freedom to express ourselves. This is the first time I've seen our students so passionate about something. So, it warms my heart that they are feeling strongly about an issue. We may disagree about it, but at least they're thinking about it." And then, I just moved on with the program.

Eventually, the committee finally reached a consensus on a new mission statement. We were able to meet the March deadline set by the USG. It did not include wording about the historically black designation.

Instead, "HBCU" would appear in the Guiding Principles section. In remarks to the implementation committee, I commended their decision: "We have the HBCU model, but we want to go beyond it. 'HBCU' has not been left out. It has just been moved. One of our guiding principles will address our historical federal designation and express our historical outreach, which we will continue. At the same time, we will be broadening the school for *all* of the community."

I left the meeting feeling that progress had been made. I gave myself a little pat on the back, thinking that I had clearly explained that "HBCU" would appear in another of our foundational documents. Before I had time to realize that not everyone on the implementation committee had understood what I thought I said, we moved forward with announcing the new mission statement. The announcement didn't mention the work being done on the guiding principles, vision statement, and official history, each still being drafted by the various committees. And it didn't say anything about what role the term "HBCU" would have in those documents. Thus, in our effort to show quick and early progress, we made a huge tactical error.

---

Not releasing all of the foundational documents simultaneously triggered a resurrection of conspiracy theories. Through social media, those theories ricocheted among Albany State alumni and supporters. By the time we explained our rationale for moving "HBCU" to another foundational section, and that we wanted a robust mission statement about the aspiration to be a high-performing regional public university, nobody believed us. People were in an uproar.

If we had just waited to present all the foundational pieces at the same time!

I should have recognized that we had functioned for so many years in an environment of distrust that people would be quick to rise to a level of fanaticism. Both sides played the race card in their reactions to the announcement.

It was a no-win situation. I have to admit that Albany State supporters were correct when they said that whites wanted the HBCU designation removed entirely. They did. Blacks, however, were loud in their cry to lead with "HBCU" before anything else. This, in turn, reinforced the white stance. They zeroed in on Albany State's desire to remain an HBCU. They would say, "That's all they want to be, so we don't want any part of the school. We don't want a degree from a place that keeps talking about 'HBCU.'" Retaining the designation as "HBCU" and the name "Albany State" were the two main concerns in the white community. The attitude was that local white students would sooner enroll at a more distant college.

This reminded me of what fellow African American students and I had encountered at the University of Alabama campus fifty years earlier. Whether we were telling the university president that the fraternity float insulted every African American student on campus, or walking onto Bear Bryant's football field, we were challenging the status quo and making an effort to normalize space and place and activity for African American students. We were active and assertive in our calls for change.

Having been on the side struggling to be represented, I could appreciate the concerns of the white community. Now at Albany State I thought, "Could we move over and create space for people, and not just always say, 'HBCU, HBCU'?" I did not want to put students of any other racial groups, not just whites, on the receiving end of not feeling invited to Albany State. Moreover, the institution's foundational documents should reflect the primacy of the academic mission not the historic mission of serving just one racial group.

Albany State supporters thought that if "HBCU" was moved from the mission statement, whites were stealing their school and their culture. What I was saying was, "I want us to hold our own against regional universities like Georgia Southern and Valdosta State." But what the black community was hearing was, "I want to sell the university out to those white folks." Albany State's black students were particularly upset. They thought the conspiracy was to take away their "HBCU experience."

To explain that being a designated historically black institution could never be removed, I found myself referencing the history of another HBCU in the country, Bluefield State College in West Virginia. The school was founded in the late 1890s as the Bluefield Colored Institute to serve the segregated coal mining area of West Virginia. Although it is an HBCU, in 2013 enrollment was 90 percent white.[3] The school, however, maintains its status in the eyes of the federal government as an *historically* black college as defined under the Higher Education Act of 1965, with the emphasis on "historic." Thus, Bluefield State is still considered an HBCU even though the demographics have flipped. The school still receives Title 3 funds under the Higher Education Act, and when I was routinely attending HBCU organization meetings across the country in the mid-2010s, Bluefield State's president at the time, a white person, was usually there, too.

"HBCU" is just an acronym, a way for the federal government to categorize institutions. It was coined in 1965. Similarly, a friend once told me, "I didn't know I was Hispanic until I got to the United States." "Hispanic" was first seen as a way to categorize people on the U.S. Census in 1970.[4] Over time, however, "HBCU" has become a cultural designation. To all the African American groups I spoke to about the consolidation, the thing they feared most was losing their cultural identification with HBCU. You would have thought the designation had been established when the earth was cooling. I told one group of students, "If we kept 'HBCU' in the mission statement, it would be like the University of Alabama saying in theirs, 'We are an historically white university.' Having attended the University of Alabama, how would I feel about that?"

The students conceded: "Well, Dr. Dunning, that would be bad if they put that in their mission statement." I continued, "Well then, why would we want 'HBCU' in ours? Think about how exclusionary that language sounds to someone who would like to come to college here but doesn't want every cultural aspect of the school defined as being historically black."

I spent months trying to broker these passions and feelings that were historic, long term, and deep. It was a struggle. I had underestimated how much "HBCU" meant culturally—how tribal it was for people on both sides, black and white. I heard some really ugly language from both sides. I did not give a pass to such language, telling the people using it, "You don't need to lead with your tribe. Lead with academic programs—associate, master's, and education specialist degrees. Even if we all decided to have a coalition of the willing to collaborate, cooperate, and leverage resources, we probably have generations of work to lift Southwest Georgia up. It's not ever going to work if we're fighting. Instead, we should be engaged and providing a vision of the future."

I realized that many did not know the history of the HBCU designation as a means to channel federal funding. They only understood what "HBCU" had come to represent—a cultural and historical designation. Rather than embrace the goal of "let's become one of the best schools in the nation," they were ready to fight to save a culture they feared was being stolen. I had to ask over and over again, "Who do you think can take it?

We're trying to elevate the institution, take it to a higher level. It's about aspirations, not clinging to one racial group's culture or another's."

I was getting a frustrating lesson in tribalism. It stemmed from distrust in a community that had been downtrodden for so long. They had reached a point, especially since the 1994 closure conspiracy by the white regent and white Albany businessmen, that they just could not take anything at face value. Things were never what they seemed to be.

The distrust that led to fanaticism had quelled any hope of Albany's black community members thinking rationally. Had that not been the case, they would not have been concerned about where in the foundational documents "HBCU" would appear. I had no doubt, however, that Albany State's federal designation was secure. Moreover, if the Albany State community focused solely on skin color for its existence, it would still be secure, as the demographic profile of Southwest Georgia was not going to change significantly over the next fifty years. As far out as most of us could see, the school would continue to have a predominantly black enrollment because of its location. It was not at risk of having the demographic profile flipped as had happened at Bluefield State.

Hanging over every conversation, however, was this feeling that there was a conspiracy to take something. That one thing that people were most worried about being taken was what was most secure. What was not secure was, "Can the university deliver quality programs?" They could not continue to say, "We're going to serve who we served in 1965, or 1978, or even 1985 with the same programs we've been offering for years." No, they had to do something different if they wanted the school to survive.

I returned to my memories of what my fellow students and I had tried to do at the University of Alabama in the late 1960s. We were pushing for the university to be for all the people of Alabama. If it was fair for us as blacks to say that calling a university "historically white" was abhorrent, then the case could be made that to have a university lead in its mission statement that it was "historically black" could—in today's society—be seen as a nonstarter.

Although Alabama didn't add "historically white" to its mission statement, it certainly didn't extend an invitation to me to enroll. I invited myself. In that historically white environment, almost all the trappings suggested that it was an historically white campus. In fact, people used creative ways to try and make me feel unwelcome, from yelling racial slurs across the quad, to getting up in class and walking out if I sat next to them, to celebrating Old South Day. But my mindset was "I don't care if people won't talk to me. I'm not going to pout. Instead, I'm thrilled to be here. Being at this university is like being at a big party. I wasn't invited, but I came anyway, and now that I'm here, I'm going to have a good time."

People who have been marginalized for long periods of time may not share my approach to adversity. Sometimes, when they finally do get invited to the party, they refuse to participate, feeling more comfortable standing by their grievances. But I had made a complete cultural and psychological shift, not living in that world since I left military service. The last moment that I had lived with anger at the unjustness of the social structure in my country was when my Hawaiian supervisor, Sergeant Wong, on Taiwan jolted me out of the mindset of being angry.

I often wondered whether his insight was because of his Polynesian background, or because he did not live in the pressure-cooker environment of the U.S. South. Whatever it was, I am forever grateful for the gift he gave me by talking me through my anger. I hate to think of what I might have become had I stayed in Alabama as angry as I was when I landed in Taiwan, where I was thrust into an environment where I had to really examine my feelings.

By the time I got to Albany State just over fifty years later, it was almost as if I had lost any memory of what it was like as an eighteen-year-old trying to navigate through my emotions about what was being done to people like me back home in Birmingham. From that time forward, I tried not to be either overtly or inadvertently uninviting to people of any background. And so, I repeated as often as I could to those at Albany State, "Can you imagine how you would feel if Valdosta State or the University of Georgia led in their mission statements, 'We are an historically white institution'? Albany State's good fortune is that the HBCU designation can *never* be taken away from us. The federal government gave us a label because they wanted to figure out a way to channel funding to schools like ours that they recognized had been underfunded since their founding. The Title 3 funding was designed to strengthen our schools academically, not turn them into cultural monoliths."

I continued, "If you get angry with that language, others could see us in the same way by what we say and how we say it. What you are telling me is, 'We've lived so long in the context of innocence and grievance and victimization, that we get a pass.' I find it hard to give us a pass when we use language that we would not accept out of other institutions." Albany State supporters, however, could just not grasp this analogy. They kept falling back on, "We're an HBCU; they can't tell us what to do." They felt that moving "HBCU" out of the mission statement was an attack on their racial identity, their history, and their culture. When they heard about the move, they went berserk. They thought there was a grand conspiracy to steal their culture.

This jump to conspiracy theories came from their history of subjugation and marginalization—from real things that happened from slavery, to lynching, to Jim Crow, to the 1994 attempt to close the school. I had empathy for their feelings. They had real reason to be suspicious, but I tried to explain, "You can't live in that lane on every issue!" It was a normal reaction. What was so interesting about this instance, however, was that I, as interim president of the university, was at the core of the conspiracy.

I was trying to have an academically inviting environment to all racial groups, but in Albany they thought "an inviting environment" meant "be nice to racist white people." No, I had in mind that we wanted to be inviting to the state's increasing Asian and Latinx population. I wanted us to be kind to all races and ethnicities of students who might show up at our doorstep wanting to get a first-rate college education. I wanted all our symbols to be inviting to the general public. Many of our students did not want that, however. Their feelings were strong that, "We don't want those white people on our campus."

This missed the point that I was acutely aware of: the institution could not survive with our current trend of enrollment decline by sticking with inviting just one historic racial group. We had to create academic and social space for other demographic groups. That was my logic. Albany State supporters did not function in a world of data and information, however. For them, it was all about feelings and emotion. And yet, for all their passion, I felt that many had lost sight of the universality of humanity. They could not see the strength and decency in people with backgrounds different from theirs.

It made me think back to Sergeant Tucker and Director Springfield. Both helped me pursue my studies out of their recognition of our shared humanity. I thought of those two when I would ask myself, "How can I do this at Albany State? How can I help these people get to a better place? Can I guide them toward adopting a common view of the future? The past is past. I don't want the struggles of the past to strangle the futures of young adults."

To secure those futures, intellectual repositories—we call them universities—could and should put a stake in the ground around teaching, research, and service, and have every discipline informed by the community that surrounds the university. It could be strategic in its applied research and service-learning courses, becoming the go-to place in the nation for research and development on topics of importance to its region. And because Albany State is situated in one of the poorest regions of a very wealthy nation, it is well positioned to lift up both the students and the community.

Thinking about how the institution could help the community, making the campus inviting to more than one racial group, and leading with a mission that aspired to create a first-rate public regional university, was neither in the minds nor hearts of many Albany State supporters. And yet, we moved forward. I cannot calculate the amount of time and energy that went into getting the mission statement completed. I commended the members of the committee for their perseverance. When the mission statement was finally completed and approved by the board of regents, the work groups and the implementation committee pressed forward over the spring of 2016 to complete the vision statement and guiding principles.[5]

---

The whole experience of wrangling over wording and placement of designations made me consider how I came to have such a strong desire for Albany State to fiercely compete with the best public universities in this country. As I pondered, I realized that it came from my military experience. There the rules were explicit, the demands were outlined, and the expectations were clarified. I found it easy when I understood some simple guideposts and guiding principles that I could leverage every ounce of my energy to compete at the highest level. As a university administrator, I learned that this mentality could be transferred to organizational behavior. I found that when people collaborated and cooperated to apply innovation, initiative, and hard work, it was easy to compete at the highest level.

At Albany State, I was weary of the school being wrongly viewed by whites and blacks alike as providing an inferior education. The consolidation was a great opportunity to catapult us to the highest level of public universities in the country. But others saw it as something altogether different, and I could not switch their mindset. In my entire academic career I had been on campuses that were always striving to be the best of their peer group and to reach the level of their aspirational institutions. But it seemed that tribalism was preventing that from happening in Albany.

At one point, I tried to bring people around with humor about the concept that geography determines one's fate. In a small group setting I said, "You know, when I was a young man, I found out something that was shocking to me. I had been harboring a deep feeling that the distribution of intellect was defined by geography: everybody north of the Mason-Dixon Line had sense; everyone to the south was ignorant. But when I got in the service, I found out that wasn't true. There I learned that there's a broad distribution of intellect." They chuckled about that.

I closed our meeting with, "So, this is our chance to prove the stereotypes wrong. We can say, 'Geography does not determine our fate, nor does skin color.' We want Albany State to be the best regional institution in the country. We can be models of engagement because we have a rich environment of challenges in Southwest Georgia that would benefit from all that our university can bring to bear to improve the area through research, teaching, and outreach." I sensed from the expressions in the room that many were still thinking, "Those white folks have done stuff to us for so long, and now they're at it again. And, Dr. Dunning, either wittingly or unwittingly, you're in there with them, too."

That sentiment showed when we got to the final piece required to complete our foundational documents—an official history of the new university, which was to include histories of the old Albany State and of Darton College. A young white faculty member in the English Department was charged with the task, which elicited a lot of passion from people. Some admonished me: "Dr. Dunning, you make sure he puts in there that Darton was created because they didn't want us desegregated. They wanted to stay segregated. Let's not whitewash that!" Albany State supporters were emphatic that the history state in black and white that the whole impetus for the creation of Darton was that white folks didn't want their students mixed in with black students.

Such comments showed the rancor I faced on almost everything. I replied, "Let's try to be subtle about it. This is not a place to get your licks in. Yes, there was a racial and historical context with Darton, but let's not replay the history of the South in public education in our foundational documents. That's not how to start a new relationship—with a fist fight." The faculty member was finally able to complete his work, and the new Albany State University official history was adopted.[6]

The impossibility of drafting a blended history that would satisfy everyone is one more example of how every inch—every step—of what we were doing to consolidate was met with tribalism because of race. It reminded me of Faulkner's writing about the past never being dead and forgotten, but always living with us.[7] This was surely playing out in Albany. I would spend the next several months trying to calm people down on both sides, especially after the mission statement setback, while at the same time taking the next step in the process—staffing the new university's colleges and administrative structures.

CHAPTER 17

# When Wounds Go Untended for Generations

I knew growing up that anyone living in the Deep South had two opposing views of history. As an adult, I had the good fortune, however, of living and working in cities in Georgia and Alabama where, through an influx of diversity and a desire to move ahead economically, people tried to rise above the history of slavery or of a glorified Confederate South. The board member who politely chided me about "the war of northern aggression" collaborated enthusiastically to make Georgia a more inviting place for all. Childhood friends who had migrated to the North were moving back to the South in retirement as they saw parts of the South becoming more open.

In my first couple of years in Albany, however, I learned that the community was trapped in a time warp. They may have known who fired the last shot in the Civil War, but the war was not over for them. Little attempt had been made to reconcile negative attitudes of whites toward blacks, or negative feelings by blacks about past wrongs by whites. The consolidation, mandated from outside, had the effect of ripping off the dressing of an old and deep wound. Covered for decades, the lesion had festered under the surface with no healing. What I experienced in Albany was more like my childhood than what I had experienced as an adult. Both sides let these old hurts infect their beliefs, attitudes, or actions toward each other.

Many in the white community persisted in holding on to stereotypes about African Americans. People inadvertently revealed their attitudes as the consolidation progressed. One instance occurred while we worked to blend the two institutions' fund-raising units. With the two earlier mismanagement instances that damaged Albany State's reputation still on everyone's minds, the people from Darton were concerned about how a combined office would be managed. One staffer told me, "As soon as we heard about the consolidation, one of the board members said, 'I don't know what we're going to do about this money in our foundation if we consolidate the two. If those guys get it over at Albany State, they're going to spend our money like drunken sailors.'"

This comment exemplified old cultural stereotypes—that African Americans lack intelligence, are shiftless and lazy, have no scruples, and are unable to handle money. People often ascribe characteristics to ethnic or cultural groups about money, and African Americans are stereotyped on the low end. Other groups have a very high reputation about managing resources. So, anytime a bad managerial situation arose, people jumped automatically to the stereotypes. The Darton people wanted an assurance that the foundation funds they received before the consolidation would be used the way they had intended them to be.

In another example of negative attitudes by whites toward blacks, several physicians spoke with me about the consolidation of the two nursing programs. In a conversation with a doctor I knew well, he said, "I just saw in the paper that they consolidated Albany State and Darton. I don't know how you're going to handle this, but don't let those Albany State people tear up Darton's nursing program. We get good nurses from them. They work in our hospital; I have two in my office. They all pass the nursing exam. But I hear other things about the Albany State program. Could you and your colleagues make sure that we have the kind of nurses we need here? Healthcare is a big deal down here. We're a poor community in a poor section of the state."

He was indirectly talking about the superiority and inferiority of programs and their graduates. I reassured him, as I had the staff in Darton's nursing program, that both programs turned out graduates who did well on the licensing exam.

"Well, you're right, but I'm talking more about the soft skills of the graduates from Albany State," he said. Again I had to read between the lines. "Soft skills" was his way of communicating what whites consider to be a "racism chip on the shoulder." It stems from a residual anger that people of color sometimes exhibit. Whites do not know how to deal with it, so it reinforces negative feelings.

A newspaper's op-ed pages offer a good civics lesson in the various ways people deal with and communicate their feelings, negative or positive. As a teenager reading the newspapers, I was fascinated by those op-ed sections—not just the letters to the editor but in particular the editorials. Maybe it contributed to my passion about the importance of the free press in setting a tone of respect and civility in the culture of a community. In particular, a good editor on a local paper could challenge readers to think deeply and clearly about an issue.

The allies for civil rights change in my generation were the federal judges and editors of newspapers like the *New York Times*, the *Atlanta Constitution*, the *Montgomery Advertiser*, and the Mississippi-based *Greenville Delta Democrat-Times*. Before the days of iPhones and 24/7 cable news, the newspaper was an extraordinarily strong ally for African American aspirations and social change. I had a deep regard for Eugene Patterson, Ralph McGill, and Hodding Carter, each Pulitzer Prize–winning newspaper editorialists.

In my youth, the Sunday copy of the *Atlanta Constitution* made its way to us via a train stop in Thomasville, Alabama, reaching the black community in Sweet Water on about Tuesday. McGill's editorials in support of the civil rights movement were heartening to us. On the other hand, whites in the community called the paper the "Lying Constitution" because they did not like what they were reading. At that time, they also considered Atlanta a Yankee city. Ernie Suggs writes that McGill, as an editor of the *Atlanta Constitution*, "used the power of the paper to become one of the most important voices of the South as he wrote against segregation and the failure of 'separate but equal.'"[1]

Unlike McGill and his peers from my youth, some in today's media outlets seem to be sabotaging the free press and social justice. In Albany, one journalist held blatant biases against Albany State. It was widely believed that he, along with some elected officials, was actively trying to undermine the consolidation.

He would periodically show up in my office, not bothering to hide his true feelings as an opponent of the consolidation. He also thought he could undermine my confidence in what I was doing, saying things like, "The System Office sent you here on a fool's errand. The consolidation is not going to work, and anybody in their right mind would not accept this because it's destined to fail." This was not the attitude I expected from someone who I thought should have an open mind in order to give a fair assessment.

I was not naive about his motives and intentions, but I stayed engaged with him. We had spirited discussions and debates about the significance of the consolidation, and how important it was for Southwest Georgia. He would always bluster aggressively, "White folks are never going to accept this! It's foolhardy! You're wasting everybody's time! All you're doing is damaging this place."

I would push back with fervor, putting facts and data in front of him and saying, "How in the world do you think the status quo is going to serve this community? We're sitting in one of the poorest sections of the state and the country. You're seriously telling me that this black and white dichotomy is something that we ought to perpetuate? I think this consolidation is the right decision, and it should have been done a long time ago. So no one pulled the wool over my eyes! The chancellor made a decision for the well-being of Southwest Georgia, and you're going to sit here and tell me you think Albany would be better off if you stayed separate forever?"

Other media types also brought their biases to the consolidation issue. Local television personalities told me about the many calls they got about what people deemed to be the failings of Albany State. "You have no idea what people call and tell us about Albany State. Every time someone stubs their toe, they come out here and tell us. They'll say, 'Here's what they're doing out there now. You need to get out there and investigate!'"

This too was not a new attempt to denigrate, shame, and embarrass those at Albany State, but it got especially bad during the consolidation. Supporters of Darton would call everyone they could think of who might publicize their case for submarining the decision. Rather than get in there, roll up their sleeves, and think about how they could make this forced marriage work, they instead shamed the old Albany State in an effort to unravel the consolidation process.

---

The consolidation announcement and effort acted like a catalyst that brought long-simmering animosities on both sides right to the surface. Whites made thinly veiled negative comments or engaged in more blatant sabotaging efforts. African Americans steadfastly refused to surrender their negative emotions born from past wrongs. Distrust, resentment, and even anger permeated the community at what felt like every turn.

It seemed to me that it was whites' negative attitudes toward African Americans—people not like them—that was causing them to fight so hard against change. When we tried to put in a walking trail connecting Albany State to downtown and beyond, apparently some whites got miffed. Just the thought of a trail connecting their white neighborhoods to the campus stoked fears based on stereotypes about lazy blacks who get drunk and "do crazy things." We could not change these negative attitudes, but our conversations about the concept were woven into others about the potential for a network of interconnected trails along the Flint River, which could be implemented over a number of years.

The breadth and depth of antagonistic overt pushing back by whites toward the consolidation was stunning to me, and sobering. I felt that if there was ever going to be any reconciliation in the community, I had to calmly and rationally keep talking to saboteurs, plying them with real data and information. Hopefully that would change their attitudes, beliefs, and behaviors, and cultivate a sense of mutual commitment toward a shared goal of helping lift Southwest Georgia.

In consolidation meetings, if I tried to talk about academic programs at Darton versus Albany State, someone loyal to the old Albany State would say, "You need to make sure they don't have more programs than we do, because they've always tried to do that to us." I countered, "Well, I would say the facilities on the West Campus, which were built in the 1960s, are newer and better."

One of the ways we tried to break old, unproductive modes of thought was to change what we called things. Since the new, combined institution would be called Albany State University, we all had to break the habit of referring to the actual physical structures of "Darton State" and "Albany State," both of which conjured "white school" and "black school." The best we could come up with at the time was to refer to the old Darton State campus as West Campus and the old Albany State campus as East Campus. This wasn't entirely successful, as most people simply transferred their old feelings to the new names. A more productive approach might have been for us to mix up the academic programming geographically.

When we moved one of the old Albany State programs in its entirety (including faculty and staff) to the West Campus, I thought the whole place would come unglued. The same thing happened when we shifted some basketball games from East Campus to West Campus, which had a better facility. From a rational standpoint, these moves made sense: the facilities and amenities on the west side of the river were, in many cases, newer and more appropriate for the particular program or activity. But people could just not get past the old wounds of race, history, and culture.

Every meeting was held hostage by those who would cry racism. This seemed to me to be incredibly disrespectful of our history.

My transformation about how I think about race, racism, and change in organizations started when I served this country. Being required to intersect with people of other races, ethnicities, religions, cultures, and people was not easy for me, but I learned how to do it. If my ancestors hadn't been slaves but were free people in the North, maybe I would have another perspective. But racism in one of the poorest and toughest parts of the nation—the Alabama Black Belt—it was not tiddlywinks.

So in those meetings, when people played the racism card, I wanted to say, "You're talking about racism, but you don't know how ugly it really was. If you had read our history, you would see that it was hard. It was inhumanity at the highest level. So don't make this a minor tactic at a meeting. Treat racism with the dignity and the enormity of what people had to endure."

As president, the only way to deal with having to choose between using my old Albany State president's office or the space that had been the office of Darton State's president was to decide to use both. The president's office at the two-year college was like a palace—it had a large waiting room, and offices for assistants, and even had a balcony. It was much more conducive to hosting visitors. The president's office at the university was more like a closet in comparison. I wondered to myself, "How does something like this happen?" I tried to be very sensitive to perceptions, and so I divided my time equally between the two. I knew I was under watchful eyes.

---

Over the years, I have concluded that there are levels of racial intensity. Stereotypes can lead to distrust, distrust to fanaticism, fanaticism to tribalism. I watched people move through these levels during the consolidation. One example was during the staffing of the new Albany State's administrative leadership. Though we would eventually realize economies of scale and a streamlining of staffing, our immediate need was to hire administrators as we consolidated institutional units. Since their responsibilities were broad and highly visible, criticisms about the hiring decisions quickly reached the level of tribalism. Contributing to the heightened tensions were several early hires whose attitudes and behaviors reinforced stereotypes and negative feelings.

One of our senior administrative hires showed a lot of promise early on. It wasn't long, however, before people started making comments about his approach to leadership. Instead of the allegations being made directly to the university, however, they were written to an elected official, who brought them to me and said, "Deal with them as you see fit." I did not know if the allegations were true and quickly turned all the information over to our legal staff for investigation.

Sadly, I later heard that, when challenged about his inappropriate behavior, he said if he had to go before the board of regents about his transgressions he would use subservient language, a tactic used to manipulate people in power, and then they would leave him alone. When I heard that, I just felt deflated. If the allegations were true, he was responding by playing the old Stepin Fetchit role of "play dumb enough and they'll leave you alone." If the allegations were false, it no longer mattered. The words were circulating; they had taken on a life of their own. He had lost the trust of the community.

When it came to staffing the consolidated institution, we followed the USG hiring guidelines for a tiered approach. There were to be three levels of consideration. One level was to use staff from each of the campuses to round out the organizational chart. Second, they asked us to consider people from other campuses in the USG. Third, we could recruit nationally. We followed these guidelines and ended up with staff from all three levels of consideration.

One of the first places where we needed to bring in new people was to the president's cabinet. Shortly after I had the positions filled, a rumor started that it was majority white. Of the nine members on the cabinet, two were white. People just could not separate fact from fiction. They were blinded by tribal loyalty.

Stereotypes of race and cries of double standards occurred on both sides. For some of our hires, I heard things like, "We hear so-and-so isn't qualified. You're demanding more credentials from your black hires than your white ones. Plus, your white hires are lazy. They won't come to work. When they do, they don't work hard, and they feel entitled." The criticisms were the same as those that had been used over the generations to describe African Americans.

Other hires were criticized as being liberal bigots. When I asked what that meant, I was told, "They act like they like black folks when they're at work here on campus, but they put us down when they're out talking to their friends." If nothing else, this showed the painful complexities of race relations.

Perhaps what I found most interesting, not to mention baffling, was how comfortable people felt coming to me to relentlessly unload their opinions about others.

For some hires we made from other USG institutions, it was clear early on that they did not have the knowledge or skill set to function at the university level. For some reason I noticed this especially with people who had only worked at state colleges. Other hires minimized their involvement in campus life. Being a racial minority in the workplace—perhaps for the first time—made them uncomfortable, so they just would not participate in or attend campus events, whether it was a sports event, a fine arts performance or exhibit, or even academic events and honors. I tried to explain to those who criticized the aloofness that "unless you are strong on the inside, being in the minority numerically is not for the faint of heart."

We even had some staff whose behavior during meetings at the USG headquarters did a disservice to the consolidation process. Ten or so two-day board of regents meetings are held each year, many of them at the USG headquarters in Atlanta. During the two days, staff from the various institutions routinely walk the halls, visiting with the USG staff and updating them on things happening on their campuses—sharing the challenges and successes.

Some comments made during these routine, informal conversations took on greater significance. Word of some of the conversations made their way back to campus, revealing that some had crossed a line from providing objective observations to making unhelpful comments with racial undertones. They were not sharing anything that USG staff and I did not already know. Their words and actions, however, strained racial relations back on campus all the more.

All this is to say that, like any organization, we had to rethink some of our staffing and make adjustments over time. It all seemed especially difficult with the added layer of racial, internecine discord.

One hire we made shocked the entire Albany community, black and white. In the spring of 2017, we hired Gabe Giardina, who is white, as head football coach for the new Albany State's Golden Rams team. As soon as the announcement was made, people in the African American community said, "My god, has he [by which they meant me] lost his mind?" It went on and on.

Then, I got it from the white community. A couple of white businessmen said, "Dr. Dunning, you act like you're serious out there trying to add a little diversity," to which I responded innocently, "What do you mean?"

I told both blacks and whites: "You know, we had about a hundred candidates. An Atlanta executive search firm handled the search. It was an open and competitive process. Gabe was on the list of finalists for the post." To those on both sides questioning my selection, I pressed, "Explain to me what you're asking me to do. You want me to hold his achievement and his color against him? At a public university? Is that what you're asking?"

"No, no, no, but you know..."

"He competed, and he won. Fair and square."

I was candid and direct with all groups when asked questions about the hiring process and the ultimate selection. After one session, an African American alumnus who loved Albany State and went to all the events but was a real gadfly, came up to me and said, "Tell that white boy—I don't know what you've done by hiring him—but if that guy can beat Valdosta [State University] and Fort Valley [State University], I'm on his side. I don't care what color he is, he's fine with me!"

"We can't promise that every year, whether it's me or Giardina coaching, but I'm glad you're that advanced in your thinking about culture and race."

"Oh, Dr. Dunning, you know what I mean."

"Well, just reverse that. Suppose somebody at the University of Georgia said the same thing you just said. You'd want to get in the street and protest and tear the place down."

"Well, I guess you've got a point."

"You know I have a point. If somebody talked about race at the University of Georgia or Valdosta State or Macon State like you're talking about it, you'd want to file a lawsuit!"

I really wanted to tie people up in knots about their prejudice toward whites. Here was an African American alumnus trying to tell me that

I should not have hired this coach—in a very joking way—because he was not African American. I challenged him: "That's the same game that's been played against African Americans for as long as we can remember. So, how in the world could you say that to me?"

As I had learned when listening to the barracks banter in Taiwan, if people have been marginalized and they consider themselves victimized, and have grievances, the very next descriptor they will add is "We're innocent. The people who are racist toward us are evil." Having been victimized and having a grievance do not give people purity, however. They can turn around and do the same thing; they can take on the habits of their oppressors. About the coach, I told any and all who would listen, "I treated this as a normal search. Gabe was on the list and made it to the short list. I interviewed all four of the finalists. He was the choice of the team's football players involved in the search process. I thought he was the best fit in terms of what I thought would be good for the community and good for the campus. He won fair and square."

And indeed, Gabe turned out to be a great fit for the program.

---

Negative attitudes and emotions about race were not confined to older members of the Albany community. They could be found in young people, too, white and black. I heard that the white peers of some black students in Albany made jokes about lynchings. I heard from employers that some young African American college graduates seemed to have chips on their shoulders about race. If a supervisor, for example, said, "You didn't get your report in on time," the knee-jerk reaction was often, "Well, you didn't say that to that white person down the hall." One Albany physician told me, "We've tried to hire some of these Albany State nursing graduates. We get them on the floor and find that the least little thing that we might have a disagreement about, they start calling you a racist."

I recognized the reaction from people of my generation, but I pondered how the attitude was instilled in young people. In my early twenties I had had a hard time adjusting to what my dad was saying about treading lightly around white people. I'd served my country for four years and thought I had the right to move around freely. But he was right when he told me not to invite trouble from police by driving home late at night.

What does growing up under such conditions do to the psyche? What toll does that take over time? What price do we pay when other children have privileges generation after generation? In many ways, living on edge is still happening today. When children grow up hearing stories from their parents and grandparents, and when they move around in an unequal world, they can develop a thin skin about past and present slights and omissions.

Thus, I understood why those Albany State nursing graduates immediately went to the "you're criticizing me because I'm black" place. I recognized, too, that young people who went to all-black high schools before attending Albany State University, a predominantly black HBCU, might never have been in an integrated environment. The shock of that immersion would come only after graduation, when they got a job as a nurse on a unit where the only other black faces were those of the cleaning staff. That would present quite a challenge.

The concept of superiority-inferiority was deeply entrenched everywhere in Albany. Because the medical community employed graduates from both schools' nursing programs, people were very aware of problems that arose when graduates got into the workplace. It was inevitable that the students from Albany State's program would be vigilantly watching for equity and fair treatment compared to those from Darton State. At the same time, the students from Darton's program may not have had opportunities to work with or administer care to people of different backgrounds. Both cases were undercurrents that the students' supervisors would always have to contend with. Having two nursing programs in the same community was a clear example of why consolidation of the two institutions was so important as a step toward reconciliation in Albany.

What I saw was an opportunity to adjust the new Albany State's academic programming to help all students in the nursing program. In a conversation with my doctor friend who obliquely referred to Albany State nursing graduates as lacking "soft skills," I walked him through my perspective about it. "This is more deeply entrenched than can be solved in one conversation." I felt we might be able to help these young nursing students through a curricular approach. I tried to explain to him: "Let's talk this through. It may be something we need to do in the nursing program curriculum around diversity. When you have people who have been isolated racially, culturally, and socially, regardless of race, and all of a sudden they turn twenty-three or twenty-four and they have to jump into an environment with all different groups, you have to develop new navigational skills."

I had seen this same thing happen when I was in Taiwan—but in reverse. There, young white men who had grown up in white communities suddenly found themselves in Taiwan. There, they worked side by side with irreverent black folks who called them "sons of bitches" every time they looked up. It unnerved them, and they didn't deal with it well.

My empathy is very deep for any person who has never experienced diversity and suddenly enters a diverse environment with no preparation. As a young adult, being thrown into the integrated environment of military service, including a couple of years halfway around the world, challenged every assumption I had held up to that point. I realize now that living in a country with a very different culture than my own was the most important variable in my transformation and growth. Thus, I remain convinced that broad exposure to the world is what can jolt people from harboring a self-righteousness about their beliefs.

In Albany, I spent a lot of time thinking about what leaders could do to help people learn to work in diverse environments when they have never experienced diversity before. As president, I hoped to accomplish much by way of academic programming. One example was in the curricular approach that could help students learn to work in a diverse environment. Black students could learn skills to help them adapt to working in a majority white medical community. White students could learn strategies for working with patients who lacked the resources to seek preventive healthcare, tried to stretch their dollars by not taking their prescription medications at the recommended frequency, or lacked trust in the medical profession.

Easier said than done in Albany. Whether it was nurses, university administrators, local ministers, or elected officials, people all too often acted like their tribe was more important than telling right from wrong.

It got to the point where every time I talked to a group, black or white, in Albany, I left feeling that if I did not laugh, I would cry. It reminded me of Little Walter's cover of "Blues with a Feelin." The song is about a relationship between a man and a woman—most blues songs delve into all the emotions of relationships: life, love, work, hate. But the words can be used to describe other types of struggles. In this case, in my mind Little Walter is singing about a university and a community grappling with change related to race.

I concluded that when wounds go untended for generations, the hopes for reconciliation and for moving forward recede from the community's grasp. If Albany State was ever going to become an intellectual repository capable of civic engagement with its community to help bring about economic change, everyone was going to have to buy into that mission. They could not cling to one tribe or the other. If they could not reconcile and move forward for the common good, what hope was there for lifting a very poor region of the state?

CHAPTER 18

# Fallout When Unreconciled

Reflecting on my time in Albany, I think there were at least four generic consequences of the community's inability to reconcile. Maybe these outcomes can be found in any community struggling to reconcile some trauma in its past. In Albany's case, the trauma was racism. The fallout of living in an unreconciled condition included resisting change, fearing a loss of culture, engaging in dysfunctional behaviors, and living with generational consequences.

I observed in Albany that, when people lived in an unreconciled environment about the traumas sustained by living for centuries in a superior-subordinate social structure in which day in and day out they are told that they are "less than" and "Other" because of the color of their skin, they often became paralyzed at the thought of change. In some cases, a cure for that is exposure to the broader world.

The eye-opening phenomenon that living abroad can have was captured nicely by an African American airman I served with in Taiwan. He said to me, "You know, I thought the whole world was full of white people. Coming out of Mississippi, I thought whites were everywhere. Now, here in Taiwan, I see that we've got all these Asians, Indians, and Africans. They're the majority of the world. These whites are a small group of folks." He was astonished by it all.

Some of the staff at Albany State had never had the opportunity to venture far from home, limiting their exposure to the wider world. They had grown up in small rural towns outside of Albany. Driving through one of these towns on the way to a meeting in Tallahassee, Florida, I saw just how isolating these small towns could be. I passed just two stores, a grocery–service station and a liquor store, several grain mills, and an old railroad track. Young people left these small towns for Albany to earn their undergraduate degrees and later got jobs at the university. Some worked there their whole career.

When I mentioned that staff would need to attend meetings in Atlanta, 175 miles north of Albany, they would almost panic: "All those cars. The traffic! We wouldn't know how to get out of there." They thought Atlanta was just too big. I wondered, "What would happen if they were dropped into the middle of Beijing?" Having been all over the world, I now pondered how I could assuage their provincial fears and nudge them to be adventurous about exploring the world beyond a thirty-mile radius of Albany. I thought, "How can we help people realize that they can learn from other places?"

When I would broach the subject, the response was often, "You're trying to get us to be like the University of Georgia or Georgia Tech," their veiled way of saying, "We're not white folks, Dr. Dunning!" Those attitudes and beliefs became especially difficult to manage when they encountered among the university's sixty or so international faculty members those who brought to their work the values and traits of many immigrants, including self-confidence, self-discipline, an openness to learning from others, and a "go-getter" attitude.

Without experience outside of one's comfort zone, people can lose self-confidence. That can lead to a normalization of feelings of being less than, and of having to make do. I saw this manifested in the young, local adults lounging on their front porches at ten in the morning when two miles down the road was Albany Technical College. There they could alter their lives by getting the skills to, say, get jobs in supply chain logistics that could pay so much more than young people in Albany could have imagined.

One city administrator who had lived in several other places before moving to Albany asked me, "How is it possible to be poor in Albany? There are postsecondary institutions that for some programs students can pay almost nothing to attend." The question spoke to the fact that people in Albany had geographical and often economical access to education, but they did not take advantage of the opportunities.

I've always felt that "If you put the rules out in front of me, that's all I need to know." Since the day Jim Crow was ended with the stroke of President Johnson's pen, I have not looked back. All the conversation we hear today about institutionalized racism, and "We can't do this. They won't let us do that," makes me think, "Are you kidding me? When I think about what it was like to live under legal segregation!"

Through their words and actions, my parents nurtured my strong sense of self. Their philosophy was "If you do what you need to do academically, you can do anything you wish to do. Start with you in terms of preparation, skills, knowledge, how you think about yourself, and the choices you make." Next to my parents, the most important factor that has helped me over time is what I learned living and working in other countries including Taiwan, Thailand, Cameroon, Tunisia, Tanzania, Croatia, Slovenia, Brazil, and Mexico. I built an aggregate set of experiences that allow me to reframe my thinking. So it was difficult at Albany State to talk with midlevel administrators, many of whom were from Southwest Georgia, about creating world-class programs when they had lived only in a make-do, wear-it-out culture.

---

A second outcome of living in an unreconciled state is a group's fear of losing its culture if the aggrieved parties set aside their differences to move forward toward common goals. At Albany State, the fear was that consolidation would cause the institution to lose its cultural essence of being an HBCU. But as we tried to placate their fears, while at the same time trying to nudge the community to be contemporary and forward thinking, we met with resistance.

For example, I gingerly approached shortening the length of commencement ceremonies. Ours dragged on for hours with prayers and gospel songs. I nudged the committee by saying, "There're people who drive in from all over Georgia and the Southeast to attend commencement. They can't sit there for three or four hours. We have to shorten the ceremony."

"Well, we've always done it this way. We always include a lot of Gospel hymns."

"Maybe we can cut some of them out," I suggested. I was not trying to offend a cultural way of doing civic life but instead trying to streamline the ceremony to a reasonable length. I tried to explain that the notions of effectiveness and efficiency, characteristics of how twenty-first-century organizations are managed, is not black or white. In today's world, time is money. People have busy lives. Trimming commencement to a time frame that is more sensitive to the demographics is not trying to change people's culture nor trying to make them be like another group.

The motive was not to change black culture to be more white. I really struggled with how to try and do this in a way that did not turn around and bite the consolidation process. I was just trying to say, "We can't stay this way. We have to be more contemporary."

The fear of losing a cultural identity can spread like wildfire in today's world of social media. With events like the 2019 premeditated social-media-streamed mass shooting in New Zealand, we know that social media can wield deadly power. In other cases, social media can wreak havoc on good intentions.

In a very nonlethal example, rumors spread on social media that we had changed the mascot and the school colors of Albany State to those of Darton State. Doctored photographs were apparently circulating. My office started fielding phone calls from panicked Albany State supporters: "You've changed our school colors? Why? How could you!" This would have been laughable if they hadn't been so upset. I wanted to respond by saying, "Whoa! Wait a minute! I'm here working to consolidate academic programs. I'm not here to take away the school's mascot, colors, and song." I got so exasperated, I thought to myself, "It used to be that there was a town crier to shout out public announcements from the street corner. Today, we have people who can manipulate images and send something around the world with the press of a button." In a fit of frustration, I *did* say, "No one is fighting with me about English literature or supply chain management. But people are fighting with me about the ram mascot, the school's colors, and school song. Something is wrong with this picture. We're a university, not a cultural icon. Let's lighten up about this."

We had never even hinted that we planned to change the school colors, mascot, or song—because there was no such plan. Once the social media rumor mill got hold of it, however, I was hard-pressed to convince people otherwise. Some even accused me of lying. Disabusing them of the notion that there was a conspiracy underfoot consumed a lot of energy. It was a wakeup call to me about the extraordinary power that social media wields in our world.

The most important lesson of the commotion about school colors was that we had to get in front of social media. If I had it to do over again, I would try to use it in constructive ways rather than let others put us in a corner by using it to manipulate people.

Social technology will continue to impact us in so many ways. It is a permanent part of our culture. It has an extraordinary potential to undermine trust, respect, and credibility of institutions. We are seeing a shift from hierarchical dissemination of information to horizontal dissemination. Everybody is a news reporter. Their phones are their voice recorders and their cameras. People can see things happening on the street, video them, and send them to the news station. As soon as people walk out of a meeting, they can post something. At that point, given the distrust of people, of organizations, and of our institutional foundations, it can immediately put decision makers on the defensive.

The role of technology and the role it plays in public policy are remaking the world. In many instances, such technology can help society. But at times, and in the wrong hands, it can be destructive. Now that social media is out there, it is something that we will live with for good or ill. The combination of social media and a growing distrust of institutions makes me wonder what we have left standing in the United States today that we have deep and profound trust in. Congress? Churches? Schools? It is very difficult now for an organization to say or write something that makes us respond with confidence, "I believe that." It is not right or wrong. It is just where we are as a nation. Technology has accelerated that. We cannot ignore it.

---

We were meeting all of the board of regents' and our accrediting body's deadlines. The intersections of race, history, and culture were, however, proving to be more difficult than the mechanical steps of consolidating academic programs and operational functions. As we drew closer to fall 2017 and the first semester as the new Albany State, the black community's conspiracy theories that the cultural aspects of "their" school were being taken from them intensified. Stereotypes, suspicion, distrust, rumors, and innuendo escalated.

On a chilly Saturday morning in October 2014, a big crowd lined the streets of town for the homecoming parade. In addition to Albany State's band and cheerleaders, the school's dance team, the Passionettes, would be performing along with high school bands and cheerleading squads, and youth dance teams. All four Dougherty County public high schools, as well as a middle school and a number of elementary schools, would be participating.

It was my job to kick off the parade with a homecoming greeting to Albany State's community, especially the visiting alumni. The theme for that year's homecoming was "We're All In." My welcome played on that theme: "Homecoming is always a grand occasion and this year, we're all in as we cherish our past through our alumni and look to the future as we continue to prepare students to become successful members of society, just like the alumni who are visiting this weekend."[1]

The parade was the culmination of a weeklong series of events and preceded a much-anticipated football game that afternoon against Clarke Atlanta University, a private HBCU in Atlanta. As with many homecoming parades, there was a competitive element to it. At a viewing platform, I was seated with the community's leading educational and governmental officials, and military and businesspeople. To the left of the viewing platform was seated a panel of parade judges. Each float and band, and each group of cheerleaders and dance teams would stop and perform in front of us and the judges.

When our Albany State dance team stopped in front of the judges' platform and performed their dance routine, I nearly had a stroke. In a state of shock, I watched the suggestive nature of the dance and the looks and comments from those on the viewing platform. Some around me looked just as stunned as I was. I understand that people have strong feelings about artistic freedom, but at a homecoming parade I was more concerned about the institution's reputation than about the right to free expression.

A remark by one spectator told me that I was not alone in my thinking. A self-proclaimed "good ol' boy" pulled me aside and chuckled, "Dr. Dunning, my wife told me, 'When you get home, don't expect me to shake my ass like that.'" I thought to myself, "Who thinks this is a good idea?" My mom and people in her community would have been horrified. She was like First Lady Barbara Bush, who was said to be "the enforcer" of the family. My mom believed in civility, respect, and manners. She was heavy on the external presentation of self. She would have dressed those young women down: "The way you present yourself reflects not only on you, the individual, but also on your family, your community, and your university. And your dance routine is not appropriate for this venue!"

Following the Albany State dance team was a middle school dance team. To my horror, the girls' routine was along the same suggestive lines as what we had all just witnessed from the college women. I am not a prude, nor do I live under a rock. Moreover, I am a strong believer in self-expression, having been denied it growing up under Jim Crow. But it was sad to watch these middle school girls doing some dance moves that simulated something they should not be practicing at their age. My heart sank as I thought about some of the most debilitating stereotypes around racial groups. One stereotype that runs deep in southern culture about African Americans is about sexual behavior. My thought was, "Clearly these young women haven't read any U.S. history!"

It was not that I wanted to be the cultural policeman for the routines. I understand that times have changed since my and my mom's generation. I understand the need for uncensored artistic expression. My concern in that moment sprang from my role as the person charged with safeguarding the reputation of the university. With that charge came a duty to guide the time and place of expression. My thoughts were of how the institution and its students would be viewed in the long term. I also felt that all members of the university community—faculty, staff, and students—shared in this duty to protect the school's brand.

In the days and weeks following the parade, the dance team's performance continued to be a subject of conversation, some approving and some disapproving. Sometimes people brought their opinions to me, and sometimes I sought out the opinions of others.

One morning, not long after the parade, as I was walking into my office on campus, a fellow came up to me and said, "I hear you've been concerned about these dancers with the band and the cheerleaders. You're going to get yourself in trouble talking about it. These are nothing but hoochie mommas."

"What in the world is that?," I asked.

"When you get a chance, take that iPhone out of your pocket and ask it to play 'Hoochie Mama,' by Bobby Rush." Later that morning, I did just that. The song made me sad. Its humor was ribald. It hit at distinctions of class in the African American community. It raised images of the ghetto. My mom would have keeled over if she had heard the song after seeing the dance routines.

What this fellow and others tried to get me to accept was that "Hoochie Mama" and suggestive dance moves were accurate representations of African American culture. My resistance to this characterization of our culture was getting me into trouble, as was my concern about the way people would perceive the university with that kind of representation.

People saw my reaction not as a quaint old-guy thing but as proof that I was a sellout to my tribe and that I was trying to remake Albany State as a white school. Others thought I was completely out of touch and didn't understand how important it was for young adults to be "authentic."

I was saddened and distressed that more than a few men approached me to convey their appreciation for the dance team's performance. They were all but leering when they said it.

At the same time that I was being hammered for being out of touch, middle-aged members of the community—both whites and blacks—were telling me how unhappy they were about the dance routine, as if I had known in advance what they were going to do. Albany State alumni were the most vocal. After all, they were the ones in the community hearing the ugly things being said about the team and about the school.

As part of my effort to protect the school's reputation and brand, I spoke with some people with responsibilities for the dance team. They dismissed alumni concerns out of hand and also managed to blame whites in the community, who they said were "out to get us." It was disappointing to still be hearing this defensiveness and distrust about whites from university staff.

Organizations have a culture that develops over time. That culture can become dysfunctional. The organization's members may know that there is dysfunction, but the culture is so deep and dear to them that change is often a struggle. That seemed to be what was happening here.

My sadness only grew as I realized the low level we had reached. A couple of folks kept hounding me that somehow the controversy about the dance routine was the fault of "those white folks who are attacking our culture." They were ignoring the fact that the people giving me the most intense comments about the inappropriateness of the dances were African American alumni. What they and I wanted the younger generation to understand was the history of women who had had centuries of things being done to them. The point of the women not doing such risqué dances was to show some respect for all of the things women had had to endure—especially African American women who were defenseless in the South.

To me, the crux of the issue came down to one question: When does free expression collide with protecting the reputation of the university? I was particularly concerned about the reputation of Albany State as an HBCU. The institution had a responsibility to counter historical stereotypes in its current set of activities. The school's reputation was not determined only by its academic programs. It was shaped by how students presented themselves on the football field, in the band, and on the dance team.

I could just hear my mom saying back when I was a teenager, "Now make sure you behave yourself. Make sure you realize that you have more than just you. You have the family name." She and I used to make fun of that. I would dash out of the house to be out of range of whatever she was saying. She would yell out, "Wait! I'm not finished talking to you yet!" Even with the teen in me trying not to hear, her words sank in.

Those memories are why I understand that people do not live in a vacuum. They intersect with the values, customs, and beliefs of other people and organizations. I struggled with this particular incident, however. I did not want to discourage these young women from potential dance careers, but I hoped to protect them from perceptions that could reflect negatively on their and their university's reputation. Discussing the whole fiasco with my wife one evening, I mused, "I wish I could help people know that I'm not puritanical. I've traveled around the world. You can't imagine what I saw in the bars and nightclubs of Southeast Asia! We young men in the lower ranks weren't on the base talking to the chaplain in the evenings. I've seen a lot of people doing a lot of things, but they weren't representing universities as part of their responsibility. I'm not trying to be the pastor of Albany State, or trying to turn the campus into a monastery. I know students will do what college students do. I'm just trying to be the president." I felt that each one of us affiliated with the university—faculty, staff, and students—had an obligation to protect and elevate the reputation of the institution.

---

As the consolidation process continued, a third outcome of being unreconciled became apparent to me: a variety of dysfunctional behaviors. I was no longer surprised that the logistics of the consolidation process was consumed by internecine racial animus. We wasted an awful lot of energy between and among groups.

Signs of dysfunction had started to appear when I first got to Albany. The feeling I got from some in the Albany State community was, "You're acting too normal around this place." They felt that way because I did not seem to wear on my sleeve "Look out for the man!" or "Look out for people who're out to get you." I was not watchful and on guard looking over my shoulder. Somehow I was unconsciously communicating that I had functioned as an American and as a human being without saying "They won't let me!" or "I can't do this."

In meetings, this paranoia of "somebody's out to get me" translated into a group-think that resulted in us rarely reaching consensus about strategic directions. The excuse people gave was, "This is just how we've always done things in Albany." It was a Balkanization of the community. It was fascinating and exhausting as I worked to understand what was behind all the comments and behaviors.

I knew the dysfunction had reached an extreme when people began to affect negative stereotypes when they were around me by saying things like, "Boss, what do you want? Whatever you say, I'll do." When that happened, all I could think was, "By gosh, that is not what we need down here! I need for you to think. Go back and come back to me with ideas."

I would be subject either to this almost pandering behavior, or dig-in-your-heels resistance, or ugly language that would come out in meetings with senior campus leadership, as well as with community members unhappy with things like the composition of the president's cabinet, the consolidation of the two foundation offices, and the blending of academic programs. The street committee was in full swing.

At one meeting, we were to work on improving our student registration process. There would be long lines curled all the way around the building. Students stood in the hot sun in ninety-degree heat for hours. It was so bad that the staff would pass out bottles of water to those waiting. Both students and parents were upset. As we discussed the problem, no one would take responsibility for the actions of the inefficient and ineffective process. The process had no paternity. I asked the staff, "What other campus in the system right now, with all the technology that we have available, would let something like this happen?"

"These kids wait to the last minute. They won't send their paperwork in on time," was the reply. The problem was the deadline. A school like the University of Georgia held firm deadlines because the demand was so high to enroll. But to cope with declining enrollments at Albany State, staff had loosened deadlines to the point where they were sliding. Students took this to mean that there were no deadlines at all. Students showing up at the last minute to enroll also indicated that Albany Sate was their fallback choice.

So, the question was, how could Albany State begin to culturally change? Could a case be made to the chancellor that if we began to impose firm deadlines, the enrollment might drop a couple of thousand students in the short term? Could the USG not penalize the school while it worked to shift the culture to firm registration deadlines? But the staff seemed unable to think innovatively about how to solve the problem.

At Albany State, the passive-aggressive pushback against change because of a history of oppression was a classic case. It cropped up in many situations, even simple things like being more efficient in the registration of students or in the administration of financial aid. Moreover, if a white person gave a suggestion, it was dead on arrival. Even if it was a good idea.

I heard over and over again things like, "Well, Dr. Dunning, they won't let us do this, and they won't let us do that," as if someone was standing over them 24/7. The staff would assign blame to "those white people." This mindset was suffocating. It was almost as if people were impotent in the process. I countered that striving for excellence and efficiency was a generic process, not a race-driven process.

This mindset was not unique to Albany State. I have had conversations with presidents, staff, and former students of other HBCU campuses where dysfunctional practices had taken hold. One student who attended an HBCU in Virginia told of having to stand in line for a couple of hours to try and make a payment to the school. When the lunch hour struck, the cashiers would pull the station shades down, leaving the students standing in line. The student said, "Why couldn't they rotate their lunch breaks? We could see all the staff sitting in the back, eating lunch while we students stood there. No other campus would do that."

In some meetings, people did not realize that everything said was in effect being spoken into an open microphone. At the close of a meeting, some would go out and call their "tribal chieftains." To those people, race was more important than being in a campus leadership role. Their thinking was not "There're good, qualified people here, and there're some mean-spirited, unqualified ones. How can we make the best of this situation?" Rather they would act out, "I'm going to stand with my tribe," black or white.

During administrative meetings, I would have liked for us to get to a place where we were thinking about the next seven to ten years and how to best serve students, rather than just sitting there talking about our tribe. I would have liked for us to talk about how to build our future on performance, achievement, and cutting-edge academic programs. I so wanted Albany State to think big.

But when I brought up adding an academic program that would help graduates get jobs at the local U.S. Marine Corps logistics base, the first responses were "Are they going to give whites the best jobs and put all the rest of us in trade jobs?" or "Will Darton get this and Albany State that?"

"No, it's a knowledge-based industry and everybody will have to function at a high level. And remember, Darton doesn't exist anymore." All of a sudden, there was a fight going on. In the meantime, the two-star general at the base was telling me, "We don't need smart people of just one category. We just need smart people, period."

The unbecoming behavior of campus administrators around the conference table reminded me of my fellow airman and basketball teammate from Tennessee, Thomas, when we were stationed in Taiwan. As you recall, he turned everything into a race issue and took his anger out on people whether they were being racist toward him or not. Our base basketball coach, our Hawaiian sergeant who had helped me come to terms with my own anger, had less success with Thomas.

I realized that when people start a relationship with the concept of Otherness and separation, they just cannot think strategically, together, about the future. That was the case in the mid-2010s in Albany, Georgia. The dysfunctional behaviors reached a crescendo when those unhappy with decisions threatened to "call the chancellor and the governor's office." They thought that such threats would make me back off, give in.

My years in the USG headquarters had given me a deep understanding of and appreciation for what the chancellor and the board of regents could do and what they could not. So, when Albany State supporters threatened to call "the bosses," I gave them the phone number and street address.

It happened so often that eventually I just did not give a damn who they called. In fact, I would try to accelerate their calling just to help people understand that they could not resist change by threatening to call an omnipotent "big bad white man" who was the chancellor up in Atlanta. I would say to them, "Please write, because I'm doing everything I can to help this university develop a strategic view of the future. We won't always get it right, but we're always going to be honest and earnest about this process."

And, in fact, there were ministers in Albany who worked hard to get a meeting with the chancellor. They had never come to my office to speak with me directly. Instead, they asked for a meeting in Atlanta on the pretext of talking about fund-raising at Albany State. That in itself was a red flag for the USG staff, as it showed they did not understand university system protocol.

The chancellor did follow protocol by inviting me to attend the meeting, as president of the university under discussion. He probably knew, as I did, that the group was more interested in getting the chancellor's ear to complain about me than they were about becoming involved in fund-raising. In any case, the group found an excuse to cancel, and the meeting never took place.

---

I understood the deep roots of these dysfunctional behaviors. Anger. Both sides had built up resentment over some 150 years since Reconstruction because no mechanisms were put in place for reconciliation. Today, we see this playing out on the national stage. Some whites have become so angry they feel emboldened to assert their feelings of supremacy as reflected in the increase of hate groups. Many African Americans of my generation harbor pent-up anger about the entrenched racism they face every day. Their feelings remind me of Howlin' Wolf's 1959 song, "I've Been Abused," in which he laments that he is "so mad" that he wants to shout because of all the scorn he's been subjected to throughout his life.

Even though we are one or two generations beyond the end of Jim Crow, our country still abounds with racism and white nationalism. Still, I am surprised to find so many young adults clinging to the anger their parents and grandparents held when they have had no direct experience living under Jim Crow. I asked some of our Albany State students to explain to me how they were so agitated about this consolidation. They responded, "Well, Dr. Dunning, you know how it is." I smiled inside, thinking to myself, "Well, I really do know how it was, but I don't think you do, so let's talk about that." Somehow, people thought I had lost the ability to understand what it meant to be black.

The anger these young students harbored made me think back to the precise moment when I chose not to ever—in any environment whether it was all white, all black, or mixed—wear my grievance, victimization, or anger on my sleeve. The transformation for me to not do that, even when

I felt I had the most legitimate reasons to do so, happened when I was nineteen years old stationed in Taiwan. There, I was angry.

That was when Sergeant Wong sat me down and gave me a hard talking to. He helped me realize, grudgingly, that my mom was right when she said, "External factors like race and economics can't take the place of personal development. If you look back at leaders like John Adams, Frederick Douglass, George Washington Carver, Booker T. Washington and others, they never used scarcity as a reason not to learn."

My sergeant and my mom taught me that I had to learn to manage my anger. I had to navigate through all the degradation of segregation and find ways to strive toward high achievement through reading, writing, and learning. Still, it was hard not to be consumed. Some of my classmates at the University of Alabama did get consumed. They had not had the chance, however, to spend time abroad. Their worldviews had been shaped only by their eighteen years growing up in Alabama. I was fortunate both to be a little older and to have had the time in another country to help me shape my identity. By the time I was on the University of Alabama campus, I had a deep sense of comfort with who I was. Years later, I would try to communicate the sergeant's and my mom's philosophy to those young students at Albany State.

If a community's residents are in a rage—full bore—and are angry all the time, it is an easy place to manipulate around gossip, innuendo, and rumor. I felt that was present all the time at Albany State, especially from some of the university's alumni. I was warned, "Dr. Dunning, these alumni are going to come after you." I responded, "I'm fiscally responsible, I'm ethically doing the right thing. I'm not violating any policies or practices. Tell me what they can do?" They said, "Well, you know how they are."

One manifestation of their anger was in the use of language. In this country, we are not surprised when we hear the language of white racists or white supremacists. It is well publicized and documented. What I find sad is when members of the African American community adopt similar debasing language. This was something I first witnessed with the African American airman in Taiwan making racist comments about the Chinese.

Since that time, I have seen it in many other instances. I have been in places where you could sit in an African American barbershop and hear people say absolutely outrageous things. They sounded liked a J. B. Stoner, the white supremacist convicted for the 1958 bombing of an African

American church in Birmingham, or a Bull Connor, Birmingham's commissioner of public safety who used billy clubs, cattle prods, and dogs to break up a nonviolent march in the 1960s.

The language of hatred can spill over into the politics of power structures like churches and government. That those black pastors used their positions to keep their congregants agitated about the consolidation underscores for me the power that words have. People can keep others stirred up by starting fights over basic things like gender, skin color, and ethnicity. In some instances, there are legitimate reasons to feel victimized. But victimization and grievance can be used by both sides as a strategy.

In my youth, Alabama governor George Wallace was a master of the tactic. He used language on the stump and on television that put whites in a frenzy thinking that they were being victimized by Washington, D.C. They were the ones with grievances because the all-powerful federal government was trying to force them to desegregate. He would refer to Frank Johnson, a federal district court judge for the middle district of Alabama, as a "lying good-for-nothing scallywag." It was an example of old-style southern political theater. He was skillful at name-calling. And, the names would stick. They appealed to people's base senses, and so people repeated them. More than half a century later, at his rallies Donald Trump resurrected George Wallace's name-calling technique as well as his ability to inflame his supporters with the self-righteousness of being victims.

In Albany, Georgia, the consolidation of two schools brought out a similarly sad side of humanity. People's emotions were so agitated that there was no purity in the process—it was never just about the consolidation but always mired in racial inferences. I heard some of the worst language from both blacks and whites. We're seeing the same thing today, but at a national level.

Words matter. People in leadership roles have an ethical responsibility to choose their words with care as everything they say—verbally or in tweets—people pay attention to and believe. It was as my dad used to say: "Son, you just can't go around telling tales. People have to trust what you're saying." Today's equivalent is the emphasis on transparency.

We are at an interesting place as a nation about what we are willing to say publicly about "difference" and "Otherness." What we went through at Albany State put us at the forefront of intense things in terms of harshness.

What I wanted to say to some of Albany's pastors was, "You're not lying about more than 240 years of slavery. You're not lying about almost one hundred years of Jim Crow. And, you're not lying about current racism. But you can't place that as a barrier against the personal development of students. Young people still have to learn."

My parents were people of faith, but they were also critical thinkers. In Albany, it appeared that some in the congregations had given up on thinking for themselves. They seemed to blindly accept what their preachers told them, which was destructive in so many ways. The pastors were creating the sort of dynamic that tears communities apart. Their words created a paralysis of action in their followers who in effect were saying, "I can't discuss Latin, history, English, math, or science because I need to make a case for my space. I need to remind you that we had almost a hundred years of legalized segregation in the United States."

The distraction of words is happening across our country and around the globe. People get so caught up in the language of hatred about difference in skin color, national origin, religion, sexual orientation, or political preferences that they cannot focus on the important topics like education, healthcare, economic equality, or environmental protection. The power of words, at times, seems to run parallel with the power of the individual. Today, we seem to have some national leaders in place who stoke the fires, in a veiled way, and sometimes not so veiled, of racism.

Sadly, I have seen African Americans use provocative language as a strategy. When I worked in the USG headquarters, HBCU presidents would get in a meeting and plead, in veiled wording, grievance and victimization; the senior staff would complain after they left. None of the USG staff ever said, "Yes, you all did get the short end of the stick, but right now we're thinking about a view of the future." If only there could have been some form of reconciliation where something could have been said like, "You know, we really are sorry about what happened during slavery and Reconstruction. We're not going to be able to give reparations, but what happened then was a wrong. Let's see what we can do together to make the future better." Then perhaps progress could be made.

At Albany State, when the USG issued a directive, often someone on my staff would say, "We're already doing that." There was almost an unconscious reaction that "If you push me to change, I'll play the race card." I would reply each time, "But we're not already doing it! Everything in the world is not about race. Some of it is about efficiency and effectiveness, which are generic concepts. They aren't tied to race." Playing the race card is unsightly in any situation. But there has not been a place for healing in the Albany community, so some of the passions run very deep.

In the late 1980s through the 1990s, Albany State leaders exhibited some of the same behaviors that I had witnessed of other HBCU leaders when they made budget appeals to the USG. When making the case for a new program, they would say something like, "If you'd allowed us to have a program that meets the emerging needs of the economy, like you gave to other USG institutions, then we could have grown and developed like they did."

What was so interesting was that at some point in time they were correct on the issue that many at the USG headquarters did not think that those at Albany State had the skills to offer some programs. What could always get hidden in a lack of capacity, or a lack of faculty credentials, or lack of support was "You're doing it because we're a black school." People were always able to pull out these instances and examples—and many could be true. But the argument could not hide inefficient or ineffective operational processes. No one at the USG was preventing Albany State from seeking excellence in all areas, from recruitment, to admissions, to student retention, to financial aid administration.

I finally had to say, "System staff in Atlanta aren't spending all their time thinking about how to disenfranchise you or take advantage of you. In fact, given the number of meetings I've been in, they don't talk about you very much at all. I don't mean any disrespect, but we're usually not high on their agenda. They aren't preoccupied with doing detrimental things to the school." Once again, I saw how living in an unreconciled condition for so long allowed anger to fester, causing distrust and even paranoia.

There are so many things in U.S. history that help people legitimize their anger. From the standpoint of mental health, racial health, and civic life, can an understanding of the past exist side by side with striving for excellence? Can people acknowledge that yes, bad things happen all the time. Parallel to knowing a history, can there still be personal development and accountability? Can those in an organization move beyond a painful past and work to create an effective, thriving organization?

I felt at times that the "I've been wronged" hand was being overplayed. Today, we hear grievance from whites claiming that others are taking their jobs, when perhaps the real causes are rapidly changing technologies, globalization, or climate change. For African Americans, the wrongs, real and sometimes imagined, can be distant or recent. At Albany State, past wrongs were often the starting point of discussions. In diplomatic and careful ways, I tried to communicate, "Don't neglect being the best that you can be by spending all your time discussing what happened in the past whether the wrong was in 1994, 1865, or in the 1700s. Don't use history as a sledgehammer to prevent change."

Somebody in Albany once asked me about reparations. I had given the subject much thought over the years and so had a ready response.

"I've read more about southern history and culture than most folks you'll meet. With all I now know about how much labor was stolen from blacks through slavery and Jim Crow, I don't think that if it was a dollar, a peso, or a ruble that it could make me satisfied about what has happened over the last three or four hundred years. It would be offensive to say you can come up with a dollar figure that equals to what I think has happened to generations of people. In fact, throwing money at me would debase the memory of the experience. That's hard for many to hear, because most want accountability, responsibility, and acceptance for deeds and actions. At this point, there may not be anybody here to do that."

"Well, you may be right," they admitted.

"I know I'm right." I continued. "Show me people who are lining up to give reparations—whether it's the Georgia or Mississippi legislatures, or the federal government. And it doesn't have to be a zero-sum game. Here in Southwest Georgia, where racism is so entrenched, it might be easier to lift the region up economically as a whole than to get someone to own up to the wrongs of slavery and then pay individuals a certain dollar amount."

On the other side, some will say, "I didn't have anything to do with slavery. I didn't own slaves. So, I don't want my tax dollars going toward reparations for something I didn't do." In 2019, Mitch McConnell, as U.S. senator of Kentucky, summed up this sentiment: "I don't think reparations for something that happened 150 years ago for whom none of us currently living are responsible is a good idea."[2] Thus, in today's discussions about reparations, we can see clearly that there are generational consequences of not reconciling our feelings about race. To me, the most egregious long-term consequence has been disengagement in the democratic process.

I was sitting in my office one day, when representatives of the Albany/Dougherty County Voter Registration and Elections office came to see me. They said, "You all have an election center on your campus, but students aren't voting. People living near the campus aren't voting, either. We can't commit four staff people to a polling station that has such low voter turnout."

I thought, "What has gone on in the socialization process where people feel that their voices don't matter—that they feel helpless and marginalized, and have such a distrust of government?" For my and my parents' generations, people were zealots about voting. It had been denied in so many ways for so long, either through innovative and creative ways like literacy tests or with violence. So, when people were pushed back in ways like that, as soon as they got the chance, they voted. They were so serious about it.

Back then, it was not a subtle suppression through underhanded means. It was just out there in your face. That time has gone. Today, no one remembers how hard people worked to prevent African Americans from voting. It is almost as if when we have something, we take it for granted.

I spoke to some Albany State students and gave them a hard time about the polling station closure. "Somehow, you guys have got to help me with this. I can't for the life of me understand how at a university they say that they are closing down an election precinct because nobody votes." I continued, "Have you ever heard of Selma, Alabama? Have you ever heard of Jim Clark? He was the sheriff of Dallas County from the mid-1950s to the mid-1960s, and a vocal and violent opponent of desegregation. He stood on the Dallas County courthouse steps in Selma, when a black man walked up and said, 'I'm here to vote, sir.' Clark punched him, knocking him off the steps."

The students shook their heads, but said, "But Dr. Dunning, our vote doesn't count."

"Well, somebody's vote is counting, guys, because we have people in these elected positions. I'm not asking you to vote one way or another. But, if you want to express your values, you better find a way to get engaged." I used to think, when I talked to students who were born in the mid-1990s to 2000s, "How can I make this not sound like the 1400s and the War of the Roses, or 1812? Rather, it's within their parents' and my memories." So, I would say something like, "Voter suppression when I was growing up was a different sort of experience. You all don't have to pass some made-up test like guessing how many jelly beans are in a jar, or how many bubbles are in a bar of soap. You don't have to recite the U.S. Constitution to the all-white election staff. My generation was subjected to literacy tests or forced to pay poll taxes. None of that exists now. So how do you deal with voter suppression when you're doing it to yourselves?"

The first time I voted was when I was stationed on an overseas military base. I cast a ballot on foreign soil for elections back at home. Since then, seared in my memory is that image of Sheriff Clark pushing that black man down the courthouse steps to keep him from registering to vote. Violence and denigration have caused me to treasure my civic right and responsibility to vote. I vote every chance I get—whether the issue is big or small.

My first chance to vote back home in Alabama was when Marengo County held a referendum on whether to go from a dry to a wet county. I was a student at the University of Alabama at the time. After I finished class at noon on election day, I drove ninety miles down from Tuscaloosa to my home county to vote in that referendum. Then I drove by my folks' house to see my mom. She said, "Why are you down here?"

"I came to vote."

"You came down here to move the county from dry to wet? Don't tell me you cut classes to come all the way down here to vote to allow alcohol sales," she smiled. "You ought to be ashamed of yourself," she laughed. She would rather I had made the long drive down to vote for something important like highway or infrastructure projects. "Don't you tell anybody you came down here to vote just so you could drink beer!"

"I do not miss a vote," I grinned back. And to this day, I do not miss an opportunity to vote.

At the meeting in Albany about closing the polling station on campus, all these memories went through my mind in a fleeting moment. All the blood, sweat, and tears that had been shed for the right to be able to vote, to have the freedom to choose where to go to school came rushing back.

These things manifest themselves for different generations. I've been struggling with what we see happening in our nation today. For my generation, the challenge was to push back against laws on the books, customs, practices, and behavior, and to protect oneself against violence.

There is a level of sophistication about this now that is very different from what my generation was exposed to. If people do not understand the history and have not felt what it is like to be disenfranchised, then it is easy to say, "I'm too busy. I don't have time to vote. That's somebody else's business," or "The place is corrupt, and all those elected officials are rascals." I understand that many do not vote because they have never had, or they have lost, trust in our governmental institutions, but people simply must get out there and exercise their right and responsibility.

Today's foot soldiers for civil rights need a new set of skills to effect change. My generation literally walked. The new generations will have an ongoing need for dignity and respect within organizations. They will need a high level of sophistication of knowledge.

I've heard it said that we cannot fight a twenty-first-century war on hatred with nineteenth-century tactics. When someone is willing to walk into a wedding with a bomb strapped to themselves and kill two hundred people, and they can radicalize people through videos on YouTube, that is not the kind of war that General Patton was fighting on the German line in World War II.

People will need advanced learning to push back against the Mitch McConnells of the world. The strategy of people standing outside the Senate chamber with signs reading "Go Home Mitch" is doomed to fail. The Capitol police will arrest them and carry them out. We need people who know how to use the legal system and who understand economic systems.

It all circles back to that most important value instilled by my parents: high academic achievement. With today's hate groups using technology, budding activists will need to start with at least sixteen years of learning and then add three more years through legal education or graduate degrees in policy or some other field in order to get the twenty-first-century version of what it takes to protect one's dignity and respect.

That is why a university like Albany State is so critical. Every single student who sets foot on the campus should leave with a college degree and be ready to take up the civil rights fight of their generation, which, today, includes a different and more subtle form of voter suppression. It is not as violent. Battles for the right to vote are now fought more often in the courts than in street marches. For example, in Georgia, in 2019, the U.S. House Oversight Committee investigated alleged problems with voter access such as polling sites being closed, consolidated, or moved;

and with voter registration, like applications being held for failing "exact match" policies that compare voter information to other state and federal documents.[3]

Today, how can we tie high performance and achievement to anger, passion, and zeal for equity and fairness? It cannot be done the way it was done in the 1960s using civil disobedience. With 24/7 news cycles, if something happens, no one is going to pay attention to a march protest. I have told students, "If you march in downtown Atlanta with 5,000 people and something happens in Croatia, or a shooting in California, you'll be off the news in an instant." In my day, if the march was covered in the newspaper, it would stay out there for people to think about. The news was not so fleeting as it is today where it is old in one or two days.

As to the students I would meet with at Albany State, I was surprised at how they would look at me and not seem to be able to connect what was happening in the nation to their decision-making, which was self-induced by their not voting or by their not wanting to complete their college education. What I was struck by was how few really understood that the way to marginalize people and to keep them from being involved politically is to discourage them from voting, prevent them from going to school, or when education is provided it is intentionally—through public policy—second rate.

With lack of education and lack of civic participation, people are essentially marginalized in a nation like ours. How do we get people civically engaged to say, "This is not who we are! We're not going to live like this—with poor education and kept from voting!"? Whether it is salaries for teachers or something else, this is how we, as a country, do our business—through people who are legally designated to represent us.

Another generational consequence of a lack of reconciliation is economic. Even places that strive to be open and inclusive today can suffer from past decisions based on racism. One example is Atlanta, the city that was "too busy to hate" in the 1960s. In 2018, Atlanta was one of twenty locations across the country in the running for an Amazon headquarters expansion. After months of exploration, Amazon chose two other cities. Two considerations for Amazon were a highly educated workforce and public transportation.

Decisions that Atlanta area residents made from the mid-1960s to the early 1970s regarding its public transportation system are partly to blame for Atlanta losing out on the Amazon headquarters fifty years later. Back then, voters in Atlanta's metropolitan counties of Cobb, Clayton, and Gwinnett twice rejected an expansion of MARTA (Metropolitan Atlanta Rapid Transit Authority). The no votes were tied more to race than to modes of transportation.[4]

Even far into the future, we as a nation pay a heavy price economically for our cultural decisions because we fail to reconcile with our past.

CHAPTER 19

# Nudges toward Healing

As the Albany State–Darton State consolidation process progressed, I was struck with the realization that I was guiding a process bigger than that of two educational institutions. I was really facilitating a reconciliation between blacks and whites in Albany. In a way, the mandate to consolidate was like ripping a bandage off a long-festering wound. Putting things out in the open, getting people to talk, and transparency were important steps for healing. Albany's citizens needed to put the issue out in the open and tell the truth about it.

I was not alone in trying to soothe the community's raw feelings about the consolidation. One ally was the editor of the local paper. A March editorial about the anger over "HBCU" being moved out of the mission statement defended me as being neither a "traitor" nor a "conqueror." The following month, the paper's editor published an opinion piece acknowledging the hard feelings by blacks and whites about the whole consolidation idea, writing that I was neither a "carpetbagger" nor a "mercenary."

That spring of 2016, I was picking up a lot of information that gave me a view about how people on both campuses, as well as in the broader community were feeling about the consolidation. I would hear things in meetings, or people would stop me in the street or in stores. I thought "this consolidation will not work very well if we can't begin to get our university to move, and to get our people understanding some of the realities that are out there." So I set out to speak to as many groups as I could, from Rotary Club meetings to town hall sessions.

In the town hall meetings, when I said "new Albany State" to historical constituents (predominantly African American), they went nuts about it. They would say, "Why do you keep saying 'new'? This is Albany State University." I would proceed to walk them through all the data that led to what was a rational decision to consolidate. It sounded harsh, but I would close with, "Albany State is at the mercy of state and federal entities. So you're in no position to tell me what to do about this. We have a board of regents. They approve budgets. I have never gotten questions from you like, 'Are we giving enough financially?' All you can give me is chatter, clutter, and irritation. If you're not providing money to support students with experiences to enrich their education, like study abroad and internships, don't come to complain to me about the regents stealing your university."

Most had to agree: "You're right, we don't give much, if any, money to the institution." I got so frustrated in one meeting, I said, "I don't mean any disrespect, but you all don't give Albany State anything to serve these students. What makes you think I'm going to listen to you?" My wife said later, "You sounded like you were telling them they have to 'pay to play.'"

"No," I replied. "They have to participate in the well-being of the institution. If all they're doing is fussing at me about band uniforms and saying that I'm trying to help the white folks attack our culture when I'm asking the young women to respect the Albany State brand—if that is all they're talking about, and they don't give the school a penny, how can they expect us to ever thrive?"

Almost to a person, Albany State's historical constituents, as well as current students, were most concerned about losing the cultural aspects of "their school." Would the school colors stay the same? The school mascot? The band uniforms? In one town hall meeting in an historic church just off campus, a student was so upset he was about to hyperventilate saying, "They're stealing our school! You're helping them steal our school! Why are we no longer an HBCU?" He was born in the early 1990s, so what had happened to him in his life that caused such deep passion and fear? How was that passed on to him with such intensity?

As he spoke, I thought, "Had he been a white student at the University of Alabama when I was there, he'd have been on national television with people calling him the most rabid racist." I was struck by the crass disrespect he showed for the senior administrators who were there with me. It was reminiscent of the 1960s when people would shout people down. Respect for people in positions of authority was just completely gone.

So I replied calmly to him, "We will continue to be an HBCU. We just won't lead with it. I want us to celebrate our HBCU heritage but not be held hostage by it." I pointed out the data to him. The demography of Albany and Southwest Georgia was such that the notion that whites would take over Albany State was nonsensical. For one thing, Southwest Georgia had one of the highest concentrations of African Americans in the state. On top of that, the university drew a large portion of its enrollment from predominantly African American high schools in the Atlanta area. He didn't listen to any of that.

"No, no. You've removed 'HBCU,'" he persisted. The racial distrust meant that everyone thought there was a conspiracy. The distrust was so strong in this young student that he had worked himself into a frenzy. I learned later that he was being coached by some of the street committee who were against the consolidation.

Neither these nor any other Albany State supporters ever chastised me about stronger academic programs. No one asked about the benefits of having a two-year college integrated with a university where students would be able to move from an associate degree to a bachelor's to a master's to an educational specialist degree.

No, they only fussed about the trappings of culture. They were upset with all those things that reflect "my tribe." They were more concerned with "the symbols on my forehead, the symbols on my arm, the clothes I wear. I'm a member of this tribe. And I don't care about facts and data about how bad off we are here in Southwest Georgia."

Interestingly, too, rarely if ever did the leaders of the street committee ever come to speak with me privately. They would get no credit for doing so by their followers. There were a couple of people that I was told said, "Well, I can't get a meeting with Dr. Dunning." When I offered to meet one-on-one, they would say, "No, I don't wanna come." But when I held a town hall session, they would come up to the mic and go on a rant. The only way they got credit with their constituents for speaking truth to power was if they did it in public.

This behavior was not limited to Albany. We see it happening today at the national level. When we are dealing with complicated and complex issues, we do not get any credit for talking privately with any given group. In fact, we are condemned for it. Moreover, people often act out thinking, often correctly, that they gain status by attempting to shame and embarrass.

It is a difficult problem. What can be done about racial hucksters—on each side—who make their livings off of racial hatred? How do we shield ourselves from people who build their status and wealth in the community by being the racial watchdogs? We are living this out with our country's highest leaders. Much the way Albany's preachers could not see how poor the people of Albany were from their perch on their pedestal from which they pontificated, our national leaders cannot see how desperately the people of our country need their help.

These games were being played as the community faced low college participation, unemployment, and high poverty rates. I tried but could not steer public discussion to these topics. Our university could have been the foundational organization to address the deep-seated challenges facing our city and our twenty-county service area. No one ever challenged me about how we could strengthen our role in those areas. It was always about the cultural trappings. I thought it was just crazy that we were in one of the poorest areas of the country, and no one ever talked to me about getting better. They could have been faced with poverty, disruption, or famine, and these constituents would still have been worried about those things that reflected on who they were, culturally.

Moreover, some people, black and white, had gotten so craven that if I pointed to data to expose some of the failings of the community, I was charged with blaming the victim. Some residents of Albany had made a cottage industry of blaming others for the community's failings rather than looking inward.

As we held these town hall meetings, I got so frustrated that I became fiercely candid, direct, and to the point in the sessions. In one small-group meeting, I said,

"Some things offer great simplicity when you think about them. When I was a child, the people I spent a lot of time around could give you very serious concepts but not in eloquent ways. One thing they told me was 'Don't close the barn door after the horses are a couple of miles down the road.' I don't know if you guys really understand what we're here to talk about. It's now about execution and implementation. The decision to consolidate is done. In all my years working in higher education in Georgia, I can't think of a single thing that has been done that's been reversed because someone got excited about it. So, we probably aren't using our time wisely here."

My wife, who was attending some of these sessions, later told me, "I think you ought to be more measured."

I told her, "I've been measured all my life, but I've been pushed to the edge here!" All I could think about were issues of complex technology facing these students, globalization, and climate change, and in the town hall sessions they were fussing about a mascot, band uniforms, the school song, and where the basketball team was going to play their games. I saw the deep-seated challenges facing young people of color in this nation that was causing so many of them to fall out of the system. I thought that there could not be a more important place to help them than a campus with an historic mission of serving African Americans. But I heard nothing about that. The silence forced me, at times, to be intemperate.

I almost lost complete patience at some of the questions when I thought about the next twenty-five to thirty years for these students. What was their work life going to be like? I was worried about the intentional, overt, and harmful ways that students of color are being challenged today. But in these town hall meetings, the fixation remained on culture: "Are we going to keep the mascot?" and "Are the crackers trying to steal our school song? Can we still sing it?"

It was almost as if the African American community in Albany had lost its way. They had been poked and pushed and battered for so long that they almost did not know how to be respectful and civil. I have never allowed myself in organizational life to be bullied, nor have I ever tried to bully others. That some in Albany had become complete bullies themselves troubled me.

Another way I tried to move the Albany State community forward was by talking with students. I quickly found that they saw me very differently than the way I saw myself. When I would walk across campus with a suit and tie on, the response I got from students, verbalized or not, was, "Dr. Dunning, you just don't understand this black stuff." What they were implying was, "The places you've been. Your career. There's no way you can understand my angst, concern, and my blackness." People just did not think that I had any empathy or understanding of their challenges. They could not imagine the earthy basic nature of existence for families in the early twentieth-century Alabama Black Belt. I had grown up watching this stuff up close and personal. But I had also tried to understand how white people felt about the South.

From day-to-day living in the Alabama Black Belt during Jim Crow, I had added—starting as far back as my memory would take me—an intellectual understanding of race in the South. I found the South such a fascinating place for its dichotomous social structure based on skin color. I was interested in all of it, so I read everything I could get my hands on to gain a better understanding.

There was a seven- or eight-year period in my life where I read everything by black authors like Richard Wright and Ralph Ellison, and white authors like William Faulkner and Robert Penn Warren. At first, I felt like I was at the mercy of hearing about "the southern lifestyle" and "southern history." My history was considered "black history." I thought, "No, mine was southern, too!" I was geographically born and raised in the South. Southern history and lifestyle were not reserved just for whites.

I learned, too, that there were certain cultural things that former slaves did in the heart of the Alabama Black Belt that were different than what freed slaves did living up in New York. The Harlem Renaissance was not like living in Marengo County. While in Taiwan, black airmen from, say, Chicago or Detroit would say, "You're not an authentic black man unless you've been arrested and have lived in the hood." This was my first introduction to the concept of racial authenticity, although I did not know the term for it at the time.

I saw then, though, that people from the same racial group can have different ideas about who is real and who is counterfeit. I also saw how people attempted to shape others' behavior through name-calling. Fortunately, I had a strong sense of self and could see now that there were multiple definitions of black authenticity, often determined by geographic location. Mine was rooted in earthy, southern, not-too-far-in-the-past plantation agriculture.

Southern authors helped me explore the paradox that "your history may not be my history, but we grew up in the same place." The roughly 581,000 square miles in the southeastern corner of the United States was the "place" where two races and cultures converged. To this day, my views are informed by that intersection. It was interesting to learn when thrown into a melting pot with forty to fifty other men from all over the United States when I was in the air force in Taiwan, that the most scorned group in the country were southerners—whites and blacks.

I have continued throughout my life to be a voracious reader trying to understand my nation, my environment, and trends. I read everything from the *Economist* to the *New York Times*. They inform me about what is happening in our country, as well as the intersections of change around the world.

Thus, at Albany State, I think my experience and knowledge was way beyond what the students realized. What I struggled to understand was how students who had no clue what it was like to grow up under Jim Crow could talk about 2018 like it was 1965. They kept saying to me, "Dr. Dunning, you just don't understand."

I would say back to them, "You were born with a cell phone in your hand. With all the freedoms you experience, you look at slights and omissions and things that people say and treat them as if the Klan is coming down the street." What I had difficulty understanding was how eighteen- or nineteen-year-olds at Albany State could be so intense about race and "our tribe" when they had devices that gave them access to the entire world of knowledge. In my day, information was hierarchical. I was barred by law from the public library. These students had never been segregated by law. Their feelings had to have been passed down to them.

Still, they persisted in telling me that I just did not understand institutionalized racism. Nor did I understand all the micro-aggressions they had to live with. I thought, "I grew up in a time when there was macro-aggression and laws. That truly was an offense, but I treated the macro as micro. I tried not to let them bother me. So today, I think I can handle micro-aggression. My reality was brutality and killings and loud racial slurs."

I tried to have sympathy for how these young students felt slighted by micro-aggressions. I found it hard, however, when I thought of my grandparents. who never lived a free existence. In my coming of age during Jim Crow, I treated the macro-aggressions as a nuisance, and even tried to counter them with humor.

For example, as a twenty-two-year-old veteran, I was a work-study student in the Sociology Department of the University of Alabama in 1966. This would have been a department of the university that considered itself pretty liberal. Even there, however, one day a professor who thought he was a fun-loving kind of guy passed me as I was sorting the campus mail. He paused and said, "Art, I've been thinking. You think black folks have a rhythm gene? Think we ought to do a study on that?" With a straight face, I responded, "I don't know. But, you know, when I went in the service, I had never been around white folks who were trying to dance. Maybe we should add to that study an investigation of the robotic gene since those airmen all looked like robots when they tried to dance. I'll work on a study like that, if we can investigate both genes!"

The professor chuckled and walked on, and I continued my rounds to deliver the campus mail. There are some people who would have just gone off the deep end if someone said that to them even in jest.

So at Albany State, I thought, "How can we help our students shrug off the slights, and not find them debilitating?" I am not suggesting that we should accept people saying and doing bad things, but how do you juxtapose what is happening today against what transpired in previous generations? Could I figure out ways to help them compare and contrast, and not become unnerved by the manifestations of today's racism?

One way to help them would be to expose them to more diversity during their formative college years. And I meant diversity broadly, not just racially. In some of my sessions with students, I would ask, "What do you think about us getting in a place where we have more diversity in who attends Albany State?" For these students, like students at many HBCUs, "diversity" was a synonym for whites.

"Oh, no, no, Dr. Dunning. We can't have that! We can't have more than four or five white folks on this campus or else they're going to try and take over." For these students, their minds automatically jumped to whites, not Asians or Latinx, or other forms of diversity other than race. Moreover, these students, in 2017, were saying to me that they wanted a segregated school. Their thinking was that somehow a half-dozen white students would change the culture of the university.

Their response transported me back fifty years to my days as a college student at the University of Alabama. That was what people there were saying when I showed up in 1966. I thought, "If the white students had said that out loud at the University of Alabama, we'd have been doing backflips."

In my college days, what we were saying when we went to meet with the school's president, was that the University of Alabama should reflect the citizens of the state—not so much a numerical reflection, but enough to reflect that it was a diverse state. Alabama was home to people from all backgrounds so it should not be a monolithic racial place.

My response to the Albany State students was, "Think about what you all just said."

"We know, Dr. Dunning. But we're an HBCU."

"Well, Darton is an historically white campus, and they could say the same thing." I felt like these students thought "We get a pass, but they don't get a pass." It was an interesting sort of mental gymnastics that people were playing around this issue.

There was also a nuance that these students did not seem to recognize. Under the umbrella of HBCU there are both private and public institutions. Private colleges like Spelman and Morehouse can define who they serve (viz., women and men of African descent, respectively). They can choose to be selective and insular.

An HBCU like Albany State, however, is a public, state-supported institution. I view it as being more like Georgia Southern, another institution in Georgia's public higher education system, than a private liberal arts institution. Thus, though many of Albany State's supporters talked as if the university was private, it was not, and therefore could not, nor should not, act like one. Georgians' tax dollars were supporting the university. Once again think back to my dad's comment about our family's taxes supporting all Alabama public schools and universities. In my mind, students of any racial background should feel welcomed at Albany State, too.

At the same time that I was trying to encourage dialogue via town hall and student meetings, almost everywhere I went when I encountered members of the white community, they told me, "You all have changed nothing at Albany State. You kept the same name, you still say you're an HBCU, you've kept the mascot, school colors, school song—all the trappings of the old school. We can't find Darton anywhere in this process." One businessman in Albany was open and candid with me, "I'm getting beat up in this community. When I drive down Gillionville Road, I don't see anything that shows that Darton State ever existed. That's driving some of my friends off the edge! What can you do about this?"

He continued, "I still don't know why the board of regents did this! Everything about Darton has disappeared. I've given money to Darton for forty years. When I drive down Gillionville Road and I see signs for 'Albany State University West Campus,' I just feel like I wasted my money."

I saw his point, and it reminded me of a conversation I had with leaders who had seen their own institutions through consolidation. To continue to emphasize one of the school's expertise in science and engineering, they used that name for one of the engineering colleges.

Knowing how important allied health and nursing was to the Albany community, it occurred to me that we may be able to reflect the economic development demands of the health professions in Southwest Georgia and also recognize the joint history of the two campuses. The new university was Albany State, but we could identify a component of the new school that was prominent. I visited the chancellor in Atlanta to propose that we create a Darton College of Health Professions. He gave us the go-ahead.

In hindsight, I wish we had thought about that earlier, and I was grateful for the idea planted by the white Albany businessman. It was a fifth college for Albany State and would house the Department of Nursing, the Department of Health Sciences, and the Department of Health and Human Performance. We had an elegant sign placed on Gillionville Road. The gesture was what I hoped would be a step toward reconciliation. The two schools had been blended, but the academic program offerings of the campus that had ceased to exist were now recognized.

I made the decision not to make whites happy but to help the economic demands of Albany for skilled health professionals. A strong health professions program would help students, both black and white, secure good jobs once they graduated. Most were hired in Southwest Georgia rather than Atlanta or farther away. For example, when I went for an annual physical, I was prepped for various tests by a young African American woman who had a two-year degree from Darton. She had a good, well-paying job with fourteen years of schooling. She could go back to nursing school at Albany State, if she wanted to.

The white community in Albany who saw all that was happening at the start of the consolidation process were angry and threw up their hands, "They've just snatched the rug out from under us. There's no sense in us wasting our time trying to change the decision." There were, however, spokespeople who were able to articulate the concerns, passions, and feelings of the white community. In this case, there was an obvious and easy solution. The decision to create the fifth college would be of benefit to all.

And so, I continued to talk with people, individually and in groups, in an attempt to broker relations between blacks and whites. There were many days when I felt like progress was painfully slow. Rumors and myths being put forth by the "street committee" continued to circulate. At the 2016 annual Albany State University Alumni Association event as part of the traditional update from the president, I addressed the conspiracies head on, directly, candidly, and with full transparency. I started by walking them through the consolidation process to date. Then, I faced the rumors and myths head on.

There is no grand conspiracy to close or forever strip Albany State of its rich legacy. Here are some things for you to remember.

I've heard that we will no longer be an HBCU. We are an HBCU and we will always be an HBCU.

I've heard that we won't have our school song. We will continue to sing the alma mater.

I've heard that Founders' Day will no longer take place. We will always have Founders' Day.

I've heard that this is the last homecoming. We will always have homecoming.

I've heard that the colors and the mascot will change. We will always be Golden Rams and don the royal blue and gold.

We will continue to celebrate and uplift our proud legacy.

In spite of the perception of a white two-year college and a black four-year university, the Darton State College student body is over 50 percent African American.

Myth: We can continue operating the way we do, when we have had five years of continuing decline in enrollment. We cannot.

Myth: We can grow and prosper without private support from alumni, and other community and corporate supporters. We cannot.

Great damage can be done to an institution and to people by the use of gossip and innuendo as a strategy instead of dealing in facts. It weakens any organization if constituents take that approach in the name of an institution that they say they love. Most importantly, it undermines the institution at every level in this state, and it weakens the value of your own degrees.

I then moved directly to updating the audience on the state of the university, and the status of search processes for various deans and directors. Finally, I introduced the new Albany State's senior staff.

I hoped with the remarks to nudge the Albany State community toward accepting their past and embracing a future together. I wondered, could we have compassion and act with restraint and generosity in dealing with each other? Today, reflecting back on the day I spoke to our alumni, I am reminded of a passage in Thomas Friedman's *Thank You for Being Late*, in which he recounts how South African president Nelson Mandela handled the raw feelings left from the formal end to apartheid. When Mandela became president of South Africa, the country's all-white national rugby team was despised by blacks. Black South Africans would routinely root for the other team. With the end of apartheid, blacks called for the team's name, emblem, and colors to be changed. Mandela refused. He said of the Afrikaners, "We have to surprise them with compassion, with restraint, and generosity."[1]

When people would get irate about the consolidation, I would give a list of what was still in place from each school. Darton had been left with almost nothing. I would say to Albany State supporters, "So it appears that you have had the short end of the stick for so long, and now you have the long end, and it still looks short to you. Look at what happened, and really be objective about it. Those images and icons—you have lost nothing. So if you are going to have a consolidation in Albany, Georgia, and you kept the name and you kept everything—HBCU, colors, song, mascot, it may be a nice time to show compassion and restraint rather than continue to spew the venom that I am hearing."

Although the process had mixed results, President Mandela was saying that in order to avoid bloodshed as the country worked through desegregation, people had to set aside their pain and hurt and not seek revenge. My thought when trying to help the Albany community was that anytime two campuses that are historically racially identifiable are consolidated into one, the key ingredient is to create conditions and circumstances that can help both campuses see a view of the future.

CHAPTER 20

# Sometimes It Takes Tough Love

As I reflect on the USG decision to consolidate Albany State and Darton State, I have come to view it as an exercise in tough love parenting. It is unlikely that the two schools would have ever worked together voluntarily to better serve Southwest Georgia. No one liked the idea of being forced to become a single institution, even though it was the right thing to do.

It was a contemporary example of what had happened throughout the civil rights movement. Then, external mandates forced change that was in the best interest of the educational, social, and economic well-being of the nation. In 1954, the U.S. Supreme Court *Brown v. Board of Education* decision forced schools to desegregate. In 1963, President Kennedy sent the National Guard to ensure the desegregation of the University of Alabama. In 1971, the Supreme Court upheld busing as a means to desegregate schools in *Swann v. Mecklenburg County*.

At Albany State and Darton, an external force (the chancellor and the board of regents) directed that the two institutions founded for racial reasons now be consolidated. My job was to see that the logistics of the process progressed in Albany in a smooth and timely fashion. Thus, while my leadership team and I tried to quell the discontent surrounding the consolidation, the implementation committee, various work groups, and the consolidation prospectus writing team pushed forward to meet the process's deadlines. Throughout the year, I kept the chancellor fully informed on our progress.

As 2016 wore on, I tried to keep everyone focused on facts and data and to steer them away from stereotypes, conspiracy theories, and tribalism. I worked to hire needed staff and made corrections when I found I had made a mistake. We resolved earlier inefficiencies and problems (like those in the financial aid and foundation offices). We tried to address legitimate concerns about curricular needs and skill development in some of the academic programs.

That July, I met with the chancellor to update him on our progress. I also discussed strategies to ameliorate a serious budget shortfall, as well as our declining enrollment numbers. A critical financial threat to the university was a budget reduction of $4 million for the coming fiscal year. The cause of the reduction was declining enrollment projections and projected repayments to the federal government for financial aid penalties.

To address the shortfall, we planned to eliminate or consolidate low-enrollment programs, not renew some faculty members, and downsize staff by about a hundred. The staff reduction would also bring our staff-to-student ratio in line with the average for USG institutions.

I also talked to the chancellor about developing a plan for future enrollment management. Over a five-year period, our graduate enrollment had increased, but our undergraduate enrollment had decreased by more, causing an overall decrease of 5 percent. This may not have seemed like much, but it was huge in terms of our federal and state funding tied to the enrollment numbers. I left the meeting with the full support of the chancellor for the steps we proposed and were undertaking.

At the end of July, the work groups' recommendations were submitted to the implementation committee for its approval by the end of August. Groups had been assigned to handle every aspect of a university. During the summer, the consolidation prospectus writing team completed its work and delivered the document to our accrediting body by mid-September, which approved the materials by early December. On December 9, 2016, the Board of Regents of the USG granted final approval for the creation of the new university.

In an open memorandum to the faculty, staff, and students announcing the board's approval of the consolidation, I strove to set an optimistic tone by celebrating the energizing effect of change and of being forced out of one's comfort zone and by setting high expectations: "Collectively, I know that we will stay true to our mission of providing a world-class education to our students and serving as a powerful catalyst for economic development in Southwest Georgia. Together, we will ensure that this is a holistic learning environment that empowers students to be great decision makers in every facet of life. We will do our part in helping to improve the quality of life for the citizens of this region by meeting unmet needs. The now seamless transition from associate's to bachelor's to graduate programs will provide greater opportunities for students to flourish through higher education."[1]

The effective date for the consolidation was January 1, 2017. On that date, the new university would have two campuses. Across the Flint River, and about four miles west of the main campus lay the previous Darton State. We would soon have a leadership team in place that would spend the next number of months completing phase 2 of the consolidation process. In the fall of 2017, students would matriculate at the new university.

The new and expanded Albany State would offer certificates, transfer associate and career associate degrees, as well as bachelor's, master's, and specialist degrees. Darton State's three schools and Albany State's four colleges would be consolidated into five colleges in the new organizational structure that would serve almost nine thousand students.

Once we accomplished the mechanics of the consolidation, I felt it was time for someone else to take the reins of leadership. I had accepted the position as president because of where I had come of age, around very bright people who did not get to realize their dreams because of a deficit of educational opportunities. Thus, I had always thought that although intellect was broadly distributed, opportunity was not. I saw Albany State as an important educational opportunity for a part of the country for which I had a deep affinity.

When asked to lead the consolidation, I felt that guiding the community through the logistics was something for which my temperament and skill set were well suited. Still, it was draining. Toward the close of 2017, I realized that it may take several years to solidify the full aspects of the consolidation, to make the university's operations efficient and effective, and to see the results of all those efforts. I thought I should step aside to allow the chancellor to select a president who could dedicate seven to ten years toward cultivating a collaborative, blended culture, and to attend to programmatic needs.

As I prepared to step down, I reflected on what we had accomplished over four years. We had worked tirelessly to review, correct, and improve business processes and operations for every academic and administrative unit, as well as worked to improve customer service—the customers being our students.

We worked to create study-abroad programs so that students could learn to evaluate their country against others, with the result of strengthening their civic participation later in life. In the summer of 2016, for example, Procter and Gamble supported the school's China study-abroad program. Albany State and Xiamen University students collaborated on reporting environmental news stories in the area around Xiamen in Southeast China.

In an effort to partner more with the business and nonprofit sectors of Albany, in ways that had not been done before, we established collaborative education and research programs with the Flint RiverQuarium. We also started a partnership with the Dougherty County Commission to develop a Rails to Trails Project connecting Albany State to downtown Albany and beyond. Foremost in my mind when working with the county commission on the project was that we, as a nation, have developed a sedentary lifestyle, which has created an obesity epidemic. Our work has shifted from outside moving around a lot to working indoors, sitting for long stretches of time. The shift has taken a toll on our health. The walking trail would give our students and the community a recreational area to exercise by long walks.

One of the most poignant moments I had while at Albany State was listening to students who had been in foster care. Karen and I invited small groups of these students to our home for dinner discussions about their experiences. Many, when they came of age and left their foster homes, had nowhere else to go. We would listen as they told of their struggles to stay in school and graduate from Albany State. People who did not hear their stories would have difficulty imagining the types of struggles these students went through.

Karen had long been an advocate for support systems dedicated to helping foster and homeless college students. As she facilitated the dinner discussions, I would listen, thankful to have had both of my parents and to have had their help through the socialization process. So, it meant a lot to help these students succeed academically, financially, and socially. We were trying to say to these young people, "You matter deeply."

---

What I was most proud of accomplishing during my time in Albany was helping to secure some $20 million for a new fine-arts building. We had been trying for over a decade, without success, to secure funding from the state legislature. The chancellor suggested that I make several trips to Atlanta while the legislature was in session to walk the halls to garner support for the project.

I went to the state Capitol to visit with many representatives of Southwest Georgia. On one visit, I was shepherded around by one who advised, "I'm going to take you 'round to see the head of one of the committees that will have sway on the decision. If I were you, I'd tell him about how long this request has been languishing. You may not get it this year. You may need to come back next year. And you need to know, he doesn't think your kind of school [an HBCU] should even exist."

When meeting with the committee chair, I gave him only the facts. Albany State was a public university. The old fine-arts building lay in a floodplain and was severely antiquated, completely inadequate for modern instruction and performances. I spoke about the number of affected majors, the condition of the existing facility, and how a new center would contribute to economic development in the surrounding area by way of jobs and bringing community members onto campus for events. The approach I took was need, not grievance or victimization. It never occurred to me to frame the funding as an issue of an HBCU having been shafted for so many years or "you haven't treated us right and so now you need to pay up." For all I know, this was the first time legislators were presented with real data about the project and hearing about it in terms of the future rather than the past.

The funding came through the following year.

The simple act of trying to secure a building that would improve the social, cultural, and economic well-being of all who lived in Albany, black and white, brought out unbecoming behavior by both sides. On one side, some of the state representatives were openly antagonistic toward Albany State.

On the other side, long-time Albany State supporters got angry, but for a different reason. When construction finally began on the new building, the contractor had to take up some space where normally we had parking available during homecoming. I got a call from an African American supporter saying, "I'm calling the president's office because I'm mad that my parking was taken away." It had taken more than a dozen years to get the building. And yet, once we broke ground, some started fussing about the construction because it interfered with football game-day parking.

It was another instance where I could hear Marvin Gaye crying out, "make me wanna holler and throw up both my hands." Still, the challenge of securing the fine-arts building for the university showed me that my process could ultimately succeed. Facts and data, together with relationships, won over the naysayers. The building was completed in the summer of 2017.

---

In early October, I announced my intention to retire at the end of January 2018. My parting words to the institution and to Albany were framed in an open letter distributed shortly before my departure.

> At the end of this month, I will retire as president of Albany State University (ASU), a position I've held for nearly five years. I came to Albany after holding various roles in the University System of Georgia (USG), and have witnessed the resilience of this university to rebuild after a natural disaster and grow from a college to a university.
>
> It has been an honor and privilege to serve as president of Albany State during such a pivotal time in the institution's history. Over these years, we have accomplished a lot together, and I am thankful for the support of the campus and Albany community for the commitment and dedication to this great institution.
>
> One of my major tasks was to guide ASU through the consolidation with Darton State College. The consolidation of these institutions was built on Albany State's Historically Black Colleges and Universities (HBCU) designation and Darton's designation as an access institution. It positioned the university to reach more students, offer more programs and have a greater impact.
>
> Change can be difficult and can take some time, but tireless efforts are continuing to be done to strengthen ASU to better serve this region and the State of Georgia.
>
> Albany State is now a larger university that offers a range of degrees. Students can earn professional certificates in less than a year or an associate's degree in two years to obtain gainful employment. They now have an easier path to achieve a bachelor's or graduate degree without transferring to a different institution.
>
> ASU is held to the same high standards as all of our peer institutions. Our governing body, the USG Board of Regents, expects the same performance and accountability from Albany State as it does from the 25 other system colleges and universities. Our students expect and deserve to receive the

highest level of customer service, innovative academic offerings and programs that position them for success.

As I prepare to leave ASU, I'm confident that the university is on the right track to becoming a game-changing leader in higher education and a catalyst for change in this community. The momentum is here, the interest is here, and the need is here.

In order for any organization to thrive, it takes a willingness to collaborate, cooperate and leverage relationships. ASU is continuing to form partnerships and build relationships with peer institutions, civic and business organizations, supporters and alumni.

Work is also being done to reimagine our academic portfolio to meet the needs of our students, the local workforce and area citizens. The college student of today doesn't look like the college student of 20 years ago. Advanced technology and access to information have reshaped the learning environment.

Colleges and universities must be in continuous quality improvement and learning mode. We have to teach differently; ensure our business processes and classrooms keep up with technology; provide exceptional customer service and diversify our financial portfolios.

We must be nimble, agile and open to accelerated change. Our graduates expect it. The vitality and survival of our region depend on it.

I have personally experienced how educational opportunities can create positive change in places and times when others didn't desire anything other than their norm. I've worked in the USG system for over thirty years, lived and worked in thirty-two countries around the world.

What I've gained through those experiences has defined who I am today and shaped my view about human connectivity, growth and development. I've witnessed how communities have grown and developed because of a unified sense of purpose.

We all should have a sense of purpose to change the economic landscape of this community. Higher education is a solution to many issues facing this region.

As Tuesday approaches, I am encouraged and excited for the future of Albany State, our students and this community.

My wife Karen and I are grateful for the time we've spent in this community. I look forward to seeing the successes that lie ahead.[2]

With that, it was now time for a new leader to partner with Albany to secure the long-term success of the new university. It was time for others to step up to the plate and do something that had never been done in anybody's memory there—create a twenty-first-century academic experience by leveraging relationships and by collaborating and cooperating to build a better future for the young people of Albany.

Martin Luther King Jr.'s words came in mind when I considered who might be Albany State University's next president: "May I stress the need for courageous, intelligent, and dedicated leadership.... Leaders of sound integrity. Leaders not in love with publicity, but in love with justice. Leaders not in love with money, but in love with humanity. Leaders who can subject their particular egos to the greatness of the cause."[3] It had taken an act of tough love to consolidate two schools founded on the basis of race. I understood how deep and persistent feelings about race were in Albany. I knew I could not make the long-term commitment necessary to continue on the difficult road toward reconciliation. That role would need a leader who could meet the standard articulated by Dr. King Jr.

# PART FIVE

# What Lies Ahead

Today, with the gift of some time to ease the emotions caught up in what was a contentious process from start to finish, I cannot help but analyze all that transpired during the four-plus years that Karen and I were in Albany. Going into the job, we knew we were there to help young people secure educations that would set them on paths to success in a world that is changing at a pace never seen before. We did not anticipate that we would have to mediate a racial healing of the Albany community as a whole. Many of the lessons we learned in the process illuminated for us keys to surviving and thriving at an individual, organizational, national, and global level. In these closing chapters, I reflect on reconciliation as a process, as well as on some, simple in concept but difficult in practice, steps that individuals and leaders can take to help educational and other institutions survive and thrive.

CHAPTER 21

# Toward Reconciliation

I have spent my professional life trying to better understand this thing called the American system of higher education. After over forty years of teaching about it, and serving as an administrator in it, I've now had time to reflect with some perspective. I am particularly interested in how my race, my own history as a southerner, and my southern culture intersected with a university and city that were abruptly forced to acknowledge their own history, and were challenged to envision a different future. The shaping of my identity was a journey. As a child, I was nurtured in an insular self-sufficient community where skills for survival and social norms were passed down from generation to generation orally through stories and direct instruction. Communal activities like hog butchering, peach picking, tree felling for firewood, and Sunday church were times for jovial social interaction, as well as for learning.

I was loved by parents who cared deeply for and respected each other, their families and neighbors, and their students. They cherished and venerated education. Intellectual curiosity, they knew, nourished the mind as well as the soul. It could open the world for people seeking to rise above the social class system into which they were born. They lived lives that personified high expectations of achievement and integrity. Most importantly, they instilled the concept that the power of the mind to think critically was to be used for the common good—for making decisions that would benefit others, particularly future generations.

My parents, neighbors, and teachers did all this while situated in a time of oppressive racial segregation and in one of the most brutally segregated regions of our country. They were two generations removed from slavery. They grew up under Jim Crow, raising a son who would come of age on the cusp of civil rights change. They maintained patience throughout the violent decades leading up to that change. At age eighteen, I did not share their stoicism. I was frustrated and angry. All around me were bright, hardworking young people who were thwarted, beaten down, hated, excluded from realizing their dreams, and barred from participating in the democratic process of picking our country's leaders—all because of the color of our skin.

In a cosmic stroke of irony, what saved me from becoming a bitter, resentful adult was the call to serve my country in the military. The U.S. Air Force gave me a chance to live and work with men from all over the country, of different racial, ethnic, religious, and class backgrounds on a level playing field. It allowed me to observe and learn from other cultures. It catalyzed my intellectual curiosity. In two short years I was transformed into a person who relished living among people different than myself, who wanted to travel the world to learn and work, and who was determined to live a personally fulfilling and professionally successful life in the Deep South. I viewed life now, in my home country, as a festive party to which I may not have been invited to attend, but to which I was going to join no matter what, and once there I was going to have a great time.

In college I discovered the major perfect for me: the study of human societies and cultures. At college I relished the concept of a university as a social institution in which its members seek knowledge, pass that knowledge on to future generations, and use that knowledge to improve the world. I went on to graduate work in higher education, the study of colleges and universities, including their history, governance, finance, organizational structures, and instructional methods. I sought out positions that combined my interest in education with living or traveling internationally, and later, positions that allowed me to encourage university faculty, staff, and students to apply their knowledge and resources to helping communities locally and globally.

All this eventually led me to Albany State University at a time when I believe it needed a leader with my background and temperament to help it transform from a cultural island in a persistently impoverished region of Georgia to a robust agent for intellectual and economic development. I grew up as a black man in a region of Alabama that was struggling to free itself from the social vestiges of slavery, so similar to the region in which Albany State is situated. The university was founded at a time when blacks could not attend white universities and in a city with a calcified social structure of separation between blacks and whites.

Many people at Albany State and in the wider Albany community lacked the opportunity I had to see the world beyond a thirty-mile radius; they lacked the opportunity to live and work on a level playing field with people different from themselves. In Albany there had been almost no opportunities for the community to reconcile the grievances of slavery, Jim Crow, or ongoing racial animus. Thus, a willingness to work together for the betterment of the community was almost nonexistent.

Instead, the town was bisected by a river that served as a physical as well as a symbolic barrier separating blacks from whites; poor from privileged. Each side tolerated the other, but each side fell victim to believing and perpetuating stereotypes about the other. There seemed to have been few opportunities to really get to know each other one-on-one or group-by-group. With little dialogue between the two, distrust of the other only grew. Each side had leaders who in effect served as tribal leaders dictating what their followers should think and believe, and who had vested interests in maintaining the racial, historical, social, and economic status quo.

When the Albany community heard of the directive to consolidate the city's historically black university with its historically white two-year college, its uneasy equilibrium was disrupted. It caused great discomfort. For some, the need to protect self-interests or tribal interests trumped strategic thinking about how to embrace this forced integration for the good of the students and the region's economy.

I am struck by the parallels of this one event with what is happening in our country as a whole. Today, the nation's status quo is being challenged by changing demographics and by calls for access to fuller participation in the democratic process called for by our Constitution. Now that I am out of the fray of day-to-day decision-making, I see things that I wish I could have done to ease the pain of the Albany State consolidation. They are things that could be attempted at a national level. In these closing pages, I hope the reader will indulge me as I lay out thoughts and ideas about how we, as Americans, can reconcile our past and forge a common, vibrant future in our universities and beyond.

What unfolded in Albany, Georgia, during the consolidation of two institutions of higher education was, I am convinced, the result of a lack of truth and reconciliation between blacks and whites. A crucial step in the process was inadvertently omitted. After the consolidation was announced to the community, and before the process of forming committees, work groups, and teams was started, I wish that the faculty, staff, and students involved in the process, as well as interested community members, could have participated in sessions to get to know one another, as individuals, and to share feelings about their collective histories. Spaces for healing can break the ice by allowing people to see each other as human beings. Such spaces can be undertaken at the individual, organizational, or national level. Recognizing that there is no specific recipe for a reconciliation process, what can we learn from examples, past and more current, about options for how to approach the process?

At a national level, the South Africans tried to make a space for healing after apartheid, their term for legal racial segregation, which ended in the early 1990s. At the time, the country was at a boiling point of anger. Newly elected President Mandela tried to let some steam out of the kettle, racially and otherwise. He felt that there had to be some formal process to reconcile the rage that the country's more than thirty million black South Africans held against some six million white Afrikaners. In 1995, the government established the Truth and Reconciliation Commission to investigate and reveal the truth about human rights violations during apartheid. It was not a judicial body that could charge individuals with past crimes. Rather, the focus was on the victims. Though the commission and its process had many flaws, it was considered to be a positive step, particularly for its emphasis on public participation.[1]

We missed that step here in our country. If something like that had been done here in the 1870s at the end of our Civil War, we would be in a different place today. As it is, we are left with the intractable subtext of race, and challenges of centuries of a superior-subordinate caste system based on skin color. Using South Africa as one model, I wonder, could we look to other times and places that have been historically polarized and examine the frameworks they used to come to terms?

For example, what could we learn from the Camp David Accords process that led to an Egypt-Israel peace treaty in the late 1970s? At Camp David, President Jimmy Carter served as an intermediary for Israeli prime minister Menachem Begin and Egyptian president Anwar Sadat as they negotiated their differences and grievances. The framework used included distilling mutual interests from a complicated hair-trigger context and agreeing on peaceful steps to achieve and monitor treaty conditions.

It required leaders who were risk-takers and were not afraid of setting aside their personal attitudes and beliefs in order to achieve something bigger and longer lasting than themselves.[2]

In another example, what could we learn from the struggle for reconciliation in the postconflict region of the former Yugoslavia? In the thirty years since the major ethno-religious conflict in the Balkan Peninsula, various groups have sought out truth-telling mechanisms to assist with reconciliation. I witnessed this firsthand in Slovenia, where I was invited to speak to a group of academic and business leaders who were interested in how the southern United States transformed itself through the civil rights era. They thought there were lessons to be learned from hearing an account of the almost a century of Jim Crow.

In thinking about reconciliation, how can people be nudged out of entrenched behaviors to take small steps in the direction of healing? At an organizational level, Karen and I participated in a celebration recognizing the fiftieth anniversary of the desegregation of the University of Alabama in 2013. The university president invited us to cochair the occasion. At one commemorative event, the university hosted the Faith and Politics Institute's annual Civil Rights Pilgrimage in Foster Auditorium, the building where Alabama governor George Wallace "stood in the schoolhouse door" to block Vivian Malone and James Hood from registering. At the event, the audience heard from Sharon Malone Holder, sister of Vivian Malone Jones, and Peggy Wallace Kennedy, daughter of the former governor.[3]

Vivian had died in 2005, but Sharon told how the whole family had worried about Vivian's safety as she made her way across the campus under federal protection to enroll for classes in June 1963, and later as she attended classes. Sharon explained to the audience how, though the school was founded in 1831, it was not truly established until it welcomed all Alabamians regardless of skin color or gender.

Peggy Wallace spoke from her perspective as a young teen at the time of her father's defiant stance against integration. She remembered understanding that something major was going on and noted that her father could talk people into doing almost anything.

At the end of their remarks, the two women walked to the podium and held each other in a long embrace. The crowd stood to give them the most serious, long ovation I had ever seen. To me, the event, with the remarks by Sharon and Peggy, represented a reconciling—a small public space for healing. It was a simple step of letting go of negative feelings. While some may equate a letting-go with giving up, others view it as a powerful means to move forward.

I was familiar with the charette process from my time at the University of Georgia. There, the Center for Community Design and Preservation used charettes with communities seeking solutions for managing stormwater, creating bike trails, planning recycling programs, or other endeavors. The charette model involves intense preparation by those leading the process, a multiday workshop for the participants where they discuss and plan, and a final outcomes session where solutions to the issue are set out and agreed on. Such efforts are not new: a municipal-level charette was held in Durham, North Carolina, in the mid-1960s to decide if the city should desegregate its public schools. The black community was led by civil rights activist Ann Atwater; the white community was led by C. P. Ellis, a white KKK leader. These two individuals went from being enemies to true friends as they worked over ten days under the charette leadership of Bill Riddick.

Asked in 2019 if the charette process would work today, Riddick responded that "bringing people together to look at the same problem but who see it very differently is something that we are going to have to start doing in our country. We bark at each other, but we don't sit down and truly listen to what the other person is saying. That was the intent of the [Durham] charrette; That we will listen and respond and listen and respond until we come up with a solution."[4]

The efforts in South Africa, Camp David, the Balkans, the University of Alabama, and Durham, North Carolina, each involved people talking to one another and listening; learning that individuals and groups have their own histories, feelings, hopes, and dreams; and putting aside differences for the betterment of their communities. The foundation that is created from a reconciliation process is trust. People cannot work together to set and achieve common goals if there is not a trusting relationship at the start. My time at Albany State convinced me that intentionally designed safe spaces for guided dialogue are needed for reconciliation of a traumatic history to take root. If we could create such spaces on an individual-to-individual, community-by-community, and institution-by-institution basis, then perhaps we could heal as a nation.

CHAPTER 22

# Looking to the Future

The United States, for good or ill, dominated the world with its values, economy, and military during the twentieth century. While we continue to struggle to reconcile the history of race in this country, however, the rest of the world has been changing, to the point where some say that in the twenty-first century Western dominance, particularly by the United States, will inevitably decline. Some of the causes of this shift include exponential increases in technology advances, globalization, population growth, mass migration, and climate change.[1] Each of these phenomena will impose serious stresses on societal institutions—governmental (local, state, and national), social (religion and family), economic, and educational. In this final chapter I suggest seven strategies that participants in these various institutions might consider in order to adapt to a new reality. As my life experiences have transpired mostly in the higher education setting, my suggestions are given in relation to universities. The essence of each, however, could be applied to any of our institutions at any level.

Topping the list is avoiding orthodoxy in any form. Traditions about almost everything were strong at Albany State. Every time I turned around, someone would tell me, "This is how we've always done it." I thought, "Well how you've always done things could be wrong. It could be that there are better ways of doing things."

Race was the most prominent form of orthodoxy at Albany State. Staff would say to me, "This university is an HBCU. This is how we do things. Case closed!" This was baffling to me. Why continue to do things wrong or inefficiently just because this is an HBCU? What they really meant was,

"This is our tribe. We've done this for generations and refuse to change." When an institution is in decline, perhaps even on its way to becoming irrelevant, change is essential for survival.

To battle that mindset, I was always challenging staff at Albany State to adopt a sense of heterodoxy. Could they assemble a rich set of ideas and experiences that could give them the ability to build a sophisticated framework for tackling complicated issues? The tribalism at Albany State played out against a backdrop of what many pundits, including Thomas Friedman, call an age of accelerated change. Things are happening so fast today that the technology we are using now will be antiquated in a few short years. We have never been pushed to adapt at such a pace. So, how do we make cultural changes when the divisions of race are so calcified?

Albany State had become a cultural island, its members living in a world that was rushing past at a distance. They clung to what they thought they had control over—their cultural items, like band uniforms and school colors—rather than risk stepping off the island and into a flow that would put them into a competition of efficiency and effectiveness. For Albany State and other institutions, the key to surviving and ultimately thriving will be tied to the relationships they can build with people who are different from themselves, people who may not even like them, as well as to their embracing technology and new ways of doing things.

---

As to embracing new ways of operating, a second key to adapting to change is to problem-solve without rejecting or accepting solutions based on where they come from. In other words, can people learn from others without being humiliated in the process? Friedman calls it "adaptability without humiliation."[2] He explains it by relating a bit of Japanese history. Until the mid-1800s, Japan remained essentially isolated from the Western world. After Commodore Matthew C. Perry pushed Japan to begin trading with the West, its leaders discovered that Western technology was quite advanced. Once the Japanese decided to interact with the West, they exploded economically because they took the best ideas from different cultures without allowing themselves to feel humiliated by doing so.[3]

One theory of why some African Americans resist functioning in modes of efficiency and effectiveness and snub suggestions from others is that they feel deep, even subconscious, humiliation about how they have been treated since the founding of our country—living under slavery, terror of lynchings, almost a century of Jim Crow, the sharecropping system, and constant indignities. But African American leaders can play a role in helping people overcome the long-simmering humiliation, frustrations, and anger. Perhaps, like the leaders of nineteenth-century Japan, they could encourage people to learn from others by taking the best of what's out there and making the most of it.

Another way of describing the dichotomy of learning, or not, from others is in two ways of responding to the concept of being behind. One way to respond is by saying, "It's your fault that I'm behind! Don't stand there and judge me. Make amends!" Another way to respond is, "I'm going to understand what happened, and I'm going to do everything I can to catch up, even surpassing what you think I'm capable of."

The chasm between these two responses was brought home to me when I asked some of Albany State's staff to observe and learn by working across organizational boundaries. While I was visiting a member of the USG staff in Atlanta, he asked me, "Why the hell do we need HBCUs if Georgia State University has more African American students than our three public HBCUs—Fort Valley, Savannah, and Albany—combined! Tell me how we can make a case to have HBCUs?" Georgia State, located in downtown Atlanta, is one of four research universities in the USG. (Although Georgia State is not an HBCU, by the spring 2019 semester, more than 40 percent of its students self-reported as black or African American.)[4]

That conversation prompted me to investigate what Georgia State was doing to achieve such high African American enrollment numbers. I found that they used something called predictive analytics to provide a safety net for all their students. This system tracked factors that could affect student success. It could trigger alerts on students who showed signs of struggling, prompting one-on-one meetings between those students and their advisors.[5]

Wanting to learn more, I pulled together seven or eight of my staff for a field trip to Georgia State to find out everything the institution was doing to attract, retain, and graduate so many African American students. Not everyone selected was eager to be part of this effort. They resented going to what they considered to be a white school to talk about how to achieve African American student success. Rather than being open to taking good ideas wherever they could be found, their attitude was "We can't, and we don't want to, learn anything from them." This seemed to me to be an arrogant and unhelpful attitude.

The team's report when they returned had all the markings of a knee-jerk defensive response: "Oh, Dr. Dunning, we're already doing the same things they are." When I pushed my team to explain how Georgia State was getting a different result to what they characterized as identical work, they had no answer.

Eventually I learned that at the heart of Georgia State's predictive analytics strategy was an understanding that students need active nurturing. Intense academic support programs helped first-year students and acclimated them to university life. Many systems were in place to show students that their university did not want them to drop out. For example, a minigrant program provided emergency funds to help students unable to pay all their tuition and fees—some shortfalls were as little as $300—which could prevent them from graduating.[6] The dedicated Georgia State administrators scanned far and wide for creative ways to support students all the way up to graduation.

I wanted my staff to be entrepreneurial rather than dogmatic so we could learn from Georgia State and others, and improve. Certainly both attitudes were already represented among Albany State administrators. One group was energizing to work with and the other draining, particularly when the latter were what Friedman and others describe as "wound collectors."[7] A wound collector's philosophy is "I'm not ever forgetting or forgiving." African American wound collectors wear an attitude that in essence declares that "we're going to remember forever what happened all those years ago in the Elmina Castle in Ghana, and what happened in Charleston, Savannah, and Mobile. There's nothing you can do to make us forget about the atrocities of slavery. We're going to treasure and wear this degradation like family jewels. And we're going to put this in your face every time we get a chance to talk."

My heart aches when I think of the horrors my ancestors endured. That pain, however, does nothing to help young people today get the education they need to succeed in our rapidly changing high-tech, global world. At Albany State in the mid-2010s, students born in the late 1990s had no firsthand, or probably even secondhand, experience with the horrors of slavery. What these students needed from us adults was not hand-wringing about the past but rather forward thinking about how to provide them with a top-notch education.

The mindset of looking to the past (e.g., blacks heartsick over a half millennium of degradation, whites longing for the fantasy "glory days" of old) does a disservice to current and future generations. In large part, it is paralyzing our nation today. So, how does a university administrator—or a nation's people—break free from being held hostage by the past? Can we move forward, setting aside differences, and work to problem-solve by scanning the world for ideas without being humiliated by learning from others?

---

A third key for surviving and thriving is to establish a healthy network of relationships internally and externally. At Albany State we had not just an unhealthy internal network of relationships, but we also had almost no healthy relationships externally, especially with other campuses in Georgia's system. I asked someone there, "Where do we get our best ideas from? Who do we aspire to be like and even exceed their standards?" Their answer was an HBCU in another state. Few at Albany State considered other schools in Georgia's university system even an option.

Any university leader at any level who wants to create ways for their institutions to be resilient will succeed when they build networks of relationships in which they cooperate and collaborate. In the political realm, it often requires stepping across the aisle to work with colleagues in another party. For example, the new fine-arts building at Albany State was funded largely because a state legislator was willing to work with members of the opposing party. A staff member in the USG later confided to me, "You made a great case, but had this legislator not been willing to collaborate with others on issues important to all Georgians, you might not have gotten the funding."

Selecting effective leaders for any post at any level is crucial in building healthy networks of relationships. Over my career in higher education, I have observed various types of leadership at both the institutional and system levels. Since the mid-1980s, I have paid close attention to the personalities and styles of USG chancellors, who have ranged from bureaucrats to bullies to visionaries. Some simply managed the day-to-day operations, a few pushed people around, and some had specific, data-driven plans to advance the system to the next level.

Poor leaders are often hostage to their memories and biases, which cloud clear thinking for good decision-making. Those who can put behind them negative feelings about the past and who have the capacity to empathize with others, rather than work for their own self-gain, can do a world of good for their people and for others. One stellar example is South African president Nelson Mandela, who governed with vision and compassion by setting aside memories of his twenty-seven years of imprisonment.

In order to live a life of dignity and integrity, and to advance through a career that eventually led to the presidency of Albany State, I had to put aside the conflicted feelings and memories of my segregated youth. When I do allow myself to reflect, however, I recall that summer evening when the intoxicated, belligerent white neighbor trespassed onto our family's land to browbeat my dad. If my dad had not diffused the situation, I might have fired my rifle at the intruder. In that world of lynchings and all-white juries, the whole trajectory of my life could have been very different from that point.

Even today, that incident symbolizes race relations in this country. I have had to suppress my family's history of slavery, Jim Crow, and racial injustice so that I could think calmly and rationally about doing what was best for students and communities, current and future.

---

My experience convinces me that those leading historically black campuses must do the same if they are to remain relevant. Administrators of these campuses have to be resilient, set aside decades of slights and omissions, and be laser-focused in the adoption of innovations and creative solutions to the rapidly changing needs of their students and the communities they serve. In addition, they must adopt a fourth key to viability and prosperity—that of cultivating a culture of high expectations and high achievement. In the long run, a culture of high expectations determines the success of a university, an organization, or a nation.

In the late 1990s I participated in a management development program organized for sitting executives by the John F. Kennedy School of Government at Harvard. While there, a colleague in the program and I shared our thoughts on what the term "elitism" meant to us. For some, the term has connotations of being snobbish. For me it means trying to be extraordinary at any and every endeavor. It does not mean being elitist and thereby exclusionary of individuals or groups. Being the most efficient and effective as one can be applies not only to individuals but to organizations also. So can a university strive for elitism without being elitist? Can it provide the highest level of quality teaching, research, and outreach?

My colleague in the program agreed, saying "one of the things that makes these folks here at Harvard so successful is they think 'if the top 1 percent need to be educated, it should be us.'" Faculty and administrators there just assume that Harvard should be the leader of higher education in this country. The institution has a culture that exudes a high level of sense of self. That contrasted sharply with what I observed at Albany State, where I frequently heard the self-defeatist rationalization "We're just an HBCU. That's why we do things this way."

That statement, not least the "just," reeks of accepting someone else's designation as being "less than," which was just about the most foreign idea I could imagine. My concept of what it means to be of a certain race in America was shaped by learning strength and dignity from people living under the most systematic and thorough exploitation of any system ever devised—Jim Crow in the Alabama Black Belt—though they managed to live their lives with a set of values that honored hard work, perseverance, endurance, and scholarship. Yet people today seem to harbor counterproductive notions about what it means to be a person of color.

The diametrically opposed comments by those at Harvard and at Albany State represent cultural statements for me. Thus, the leadership challenges I faced while at Albany State were how I could help create a culture of high expectations and how the institution could be elite without being elitist. If the diversity of the consolidated institution was going to work long-term, people had to shift from focusing narrowly on providing an HBCU experience to thinking of preparing students to reach a generic set of rigorous, academic standards. I'll use a football metaphor to illustrate this: when the University of Alabama's football coach, Nick Saban, was asked how he prepared his team to play against a big rival, he said something along the lines of "We don't ever prepare to play against a particular team. We have an identified standard of excellence that we prepare for. We don't think, 'Are we playing a lesser team or a big team?' We fight against our own standard of excellence."

Another way of thinking about reaching for excellence is succinctly captured by Lexus's first advertising slogan for its luxury vehicles: "the relentless pursuit of perfection." That was exactly my goal for Albany State. I wanted us to honor and treasure the institution's HBCU history while improving inefficient systems and business processes and increasing retention and graduation rates.

In the pursuit of excellence, leaders often have to help some in the organization face hard realities. Shortly after the consolidation was announced, I went on a speaking tour around the state, including Columbus, Atlanta, Augusta, and Savannah. The purpose of the tour was to give a comprehensive update about the steps we would be taking and of the benefits the consolidation would bring to the school's students and to Southwest Georgia.

Many of the attendees of these sessions were skeptical of the consolidation. My candid, tough-love approach didn't always go over well, as when I spoke to an all-black group of Albany State supporters: "You just can't do trading on race. It's not a hard currency. The people [USG administrators, corporate donors] I deal with not only do not want to hear it, they start looking for the exit. So help me think through how to make the case for Albany State to retain and graduate young people to compete in any environment. It pains me to tell you that the gap between what Albany State has been doing to prepare graduates and what other institutions in Georgia's system are doing is wide. I know that causes you all angst to hear me say that. But look, there's a reality out here, and you need to mobilize to work in that reality, not the one you create in your mind." Supporters also needed to understand that the university would have to adapt in order to survive.

Especially when it serves minorities, how the institution defines itself and its mission are crucial. Many may push back against leading with high academic expectations rather than with historical racial background. They certainly did in Albany. My view ran counter to everything that I was seeing and hearing there. It got to the point where people in the Albany State community were questioning whether I was "black enough," by which they meant "he doesn't think the way we think."

For a university to thrive in the long term, however, it must lead with statements about performance, high achievement, and strong academic programs. References to the cultural aspects important to its history come second. Such an approach allows students of all backgrounds to feel welcome at the institution. When a school earns a reputation for being welcoming and supportive of student success, demand increases—enrollments go up. When enrollments increase, especially in public institutions, funding increases. When funding increases, leaders can expand program offerings and support services.

The USG gave Albany State a gift by consolidating it with Darton State because the resulting new university had a rare opportunity to reinvigorate its previously separate parts. It could strive to become one of the most outstanding regional universities in the country. It could set standards for high achievement and high performance, develop strategies to meet those standards, and continuously measure and evaluate its progress toward its goal.

---

The school also was given the gift of automatically diversifying and expanding its enrollment, which brings me to a fifth key to surviving and thriving. Individuals, groups, communities, organizations, and nations must embrace diversity. For Albany State, that meant doing some deep soul-searching: Rather than focus on the skin color of faculty, staff, and students, could we as members of a new institution focus on creating a rich and rigorous educational experience? Moving "HBCU" from Albany State's mission statement to another of the institution's foundational documents was the right thing to do in order to recruit students of all backgrounds. Perhaps more than anything else, that one decision will determine the long-term success of Albany State.

Most college students probably pay little attention to the mission statements of institutions when they are surveying possible universities to attend. They may tour a campus, sample life around the school, and peruse the school's website. Few, I suspect, seek out the institution's mission statement and think deeply about what it hopes to convey. To test this hunch while at Albany State, I would sometimes ask students if they knew what our mission statement said—most did not. During the consolidation, however, the decision to shift "HBCU" out of the mission statement created an uproar among staff, students, and the greater community. The move was seen as something that would change the DNA of the campus. In reality, the shift was irrelevant to daily campus life, though I hoped it would help the institution diversify its enrollment over time. Diversifying enrollment in all educational settings will be crucial for our country as it grapples with accepting "Otherness" and "difference."

Population diversity is already a fact that is here to stay in this country, and a border wall no matter how high or impregnable cannot change that fact. It's been well established for at least twenty years that the United States will cease to have a white majority before 2050, making ours a multiracial nation, which we should celebrate and be thankful for.[8] Rather than diminish, diversity enriches a community, a university, a state, or a nation. In a diverse nation, we need leaders that serve all their constituents, not just one group or another. They need to think and act on the questions, "Where are the common threads in this multiplicity of people in terms of how people feel and what they believe? How can we take the common threads and weave them into a promising future for all?" Each person has a unique lens through which they look at the world. And yet, all seem to want a future that is supportive, strong, and healthy—a future that allows them and their children and grandchildren to survive and prosper.

Skeptics say that diversifying a university's enrollment can't happen without lowering admissions standards. It doesn't have to. It's possible to retain high standards by focusing on identifying and bringing in high-achieving, academically prepared students. Institutions should offer help to students who have difficulty adjusting to college life, as I related earlier about Georgia State's success in retaining African American students, but in that case, too, the students had the academic chops to be successful. The same things that had been said for generations about African Americans were later said about other groups. Contrary to these stereotypes, and as I said earlier, I have always believed that there is no scarcity of intellect in any group or community—there is only scarcity of opportunity.

While university enrollments can, and should, be made more inclusive of race, gender identity, ethnicity, religion, and socioeconomic status, they can also seek geographic diversity, as the University of Alabama has done. Until recently, the university had tried to stay the course as a southern school serving predominantly students from Alabama. Demographic projections, however, indicated that the number of Alabama high school graduates was poised to decline in the coming years.

Another reality the university faced was a significant decline in state funding, making the university more "state located" than "state supported." Alabama's leadership recognized that one way to address declining state support was to enroll more out-of-state students. To attract such students, the university modernized the campus, built new residence halls, and established scholarships to help ease the burden of out-of-state tuition. Finally, by attracting highly qualified students, the university hoped to enhance its academic standing. The University of Alabama has been extremely successful with this approach; in 2018, almost 60 percent of the student body was from outside Alabama.[9]

Not long ago, I had a chance conversation with one of these out-of-state students. On a Sunday evening, a current undergraduate working the phone bank of the university's alumni association called to ask if I was planning to continue my membership with the association. Always interested in hearing the paths that students take to get where they are, I inquired where she was from and what she was studying. She said, "I'm from Northern California."

"How did you find your way to Tuscaloosa?," I asked. She responded, "Well, I have so many family members in California. I wanted to be independent. Alabama has a program called New College where you can create your own major. I was able to come here and design my own environmental studies degree." The New College program allows an independent student to work closely with faculty advisors in putting together a thoughtful academic program, and this young woman from California had found her way there.[10]

The benefits that can accrue to the state when its flagship university seeks students from other states, and even countries, are exponential. Some graduates will remain in the state after graduation, enriching the state's economy and quality of life. For this reason alone, every college and university would benefit by diversifying its enrollment. I especially believe that the benefits far outweigh any perceived costs for minority-serving institutions that diversify their student body. I would make the case that if the just over one hundred HBCUs in the country want to survive financially, they must diversify their enrollments with more white, Latinx, and Asian students, among others.

When I talked about diversifying the Albany State student profile, some responded defensively, "We've never been segregated." Although that was true, I patiently explained that Albany State was so culturally compacted in terms of what people think, believe, and do that it was hard for others to find themselves in this culture. I felt strongly that if, as an HBCU, we aligned ourselves with the country's changing demographic profile, we stood a better chance of surviving in the long term.

There are in fact few instances in any context where diversity is not an asset. From the conference table to communities, to cities, to regions, to countries, the long-term benefits of diversity across a variety of measures are immense. For one, such wide-ranging diversity ensures that decisions take in a wide variety of opinions and perspectives. I have always felt that some of the best decisions—whether about geopolitics, foreign policy in the Middle East, or consolidation of two schools in Albany, Georgia—emerged from diversity.

While shepherding Albany State through the merger, I felt that a diversity of opinions was missing from many discussions. In retrospect, I see that response may have been fueled by fears of change and of loss of self-identity. Many leaders during times of change face similar resistance, particularly when the inner community includes unreliable translators of reality regarding challenges and issues facing the organization, and especially if those unreliable voices tout a false reality to others.

Today in the United States, demographic diversity is a flashpoint centered on race. As strongly as I feel about the benefits of diversity, I am equally sober about the strain that demographic change can cause. We see this today as our country approaches becoming one in which the majority are nonwhite. Many people feel threatened. The transition is difficult both for those who think the shift away from majority white is hurting them and for nonwhites facing a knowledge-based economy without always having the skills to enter it.

Not embracing diversity, however, can have negative effects well into the future. The Atlanta-Birmingham example I offered from the 1960s is a glaring contrast of the consequences of the two cities' business, educational, and governmental leadership. Atlanta chose in a way that made it the economic center of the southeastern United States. Atlanta's leaders said, "We're not ready for all this integration, but we're not going to destroy the city over it." Its "too busy to hate" slogan was not completely accurate. Racism was still there, for example in the votes to not extend the metro system to the white-dominated suburbs. Still, its positive tone led to economic growth and a more cosmopolitan feel compared to the rest of the Southeast. On the other hand, Birmingham's leaders fought change tooth and nail. Were it not for the University of Alabama–Birmingham in downtown Birmingham, I'm not sure what the city would be like today, more than a half-century after those fateful decisions. My point here is that decision-making based on animosity has generational outcomes.

A more current example is my home county, Marengo. Linden, the county seat, has been a tough, dangerous place since my youth. It was a two-traffic-light town, where the police chief sat in his car ready to pull people over at one or two in the morning just because they were black. That's just one reason my dad did not want me driving through there late at night on my visits home from college.

Over the years, Linden has for the most part kept its schools segregated. It is home to Marengo Academy, founded in 1969 as a segregation academy—that is, a private school founded so whites could avoid having their children attend desegregated public schools. It is home to the *Democrat-Reporter* newspaper, whose editor in 2019 called upon the Ku Klux Klan to ride again to conduct lynchings to "clean up Washington, D.C.," and to kill the "socialist communists" who exposed his habit of writing racist editorials. Today, many would describe Linden as a racially divided town that watches as the world passes it by.[11]

Two nearby cities offer contrasting strategies. Demopolis, about fifteen miles north of Linden, has a desegregated city school system that is striving to become one of the top ten in the state. About thirty miles south of Linden, Thomasville is being intentional in preparing students, from elementary school through dual-enrollment programs between the Thomasville High School and Coastal Alabama Community College, to work in the high-tech industries it is actively working to attract. Both cities are thriving.[12]

Richard Florida, a professor who uses social and economic theories to study urban areas, talks about diversity spurring economic development and how homogeneity slows it down. He writes in *The Rise of the Creative Class* that economically thriving areas attract people and organizations that value diversity in a variety of manifestations. For a number of reasons, people in the Albany community were wary of "Otherness" and "difference," which inevitably made them resistant to embracing diversity. In that community with rather rigidly drawn lines, even which church a person attended tended to reveal their race, economic status, and culture. Unfortunately, few people saw the connection between their tribalism and the region's lack of development. The long-term economic impact of the region's resistance to diversity, however, was inevitable—and reminiscent of how the nation and the South dealt with the aftermath of the Civil War.

After the Civil War, although racial division continued, there was measured progress toward constitutional equality for African Americans. In the mid-1870s, the political winds shifted, however, leaving the South to set its own laws and practices. The result was almost a century of Jim Crow laws and practices and of economic stagnation in the South. In the 1950s, with the public participating in calls for change, politics began to shift toward support of civil rights, although segregationist members of Congress fought against federal legislation. When the Civil Rights Act was finally passed in 1964, it became the external push needed to change southern society. Helped along by innovations in technology, especially air-conditioning, the South's economy, which had been stagnating for the previous century or more, took off.

Like the South in the century after the Civil War, the Albany community was frozen in time in its racial division. This was made possible, unfortunately, by the USG's willingness to treat Albany State with benign neglect, which went on for so long that the school stagnated, falling behind the state's other regional institutions. When the USG did finally make up for its long inaction in 2015, the consolidation process was a logistical success, but we could have done better at managing reconciliation. In our haste and concern for administering the process itself, we overlooked creating support mechanisms to help ease people into change, and for that I accept responsibility.

---

Thus, a sixth strategy for surviving and thriving is providing support structures to help those entering the mainstream, as well as spaces for civilized dialogue to understand and acclimate to diversity. I have seen each have a positive impact in the academic environment. There, the support can be academic, social, financial, and enrichment outside of the classroom. For example, study skills centers can help with academic need. Some universities have support programs for first-generation college-attending students. Other examples include programs like the one Karen and I supported at Albany State for students who had grown up in foster care, and Georgia State University's microgrants program to help students avoid dropping out of school due to financial hardship.

While these programs help all students, I have over the years given a lot of thought to students of color, particularly young men, because of my own experience growing up. I worry about them because of the way our society has responded to them, culturally, politically, and socially. Young men of color are often faced with few or substandard educational opportunities and with high rates of incarceration. This is a regrettable but undeniable fact in U.S. life and culture. Over the years, I have had many conversations about the stresses of parenting African American young people in a society still dealing with the legacy of slavery, Jim Crow, and de facto segregation. Such ignominious historical facts will cast a long shadow over parenting or managing organizations.

Albany State would have benefited from campus conversations on these topics. I regret now that I didn't invite some of the best minds and thinkers to campus to lead students, faculty, administrators, and community members in discussions on important topics like "growing up black in America." An HBCU is the ideal place to tackle head-on these and other issues related to marginalization. And all colleges and universities should consider what support structures can be put in place to encourage lively dialogues about complicated issues facing today's students from navigating in a world of racism, to globalization, to climate change. Having such campus dialogues is one way of creating a vibrant, enriched experience for students outside of the classroom. It is a credit to an institution when its graduates can say that they learned as much outside of class as they did inside the classroom.

Deep reflection could occur in these rich campus-based conversations, as well as in service-learning classes and internships. Far from campus, study abroad is another support mechanism to enhance academic learning and personal development. Students are stretched when their cultural assumptions are challenged. I have often found that when people travel to Asia, Africa, or Latin America, many of their feelings and beliefs—whether about the major world religions, music, cuisine, political structures, or organizational values and behaviors—are challenged by sheer observation.

While I was at Albany State, one pastor asked me why I frequently mentioned my time in Asia. His question led me to understand that it was not the region per se that was memorable, but rather the exposure to very different cultures that stayed with me and influenced by thinking. That perspective-altering experience made me passionate about creating service-learning-based study-abroad experiences in countries like Tanzania and Thailand. I felt it was one of the best ways to help young people discover themselves.

To fund student support structures like these, as well as help with other needs, institutions need robust endowments. In fact, most public universities today need a broad donor base if they want to go from marginal to good to great, and remain great. They need corporate donors, and they also need support from alumni. Schools with degree programs (e.g., engineering, medicine, law) can produce graduates who thirty years into their careers are in positions to give large sums to the institution. For example, G. Wayne Clough, the president of Georgia Tech (the Georgia Institute of Technology), established the Tech Promise Scholarship program in 2007 to raise $50 million to provide "a debt-free Georgia Tech education to students whose only obstacle to success was a lack of financial resources." With his legacy carried forward by later presidents, the program endowment exceeded $60 million, a substantial portion donated by alumni.[13]

Small, regional universities like Albany State with programs in social work, education, arts and sciences, and business are unlikely to ever develop a wealthy donor base among its graduates. It stands to reason that they must approach corporate donors and wealthy individuals to take an interest in enhancing programming for their students. Endowment funds have the added benefit of providing flexibility on how the funds are used. State funding is more restrictive.

In my efforts to raise private donations, I also communicated to Albany State's supporters that Georgia has one of the most robust publicly supported systems of higher education in the nation. When I joined the USG office in the late 1980s, the state paid about 75 percent of what it cost to educate a student, with students paying about 25 percent. Today, the ratio is about even, which still represents a high state contribution compared with elsewhere. As of this writing, in Alabama, Virginia, and Michigan, for example, state funding is much lower now for its public universities and colleges. One of my greatest frustrations as an educator is the decline in support for higher education across the country in general and for HBCU institutions in particular. Today, private giving is essential for a university to grow.

While building endowments is one means of helping fund universities, another is to leverage with collaborating partners just as how my grandfather partnered with the Rosenwald Foundation and the local school board. I watched this same strategy unfold a number of times when I worked in the USG headquarters. For example, a president of one of the research universities came to one budget hearing proposing to build a multimillion-dollar science building, raising half from private and corporate donors if the USG would raise the rest. Such determined self-sufficiency energized the system staff and regents, who too often were being asked to do all the heavy lifting.

---

Generously publicly and privately funded universities are incalculably important in helping our world. This brings me to my seventh, and final, suggestion for how colleges and universities can survive and thrive. They must be civically engaged in their research, their teaching, and their public service and outreach. More so than for other major social institutions like religion and government, their mission is to seek new knowledge through research, to disseminate that knowledge through teaching, and to apply that knowledge in ways that help local and global communities.

In fact, universities may soon be one of the last remaining institutions that people can trust, as I feel many have lost trust in our country's institutions, including our legislative, judicial, and executive branches of government. Moreover, in a world now inundated with an infinite amount of information, universities are perhaps one of the few remaining spaces where the skills of analysis and synthesis are applied to evaluate information. Time-intensive, deep study of information can, in turn, help people make informed decisions on a wide variety of topics.

Thus, universities can address topics critical to our world's future. For example, I mentioned earlier that between 1990 and 2000, the Latino population rose by some 300 percent in Georgia. That rapid growth rate had a huge impact on those people migrating in, as well as on Georgia's economy. Those newly arriving in Georgia faced challenges related to language, culture, education, transportation, housing, and healthcare. Georgia's infrastructure strained to meet the demand. Many individuals, government officials, and nongovernmental organizations worked to ameliorate the situation.

Part of the cache of a good university is as a place to convene for conversations on difficult topics. The University of Georgia, as the state's land-grant institution, had the infrastructure and faculty expertise to provide leadership on what we called a Latino Initiative. Held in high esteem around the state, the university could bring people to the table who otherwise might not show up. We held our first Latino Conference, "Power of Latinos for a Stronger Georgia," in 2001, and subsequently launched a number of campus initiatives to address the issues raised in the sessions. Like the 1970s television commercial for the E. F. Hutton stock brokerage firm, "When E. F. Hutton talks, people listen," when the university invited people to the campus, people came.

A university's applied research efforts have great potential for helping communities. Not long ago I was reminded of the proactive efforts that university outreach can play. A faculty member in Alabama's Cooperative Extension Service (a collaboration among Alabama A&M University, Auburn University, and Tuskegee) found my name in the deed records in the Linden County Courthouse and called me to share the results of aerial surveys he was conducting on pine beetle damage to timberland in Marengo, Clarke, and Choctaw Counties. Aerial photos showed that trees on land adjacent to mine were infested with the beetle, which can kill trees weakened by droughts and by warmer-than-average winters. I was grateful that he reached out to warn me, "If you're not ready to harvest the timber on your land, you should do something to prevent the spread of the beetle to your trees." This was an example of the faculty personally reaching out to the community to share information gathered by an academic research endeavor.

In teaching, universities can adjust curricula to meet student content-learning needs, as well as community needs. For example, while at Albany State, I talked to one of the nursing program administrators about addressing some common healthcare issues in the community, which included mistrust in the allopathic medical system, reliance on home or folk remedies, poor diet, and low income, which put medical attention out of reach for some people. We considered changes to the curriculum that could help train nurses to be alert to and responsive to the particular culture and needs of a particular community. My hope was that, over time, we could establish advisory boards with members of the professional community who could share their expertise and knowledge to help us shape our academic programs. The goal was to enhance our nursing curricula in ways that would help both the students and the communities they lived in. Then I took a similar approach with the other disciplines.

With applied research and service-learning—an instructional method in which students learn content while engaged in activities that address a community need—a university has a huge capacity to help with the economic development of the community surrounding it. With an estimated seventy-five thousand residents, Albany has a shrinking population, whereas Greenville, South Carolina, where I live now, is growing at a remarkable rate.[14] Albany is ripe for growth and development, while Greenville has already transformed itself. It has great restaurants, a thirty-two-acre park on the edge of Reedy River Falls in the center of town, an art museum with an annual Shakespeare festival, and the Peace Center, a performing arts center that also hosts educational and community events. The town is a magnet.

When town and gown—town and higher education—join forces, magnificent things can transpire. One very basic step is to get the students off campus and into the city itself. The attractions in downtown Greenville, for example, draw the city's higher-education students, who spend their money in the local businesses, injecting money into the local economy. The same could happen in Albany, particularly if we could get consensus among university and community stakeholders about what to focus on in revitalization efforts.

Another way to join town and gown is to involve students with communities through service-learning. On a small scale while at Albany State, Albany's city manager and I talked about finding space in downtown Albany in which to offer academic programs, thereby embedding and immersing students in the heart of the city. As our planning progressed, I suggested the idea of creating a town and gown service-learning and student-internship project. We could establish a center for innovation and creativity housed in a jointly supported downtown location.

There, students could work with faculty and city administrators to tackle intractable local issues. For example, if Albany was having trouble with housing in a particular zip code, students guided and mentored by faculty and municipal staff could research best practices and propose solutions and strategies. The process, we felt, would help build a level of town-gown collaboration and trust around problem solving for the twenty-county service area of Albany State. We could help those counties match up economic development with their workforce options. We could build a ladder with a two-plus-two program with the local technical school. In the program, we would get students involved in research, analysis, and writing as part of the application of their content learning.

The first step in implementing our plan was to create space just for people to get to know each other, and to build some trust. Historically, there was little interaction between Albany State and municipal administrators. Without trust, little would be accomplished, but if we could help build relationships, the idea might take hold. We brought our senior leadership teams together for an all-day get-acquainted workshop. We hoped it would get people talking, listening, and building a level of trust and respect. That would be the groundwork on which plans for the innovation center could be built.

Another place ripe for collaboration was the U.S. Marine Corps Logistics Base, one of only two such bases in the entire country. All U.S. military equipment that has been repaired or retrofitted moves through either this base outside Albany or a base in California on its way to overseas operations. More than four thousand civilians, contract employees, and marines work at the Albany base.

That substantial workforce a stone's throw from the university was sufficient reason for me to want Albany State to establish a relationship with the base. When I met with the base commander, they were just as interested in a partnership: "If we could get people who have two years past high school in robotics out at this logistics base, and if they could pass the drug test, they could make $60,000 to $70,000 a year." The base was a perfect setting for internships to act as a supply chain into those good-paying jobs.

Universities can also advance economic development efforts beyond their regional area. In my role at Kennesaw State University, I was able to support programs for adults in the community. For example, to help the Cobb County Chamber of Commerce prepare a business delegation for an economic development mission to Japan, Korea, and Taiwan, I arranged for a professor of Asian history to develop an orientation program. The training gave the group an understanding of not just the political, economic, and social structures in the countries they would visit but also the social conventions and appropriate business behavior.

On a larger scale, while I was at the University of Georgia, Mel Garber, at the time a leader in the institution's Cooperative Extension Service, and I worked to create a framework administratively, organizationally, and culturally to extend all aspects of the university—not just the College of Agricultural and Environmental Sciences—to solve complex problems in communities across Georgia. Playing off of the university's symbol of the Arch, the gateway from downtown Athens to the north campus, we named the endeavor the Archway Partnership Project. Through it, university staff and faculty worked with targeted communities to address self-identified community needs. Archway professionals served as bridges to the huge repository of knowledge scattered across the university's seventeen schools and colleges that range from pharmacy and social work to public health and engineering.

The program continues today as an efficient conduit to connect the state's land-grant institution to the people of the state.[15] It has given life to the application of scholarship and provided a laboratory for student learning. My hope is that this twenty-first-century model can be extended to all types of institutions, including regional universities like Albany State.

This is a good place to point out, however, that educational institutions are made up of individual people. Each of us has a personal history, and each of us has our unique set of strengths and weaknesses. Although the institutions of slavery and Jim Crow have been broken, each of us still deals with the unreconciled issue of race, now often in the guise of political demagoguery, blind nationalism, and proliferating hate groups.

What is also true for each of us, however, is that as individuals we are more interconnected with one another around the globe than ever before. There is hope for our mutual future if each of us, each day, can get up and live up to Nelson Mandela's challenge to surprise the world with compassion, restraint, and generosity. I am convinced that education at all levels—K–12, technical schools, and colleges and universities—and for students of all ages is the most powerful catalyst for social change, for political stability, and for the economic development of communities locally and globally.

# Notes

PART ONE. Coming of Age in the Alabama Black Belt of the 1950s

1. McDonald and Burnes, *Visions of the Black Belt*, viii.

CHAPTER 1. The Alabama Black Belt

1. Zinn, *People's History*, 29.
2. Elmina Castle's history is well-known, but see, for example, Deb and Akande, "Inside Ghana's Elmina Castle," and Diarra, "Ghana's Slave Castles."
3. Eltis and Richardson, *Atlas*, 205–208. See also Diouf, *Dreams of Africa in Alabama*, 14–15.
4. Hebert, "Slavery."
5. Zinn, *People's History*, 199.
6. Archer, *Growing Up Black*, 62.
7. Hebert, "Ku Klux Klan in Alabama."

CHAPTER 2. A Sense of Southern Place

1. Holt, "Black Life," 137.
2. Ibid., 137.
3. Shell, *Evolution of the Alabama Agroecosystem*, 376.
4. Van West, "WLAC."
5. Encylopaedia Britannica editors, "Blues Music."
6. Cobb, *Redefining Southern Culture*, 93.

CHAPTER 3. Navigating Jim Crow

1. O'Neill, "Sheila Oliver Says 16 States"; Richter, "Alabama's Anti-Miscegenation Statutes."
2. Little Known Black Library Facts, "Integration."
3. King, "Letter from Birmingham Jail," 78–88.

## Chapter 4. The Will to Learn

1. Flint, *Alabama in the Twentieth Century*, 221.
2. Gavins, *Cambridge Guide*, 87.
3. Ascoli, *Julius Rosenwald*, 87.
4. Ibid., 56.
5. Ibid., 225.
6. National Museum of African American History and Culture, "Emmett Till's Open Casket Funeral."

## Chapter 5. The Great Migration

1. Wilkerson, *Warmth of Other Suns*, 9.
2. Museum of Modern Art, "Visualizing the Great Migration."
3. Smith, "Boll Weevil in Alabama."
4. Michaeli, "Bound for the Promised Land."
5. Wilkerson, *Warmth of Other Suns*, 190.

## Chapter 7. Anger Becomes Resolve

1. Obama, *Becoming*, 259.
2. Dan T. Carter, *Politics of Rage*, 149.
3. For more on this, see Federal Bureau of Investigation, "Medgar Evers."
4. See, for example, Pettus and Santana, "Man Convicted."
5. See, for example, Fiffer and Cohen, *Jimmie Lee & James*, 50.
6. See, for example, Stanford University, "Selma to Montgomery March."
7. Ibid.
8. American War Library, *Allied Troop Levels*.

## Chapter 8. Taxes Aren't Segregated

1. Freemark et al., "Segregation Now, Segregation Forever."
2. University of Alabama, "Presidents of the University."

## Chapter 9. Lessons Learned along the Way

1. Wilder, *Son of Virginia*, 185.
2. See, for example, Bain-Selbo, "From Lost Cause to Third-and-Long."

## Chapter 11. Albany, the Egypt of the Confederacy

1. Samuel, "River Flows under Atlanta's Airport."
2. Morris, "Flint River."
3. Ibid.
4. Worthy, "Creek Indians of Georgia."

5. Du Bois, *Souls of Black Folk*, 121.
6. Ibid., 57.
7. Ibid., 57–58.
8. Stanford University Press, "Cotton Revolution."
9. Du Bois, *Souls of Black Folk*, 62.
10. Ibid., 63.
11. Ibid., 73.
12. Ibid., 63.
13. Clive, Davis, and Liner, *Glancing Backward*, 57.
14. Du Bois, *Souls of Black Folk*, 69.
15. Ibid., 69–70.
16. Clive, Davis, and Liner, *Glancing Backward*, 64, 69, 109.
17. Ibid., 68–70.
18. Ibid., 108–134.
19. Ibid., 140–141.
20. MilitaryBases.com, "MCLB Albany Army Base."
21. Clive, Davis, and Liner, *Glancing Backward*, 145.
22. Carson, "SNCC and the Albany Movement," 15–16, 16.
23. Ibid., 18–20. See also Formwalt, "Albany Movement."
24. Mieder, *Making a Way*, 90.

CHAPTER 12. A City Held Hostage by Its Past

1. Knight, "Facebook SOTD."
2. Carl Vinson Institute of Government, *Dismantling Persistent Poverty in Georgia*, 4.
3. Martin, "Georgia Farmers Face Long Recovery."
4. Burke, "Nine Standout Lodges."
5. Barry, "Ivan Allen Jr. Helped Build."

CHAPTER 13. A University with Unsinkable Determination

1. Much of this part about the history of Albany State University is from the official history that is part of the ASU foundational documents.
2. Woolley and Peters, "Remarks."
3. U.S. Department of Education, "What Is an HBCU?"
4. Williams and Ashley, *I'll Find a Way*, 72.
5. WALB News10, "Albany State Proves 'Unsinkable.'"
6. Lewis, "Flood of 1994."

CHAPTER 14. The Calm before the Storm?

1. Staff Report from Albany CEO, "ASU Interim President Art Dunning."
2. Thomas Friedman does a good job of describing the accelerated rate of change in these forces and their impact on individuals and communities, our workplaces, and our politics locally and globally. See Friedman, *Thank You for Being Late*.
3. See more on this in Davis, "Albany State Financial Aid Audit."
4. "ASU Interim President Art Dunning and Wife."
5. Hurst, "Stepin Fetchit."
6. Pilgrim and Gates, *Understanding Jim Crow*, 144.
7. Goldstein, "Earl L. Butz."

PART 4. Never before in Our Nation's History

1. University System of Georgia, "Regents Approve Principles for Consolidation."
2. Albany State University and Darton State College, *Consolidation Prospectus*, 27.
3. University System of Georgia, "Previous Campus Consolidations."
4. Jarrett Carter, "Benefits of College Mergers."
5. Albany State University, *ASU/DSC Consolidation Overview*.

CHAPTER 15. Pushback in Black and White

1. Albany State University and Darton State College, *Consolidation Prospectus*, 39.
2. University System of Georgia, "Huckaby Recommending Consolidation."
3. Gaye, "Inner City Blues."

CHAPTER 16. A Near Derailment at Square One

1. Albany State University, *ASU/DSU Consolidation Timeline*.
2. Albany State University and Darton State College, *Consolidation Prospectus*, 31.
3. For more on Bluefield State College, see Meraji and Demby, "Whitest Historically Black College."
4. Pew Research Center, "Social & Demographic Trends."
5. Albany State University, *Vision, Mission, and Guiding Principles*.
6. Albany State University and Darton State College, *Consolidation Prospectus*, 101–104.
7. Faulkner, *Requiem for a Nun*.

CHAPTER 17. When Wounds Go Untended for Generations
   1. Suggs, "Civil Rights Champion."

CHAPTER 18. Fallout When Unreconciled
   1. Parks, "Homecoming Parade."
   2. Barrett, "McConnell Opposes Paying Reparations."
   3. Lockhart, "House Democrats."
   4. Monroe, "Where It All Went Wrong."

CHAPTER 19. Nudges toward Healing
   1. Friedman, *Thank You for Being Late*, 311.

CHAPTER 20. Sometimes It Takes Tough Love
   1. Dunning, "Celebrating the New Albany State University—BOR Finalizes Consolidation," memo to faculty, staff, and students Albany State University and Darton State College, December 9, 2016.
   2. Dunning, "Art Dunning."
   3. King, "Desegregation and the Future."

CHAPTER 21. Toward Reconciliation
   1. Truth and Reconciliation Commission, *Official Truth and Reconciliation Commission Website*.
   2. Barron, Kurtzer-Ellenbogen, and Yaffe, "Middle East Peace."
   3. University of Alabama News Center, "Faith and Politics Institute's Civil Rights Pilgrimage."
   4. Owusu-Ansah, "Best of Enemies." See also Davidson, *Best of Enemies*.

CHAPTER 22. Looking to the Future
   1. Friedman, *Thank You for Being Late*, 244–250.
   2. Ibid., 313.
   3. Ibid., 313–314.
   4. University System of Georgia, "Semester Enrollment Report."
   5. Georgia State University, "Leading with Predictive Analytics."
   6. Georgia State University, "Panther Retention Grants."
   7. Friedman, *Thank You for Being Late*, 315–316.
   8. See, for example, Frey, "U.S. Will Become 'Minority White.'"
   9. University of Alabama, "Quick Facts."
   10. University of Alabama, "New College."
   11. Scarborough, "Linden."

12. Estes, "There's No Doubting Thomasville."
13. Georgia Tech, "Tech Promise Challenge Exceeds Goal."
14. Population figures from "Albany, Georgia," and "Greenville, South Carolina."
15. University of Georgia, "Archway Partnership."

# Bibliography

"Albany, Georgia." *Wikipedia.* https://en.wikipedia.org/wiki/Albany,_Georgia, accessed April 1, 2020.
Albany State University. *ASU/DSC Consolidation Overview.* https://www.asurams.edu/presidents-office/consolidation/, accessed October 7, 2019.
——— . *ASU/DSU Consolidation Timeline.* https://www.asurams.edu/presidents-office/consolidation/asudsu-consolidation-timeline.php, accessed October 8, 2019.
——— . *Vision, Mission, and Guiding Principles.* https://www.asurams.edu/vision-mission-guiding-principles.php, accessed October 9, 2019.
Albany State University and Darton State College. *Consolidation Prospectus.* September 15, 2016.
American War Library. *Allied Troop Levels—Vietnam, 1960 to 1973.* December 6, 2008. https://www.americanwarlibrary.com/vietnam/vwatl.htm, accessed October 3, 2019.
Archer, Chalmers, Jr. *Growing Up Black in Rural Mississippi: Memories of a Family, Heritage of a Place.* New York: Walker and Company, 1992.
Ascoli, Peter Max. *Julius Rosenwald: The Man Who Built Sears, Roebuck and Advanced the Cause of Black Education in the American South.* Bloomington: Indiana University Press, 2006.
"ASU Interim President Art Dunning and Wife Make Major Donation to ASU." *Albany CEO,* September 23, 2015. http://albanyceo.com/news/2015/09/asu-interim-president-and-wife-make-major-donation-asu/, accessed June 5, 2019.
Bain-Selbo, Eric. "From Lost Cause to Third-and-Long: College Football and the Civil Religion of the South." *Journal of Southern Religion* 11 (2019). http://jsr.fsu.edu/Volume11/Selbo.htm, accessed May 18, 2020.
Barrett, Ted. "McConnell Opposes Paying Reparations: 'None of Us Currently Living Are Responsible' for Slavery." *CNN.com,* June 19, 2019. https://www.cnn.com/2019/06/18/politics/mitch-mcconnell-opposes-reparations-slavery/index.html, accessed October 11, 2019.
Barron, Robert, Lucy Kurtzer-Ellenbogen, and Michael Yaffe. "Middle East

Peace: What Can We Learn from Camp David 40 Years Later?" *United States Institute of Peace*, March 25, 2019. https://www.usip.org/publications/2019/03/middle-east-peace-what-can-we-learn-camp-david-40-years-later, accessed October 11, 2019.

Barry, Tom. "Ivan Allen Jr. Helped Build, and Heal, Atlanta." *Atlanta Business Chronicle*, November 11, 2002. https://www.bizjournals.com/atlanta/stories/2002/11/11/focus2.html, accessed October 4, 2019.

Burke, Monte. "Nine Standout Lodges for the Southern Quail Hunter." *Garden & Gun*, December 2017/January 2018. https://gardenandgun.com/feature/bobwhite-bellwethers/, accessed August 5, 2019.

Carl Vinson Institute of Government. *Dismantling Persistent Poverty in Georgia: Breaking the Cycle*. Athens: Carl Vinson Institute of Government, University of Georgia, 2003.

Carson, Clayborne. "SNCC and the Albany Movement." *Journal of Southwest Georgia History* 2 (1984): 15–16.

Carter, Dan T. *The Politics of Rage: George Wallace, the Origins of the New Conservatism, and the Transformation of American Politics*. 2nd Louisiana pbk. ed. Baton Rouge: Louisiana State University Press, 2000.

Carter, Jarrett. "Benefits of College Mergers Don't Always Add Up: Despite Successes, Consolidation Doesn't Always Balance Campus, Community Cost in the Long Run." *Education Dive*, August 1, 2016. https://www.educationdive.com/news/benefits-of-college-mergers-dont-always-add-up/423561/, accessed October 7, 2019.

Clive, C., F. Davis, and T. Liner. *Glancing Backward: Albany, Georgia, 1836–1986*. Albany, Ga.: Dougherty County School System, Sesquicentennial Publication Committee, 1986.

Cobb, James C. *Redefining Southern Culture: Mind and Identity in the Modern South*. Athens: University of Georgia Press, 1999.

Davidson, Osha Gray. *The Best of Enemies: Race and Redemption in the New South*. Chapel Hill: University of North Carolina Press, 1996, 2018.

Davis, Janel. "Albany State Financial Aid Audit Finds Misconduct; Four Fired." *Atlanta Journal-Constitution*, October 22, 2015. https://www.ajc.com/news/local-education/albany-state-financial-aid-audit-finds-misconduct-four-fired/STlNVQXg2IDpkoeE7nc3cP/, accessed October 7, 2019.

Deb, Tanni, and Segun Akande. "Inside Ghana's Elmina Castle Is a Haunting Reminder of Its Grim Past." *CNN Inside Africa*, July 30, 2018. https://www.cnn.com/2018/07/27/africa/ghana-elmina-castle/index.html, accessed April 29, 2019.

Diarra, Lilian. "Ghana's Slave Castles: The Shocking Story of the Ghanaian Cape Coast." *Culture Trip*, January 24, 2017. https://theculturetrip.com/africa

/ghana/articles/ghana-s-slave-castles-the-shocking-story-of-the-ghanaian-cape-coast/, accessed April 29, 2019.

Diouf, Sylviane A. *Dreams of Africa in Alabama: The Slave Ship Clotilda and the Story of the Last Africans Brought to America.* New York: Oxford University Press, 2007.

Du Bois, W. E. B. *The Souls of Black Folk: Essays and Sketches.* Chicago: A. C. McClurg, 1903.

Dunning, Art. "Art Dunning: Albany State University Is Poised for Success." *Albany Herald*, January 27, 2018. https://www.albanyherald.com/opinion/art-dunning-albany-state-university-is-poised-for-success/article_6406c8d8-78a1-5a30-a6f3-b2b9b0b6fe64.html, accessed October 11, 2019.

Eltis, David, and David Richardson. *Atlas of the Transatlantic Slave Trade.* New Haven, Conn.: Yale University Press, 2010.

Encyclopædia Britannica Editors. "Blues Music." *Encyclopædia Britannica*, April 4, 2019. https://www.britannica.com/art/blues-music, accessed April 29, 2019.

Estes, Cary. "There's No Doubting Thomasville as an Alabama Community of Excellence." *Alabama NewsCenter*, August 9, 2017. https://alabamanewscenter.com/2017/08/09/theres-no-doubting-thomasville-as-an-alabama-community-of-excellence/, accessed September 23, 2019.

Faulkner, William. *Requiem for a Nun.* London: Chatto & Windus, 1953.

Federal Bureau of Investigation. "Medgar Evers." *FBI.gov.* https://www.fbi.gov/history/famous-cases/medgar-evers, accessed October 3, 2019.

Fiffer, Steve, and Adar Cohen. *Jimmie Lee & James: Two Lives, Two Deaths, and the Movement That Changed America.* New York: Regan Arts, 2015.

Flint, Wayne. *Alabama in the Twentieth Century.* Tuscaloosa: University of Alabama Press, 2004.

Florida, Richard. *The Rise of the Creative Class: Revisited.* 2d ed. New York: Basic Books, 2012.

Formwalt, Lee W. "The Albany Movement." *New Georgia Encyclopedia.* December 2, 2003; last updated March 1, 2019. https://www.georgiaencyclopedia.org/articles/counties-cities-neighborhoods/albany, accessed April 19, 2020.

Freemark, Samara, with Joe Richman, Sarah Kramer, Ben Shapiro, Nellie Gilles. "Segregation Now, Segregation Forever: The Infamous Words of George Wallace." Edited by Deborah George, *Radio Diaries.* http://www.radiodiaries.org/segregation-now-segregation-forever-the-speech-that-changed-american-politics/, accessed October 3, 2019.

Frey, William H. "The U.S. Will Become 'Minority White' in 2045, Census Projects: Youthful Minorities Are the Engine of Future Growth." *Brookings the Avenue*, September 10, 2018. https://www.brookings.edu/blog/the-avenue

/2018/03/14/the-us-will-become-minority-white-in-2045-census-projects/, accessed September 24, 2019.

Friedman, Thomas L. *Thank You for Being Late: An Optimist's Guide to Thriving in the Age of Accelerations.* New York: Farrar, Straus & Giroux, 2019.

Gavins, Raymond. *The Cambridge Guide to African American History.* New York: Cambridge University Press, 2016.

Gaye, Marvin. "Inner City Blues (Make Me Wanna Holler)." *What's Going On.* Tamla Records. 1971.

Georgia State University. "Leading with Predictive Analytics." *Student Success Programs.* https://success.gsu.edu/approach/, accessed September 22, 2019.

———. "Panther Retention Grants: A Strategic Approach." *Student Success Programs.* https://success.gsu.edu/initiatives/panther-retention-grants/, accessed September 22, 2019.

Georgia Tech. "Tech Promise Challenge Exceeds Goal." Office of Development. http://development.gatech.edu/why/impact-stories/tech-promise-challenge-extended, accessed July 23, 2019.

Goldstein, Richard. "Earl L. Butz, Secretary Felled by Racial Remark, Is Dead at 98." *New York Times*, February 4, 2008. https://www.nytimes.com/2008/02/04/washington/04butz.html, accessed October 7, 2019.

"Greenville, South Carolina." *Wikipedia.* https://en.wikipedia.org/wiki/Greenville,_South_Carolina, accessed April 1, 2020.

Hebert, Keith S. "Ku Kux Klan in Alabama from 1915–1930." *Encyclopedia of Alabama*, November 7, 2013. http://www.encyclopediaofalabama.org/article/h-3221, accessed February 13, 2019.

———. "Slavery." *Encyclopedia of Alabama*, August 22, 2017. http://www.encyclopediaofalabama.org/article/h-2369, accessed September 13, 2019.

Holt, Thomas. "Black Life." In *The Encyclopedia of Southern Culture*, edited by Charles R. Wilson, William Ferris, Anne Abadie, and Mary Hart. Chapel Hill: University of North Carolina Press, 1989.

Hurst, Roy. "Stepin Fetchit, Hollywood's First Black Film Star." National Public Radio, March 6, 2006. https://www.npr.org/templates/transcript/transcript.php?storyId=5245089, accessed October 7, 2019.

King, Martin Luther, Jr. "Desegregation and the Future." Address Delivered at the Annual Luncheon of the National Committee for Rural Schools. Martin Luther King, Jr. Research and Education Institute, Stanford University. https://kinginstitute.stanford.edu/king-papers/documents/desegregation-and-future-address-delivered-annual-luncheon-national-committee, accessed October 11, 2019.

———. "Letter from Birmingham Jail." *Atlantic Monthly*, 212, no. 2 (August 1963). http://web.cn.edu/kwheeler/documents/letter_birmingham_jail.pdf, accessed October 1, 2019.

Knight, Ashley. "Facebook SOTD: 'How Did Albany Get the Nickname "The Good Life City"'?" WFXL Fox 31, July 12, 2011. https://wfxl.com/news/local/facebook-sotd-how-did-albany-get-the-nickname-the-good-life-city, accessed October 4, 2019.

Lewis, Terry. "Flood of 1994 Spurred Building Boom at Albany State University." *Albany Herald*, June 26, 2014. https://www.albanyherald.com/news/flood-of-spurred-building-boom-at-albany-state-university/article_f92479bb-085e-5ace-b93d-319dd4713e5f.html, accessed October 5, 2019.

Little Known Black Library Facts. "Integration and the Anniston Public Library, Anniston, Alabama." *Little Known Black Library Facts*, November 2, 2014. https://littleknownblacklibrarianfacts.blogspot.com/2014/11/integration-and-anniston-public-library.html, accessed October 14, 2019.

Lockhart, P. R. "House Democrats Have Launched an Investigation into Voter Suppression in Georgia." *Vox*, March 6, 2019. https://www.vox.com/policy-and-politics/2019/3/6/18253689/voter-suppression-georgia-kemp-investigation-cummings, accessed August 7, 2019.

Martin, Jeff. "Georgia Farmers Face Long Recovery from Hurricane Michael Crop Losses." *Insurance Journal*, November 2, 2018. https://www.insurancejournal.com/news/southeast/2018/11/02/506416.htm, accessed October 4, 2019.

McDonald, Robin, and Valerie Pope Burnes. *Visions of the Black Belt: A Cultural Survey of the Heart of Alabama*. Tuscaloosa: University Alabama Press, 2015.

Meraji, Shereen Marisol, and Gene Demby. "The Whitest Historically Black College in America." National Public Radio, October 18, 2013. https://www.npr.org/sections/codeswitch/2013/10/18/236345546/the-whitest-historically-black-college-in-america, accessed October 9, 2019.

Michaeli, Ethan. "'Bound for the Promised Land': African Americans Devised a Mass Exodus from the Jim Crow South Largely at the Urging of *The Chicago Defender*." *Atlantic*, January 11, 2016. https://www.theatlantic.com/politics/archive/2016/01/chicago-defender/422583/, accessed October 2, 2019.

Mieder, Wolfgang. *"Making a Way Out of No Way": Martin Luther King's Sermonic Proverbial Rhetoric*. New York: Peter Lang, 2010.

MilitaryBases.com. "MCLB Albany Army Base in Albany, GA. https://militarybases.com/georgia/mclb-albany/, accessed October 4, 2019.

Monroe, Doug. "Where It All Went Wrong: If Only We Could Undo the MARTA Compromise of 1971." *Atlanta Magazine*, August 1, 2012. https://www.atlantamagazine.com/great-reads/marta-tsplost-transportation/, accessed October 11, 2019.

Morris, Susan D. "Flint River." *New Georgia Encyclopedia*, July 26, 2017. https://www.georgiaencyclopedia.org/articles/geography-environment/flint-river, accessed October 4, 2019.

Museum of Modern Art. "Visualizing the Great Migration, One-Way Ticket Jacob Lawrence's Migration Series." Moma.org. https://www.moma.org/interactives/exhibitions/2015/onewayticket/static/visualizing-the-great-migration/, accessed October 15, 2019.

National Museum of African American History and Culture. "Emmett Till's Open Casket Funeral Reignited the Civil Rights Movement." Smithsonian.com. https://www.smithsonianmag.com/smithsonian-institution/emmett-tills-open-casket-funeral-reignited-the-civil-rights-movement-180956483/, accessed October 15, 2019.

Obama, Michelle. *Becoming*. New York: Crown, 2018.

O'Neill, Erin. "Sheila Oliver Says 16 States Prohibited Interracial Marriage in 1958." *Politifact*, January 15, 2012. https://www.politifact.com/new-jersey/statements/2012/jan/15/sheila-oliver/sheila-oliver-says-16-states-prohibited-interracia/, accessed May 14, 2019.

Owusu-Ansah, Donna Olivia. "The Best of Enemies." Interview with Bill Riddick. *Urban Faith*. https://urbanfaith.com/2019/04/best-of-enemies-interview-with-bill-riddick.html/, accessed July 19, 2019.

Parks, Jennifer. "Homecoming Parade Brings in Albany State University Supporters and Alumni: Pine Avenue Was Crowded with Those Catching a Glimpse of Albany State's Homecoming Parade." *Albany Herald*, October 22, 2016. https://www.albanyherald.com/news/local/homecoming-parade-brings-in-albany-state-university-supporters-alumni/article_4b674a84-548f-5385-9774-6e273a092eec.html, accessed October 9, 2019.

Pettus, Emily Wagster, and Rebecca Santana. "Man Convicted of 3 Killing Civil Rights Workers Dies in Jail." *AP News*, January 12, 2018. https://www.apnews.com/3d82e778b5d643088268c3214ae904f8, accessed October 3, 2019.

Pew Research Center. "Social & Demographic Trends." June 10, 2015. https://www.pewsocialtrends.org/interactives/multiracial-timeline/, accessed October 9, 2019.

Pilgrim, David, and Henry Louis Gates Jr. *Understanding Jim Crow: Using Racist Memorabilia to Teach Tolerance and Promote Social Justice*. Oakland, Calif.: PM Press, 2015.

Richter, Jeremy W. "Alabama's Anti-Miscegenation Statutes, Part 7." *Jeremy W. Richter*, June 14, 2017. https://www.jeremywrichter.com/2017/06/14/alabama-anti-miscegenation-statute/, accessed May 14, 2019.

Samuel, Molly. "A River Flows under Atlanta's Airport, and People Hope to Make It a Destination." Wabe.org, September 13, 2018. https://www.wabe.org/a-river-flows-under-atlantas-airport-and-people-hope-to-make-it-a-destination/, accessed October 4, 2019.

Scarborough, Alex. "Linden, a Town Divided by Race." *Tuscaloosa News*, September 25, 2011. https://www.tuscaloosanews.com/article/DA/20110925/NEWS/605312046/TL/, accessed September 23, 2019.

Shell, Eddie Wayne. *Evolution of the Alabama Agroecosystem: Always Keeping Up, but Never Catching Up*. Montgomery, Ala.: NewSouth Books, 2013.

Smith, Ron. "Boll Weevil in Alabama." *Encyclopedia of Alabama*, December 3, 2018. http://www.encyclopediaofalabama.org/article/h-1436, accessed October 2, 2019.

Staff Report from Albany CEO. "ASU Interim President Art Dunning and Wife Make Major Donation to ASU." *Albany CEO*, September 23, 2015. http://albanyceo.com/news/2015/09/asu-interim-president-and-wife-make-major-donation-asu/, accessed October 5, 2019.

Stanford University. "Selma to Montgomery March." Martin Luther King, Jr. Research and Education Institute. https://kinginstitute.stanford.edu/encyclopedia/selma-montgomery-march, accessed October 3, 2019.

Stanford University Press. "The Cotton Revolution." *American Yawp*. http://www.americanyawp.com/text/11-the-cotton-revolution/, accessed October 4, 2019.

Suggs, Ernie. "A Civil Rights Champion Used the Power of Media." *Atlanta Journal-Constitution*, January 4, 2017. https://www.ajc.com/lifestyles/reasons-celebrate-black-history-month-ralph-mcgill/HcsE6JOZ1gFAFA8isLSMAK/, accessed October 9, 2019.

Truth and Reconciliation Commission. *The Official Truth and Reconciliation Commission Website*. http://www.justice.gov.za/trc/, accessed October 11, 2019.

University of Alabama. "New College." https://nc.as.ua.edu/, accessed October 13, 2019.

———. "Presidents of the University of Alabama." *University Libraries*, November 26, 2018. https://www.lib.ua.edu/libraries/hoole/the-universty-of-alabama-presidents/, accessed October 3, 2019.

———. "Quick Facts: Did You Know?" https://www.ua.edu/about/quickfacts, accessed October 13, 2019.

University of Alabama News Center. "The Faith and Politics Institute's Civil Rights Pilgrimage." June 13, 2013. https://www.ua.edu/news/2013/06/the-faith-and-politics-institutes-civil-rights-pilgrimage/, accessed September 30, 2019.

University of Georgia. "Archway Partnership." https://www.archwaypartnership.uga.edu/, accessed October 13, 2019.

University System of Georgia. "Huckaby Recommending Consolidation of Albany State University and Darton State College." November 6, 2015. https://www.usg.edu/news/release/huckaby_recommending_consolidation_of_albany_state_university_and_darton_st, accessed October 7, 2019.

———. "Previous Campus Consolidations." https://www.usg.edu/consolidation/, accessed October 7, 2019.

———. "Regents Approve Principles for Consolidation of Institutions." November 8, 2011. https://www.usg.edu/news/release/regents_approve_principles_for_consolidation_of_institutions, accessed October 7, 2019.

———. "Semester Enrollment Report: Spring 2019." Research and Policy Analysis. https://www.usg.edu/research/enrollment_reports, accessed October 13, 2019.

U.S. Department of Education. "What Is an HBCU?" *White House Initiative on Historically Black Colleges and Universities*. https://sites.ed.gov/whhbcu/one-hundred-and-five-historically-black-colleges-and-universities/, accessed October 5, 2019.

Van West, Carroll. "WLAC." *Tennessee Encyclopedia*, March 1, 2018. http://tennesseeencyclopedia.net/entries/wlac/, accessed, April 29, 2019.

WALB News10. "Albany State Proves 'Unsinkable' in Flood of '94." WALB.com, July 12, 2004. https://www.walb.com/story/2025395/albany-state-proves-unsinkable-in-flood-of-94/, accessed October 5, 2019.

Wilder, L. Douglas. *Son of Virginia: A Life in America's Political Arena*. Lanham, Md.: Rowman & Littlefield, 2015.

Wilkerson, Isabel. *The Warmth of Other Suns: The Epic Story of America's Great Migration*. New York: Random House, 2010.

Williams, Juan, and Dwayne Ashley, with Shawn Rhea. *I'll Find a Way or Make One: A Tribute to Historically Black Colleges and Universities*. New York: Amistad, 2004.

Woolley, John, and Gerhard Peters. "Remarks at Southwest Texas State College Upon Signing the Higher Education Act of 1965 on November 8, 1965." *The American Presidency Project*. https://www.presidency.ucsb.edu/documents/remarks-southwest-texas-state-college-upon-signing-the-higher-education-act-1965, accessed October 5, 2019.

Worthy, Larry. "The Creek Indians of Georgia." *Our Georgia History*. http://www.ourgeorgiahistory.com/indians/Creek/creek01.html, accessed October 4, 2019.

Zinn, Howard. *A People's History of the United States*. 1980; rpt., New York: HarperCollins, 2015.

www.ingramcontent.com/pod-product-compliance
Lightning Source LLC
Chambersburg PA
CBHW021339230426
43666CB00006B/339